ENOUGH

CASSIDY HUTCHINSON

Simon & Schuster

NEW YORK LONDON TORONTO
SYDNEY NEW DELHI

Simon & Schuster
1230 Avenue of the Americas
New York, NY 10020

First Simon & Schuster hardcover edition September 2023

SIMON & SCHUSTER and colophon are registered trademarks
of Simon & Schuster, Inc.

For information about special discounts for bulk purchases,
please contact Simon & Schuster Special Sales at 1-866-506-1949
or business@simonandschuster.com.

The Simon & Schuster Speakers Bureau can bring authors to your
live event. For more information or to book an event, contact the
Simon & Schuster Speakers Bureau at 1-866-248-3049
or visit our website at www.simonspeakers.com.

Manufactured in the United States of America

5   7   9   10   8   6

Library of Congress Cataloging-in-Publication Data has been applied for.

ISBN 978-1-6680-2828-5
ISBN 978-1-6680-2830-8 (ebook)

To Bill Jordan and Jody Hunt

Contents

PART IV: ENOUGH

Acknowledgments

Writing this memoir has deepened my appreciation for my family's support and often uncelebrated sacrifices—a narrative that surpasses the limits of these pages.

I owe a debt of gratitude to my mother. Her refusal to accept anything less than my best nurtured the fire within me, and she provided a home to my passion for life and bravery to speak the truth.

Jack, my brother and eternal friend, has revealed the virtue of patience and deepened my capacity for love. When confronted with adversity, we had each other to light the way.

My chosen father, Paul, has enriched my life more than I can express. Paul exemplifies that the true essence of family lies in bonds forged through commitment and love, and demonstrates that not every successful man is a good father, but every good father is, undoubtedly, a successful man.

My beloved grandmother, a paragon of resilience and grace, encouraged me to search for miracles in the overlooked corners of the world. She taught me that a single act of courage can have a reach beyond one's imagination.

Aunt Steph and Uncle Joe breathed life into my greatest aspirations, taught me the power of compassion, and showed me how to embrace hardship as an opportunity for growth.

I pay tribute to the lessons and spirit of my dad. He imparted to me a warrior spirit—mental fortitude and perseverance—qualities that have shaped my path toward success. Despite the complexities of our relationship, he will always have a special place in my heart.

To the family, friends, and mentors, past and present, whose names and stories are not mentioned: thank you. Your memory and love is with me, always.

Enough would not have been possible without the village that saw purpose and value in this project long before I did.

Mark Salter, my collaborator, source of strength, and dear friend. Mark's appetite for understanding and belief in my potential allowed this memoir to reach greater heights. Thank you for being a beacon of confidence and ensuring my fingerprints are on every page.

Robert Barnett and Emily Alden of Williams & Connolly provided invaluable guidance during an unfamiliar, daunting journey. Bob, it is an honor to work with and learn from you. You are my National Treasure.

I am forever indebted to the support of Simon & Schuster for bringing this project to life. When I first met my editor, Stephanie Frerich, I trusted that her passionate mind and eye for detail would bring life to my memoir. My admiration for Steph has grown tremendously as an editor and, I hope, as a lifelong friend.

Thank you to Jonathan Karp, Priscilla Painton, Julia Prosser, Jackie Seow, Janet Byrne, and Carolyn Levin for your commitment to this project. And many thanks to the full book publishing team: Brittany Adames, Stephen Bedford, Mikaela Bielawski, Susan Bishansky, Lyndsay Brueggemann, Ray Chokov, Samantha Cohen, Paul Dippolito, Marie Florio, Debbie Friedman, Mike Goehler, Lauren Gomez, Kayley Hoffman, Navorn Johnson, Zoe Kaplan, Irene Kheradi, Sara Kitchen, Erin Larson, Winona Lukito, Beth Maglione, Dominick Montalto, Nicole Moran,

Amanda Mulholland, Meryll Preposi, Jamie Selzer, Emma Shaw, Elisa Shokoff, Tom Spain, Mabel Taveras, and Christina Zarafonitis.

In the fabric of our nation's history, there is a body of guardians who protect the sanctity of our republic.

I extend heartfelt gratitude to the United States Capitol Police. Your courageous defense of the Capitol, and the democratic principles it represents, is an enduring reminder of the sacrifices made by those who preserve the ideals of freedom and justice.

Thank you to the members of Congress and staff who served on the January 6th Committee. These individuals shone light on the perils our nation faced that day. Their commitment to the task at hand, regardless of political affiliation, exemplifies the strength of our institutions. A special thank-you to Kristin Amerling, Dan George, Tim Heaphy, Joe Maher, John Wood, and Hannah Muldavian for your professionalism and intellect.

Alyssa Farah Griffin is a true American patriot who I am fortunate to call my dear friend. When courage was scarce, Alyssa chose to speak out—a testament to her fidelity to our nation.

I cannot overstate the impact that Alexander Butterfield has had on my life. His allegiance to the oath he swore is a reminder that the pursuit of justice is an obligation that should never waver. May his legacy continue inspiring future generations to find their moral compass in the face of adversity.

This journey would not have been possible without the generosity of Alston & Bird. Beyond their legal expertise, the entire law firm became a source of encouragement and support—a reminder that no one should face the challenges of life alone. Richard Hays, Mary Benton, Stephen Simrill, Alicia Badley, Mary Fertitta, Dayle Foster, and Alex Wolfe: thank you for renewing my sense of resilience and transforming my perspective on the power of community.

Bill Jordan and Jody Hunt, you changed the trajectory of my life for good. Thank you for representing and caring for me as though I were your own. My love for you two and your families is forever, always.

And finally, I want to extend my deepest appreciation to Liz Cheney. Liz reminds us that true leadership is grounded in principle, and that change can be achieved through unyielding loyalty to our democratic ideals. May this book serve as a testament to the transformative power of leaders like Liz, who inspire us to be agents of the truth in our republic, and beyond. That we, as individuals, are enough.

Author's Note

As I write this, it has been just over a year since I testified before the House Select Committee to Investigate the January 6th Attack on June 28, 2022. I chose to come forward to provide the committee—and country—with my truthful and candid observations of events that preceded the attack on the United States Capitol. I chose to come forward in *Enough* to share how I arrived at that moment, and what happened afterward.

I relied on information both personal and public to write this memoir: my memory, text messages, call logs, journal entries, notes, calendars, and government interview transcripts. The essence of moments and dialogue are rendered according to my best recollections.

Names and identifying characteristics of some individuals have been changed.

Prologue

HOW HAD I GOTTEN HERE? What had I done to wind up in this predicament, a featured player in a Washington political scandal, struggling to keep my composure under the glare of television lights as I became, depending on your political allegiance, briefly famous or infamous?

The Cannon Caucus Room is one of the largest and grandest rooms in any of the House office buildings. With its high, ornate ceilings and chandeliers, it looks like a Hollywood set that's meant to transform the often cramped and dingy reality of government office space into a majestic hall of power. As Rep. Liz Cheney, of Wyoming, would observe in a subsequent hearing, it had been home to the historic talks for women to be able to vote a century earlier; Cheney noted, "In this room in 1918, the Committee on Woman Suffrage convened to discuss and debate whether women should be granted the right to vote." I would estimate its generous proportions could accommodate five hundred or more people comfortably.

On June 28, 2022, I entered from the back of the chamber with my lawyers, and we wound our way down a security-cleared path to the witness table, past a row of US Capitol Police officers. There wasn't an empty seat in sight. House staffers who couldn't find a seat stood along the walls. Photojournalists pressed against the table, clicking away. I blinked and tried to adjust my eyes to the bright lights needed by the many C-SPAN cameras that were providing the live feed to the news networks. I had wanted to arrive at the same time that the members of the committee did, so I wouldn't have to endure prolonged, awkward minutes of being frantically photographed as I tried not to return people's stares. But still the seconds ticked by excruciatingly slowly as I waited for the hearing to start.

The atmosphere was charged, to say the least. Everyone in the room—committee members, reporters, spectators—seemed attuned to the sense that something dramatic and important was about to happen. So was I, the hearing's sole witness. The committee had been methodical in planning its five previous hearings. Today's hearing had been rushed, out of concerns for my safety, news reports claimed, and, I expect, out of concern that I might back out at the last minute.

I just might have. I had been episodically panic-stricken for the last twenty-four hours. The night before, I had pleaded with my lawyers, Jody Hunt and Bill Jordan, that I wasn't ready and needed more time. I had threatened to bolt on the car ride to the hearing, and again as I peered from a holding room into the bright, bustling hearing room.

As members of the select committee looked down at me from the dais, I could sense myself trembling, and I worried someone would notice. I could feel that my necklace wasn't straight, which Mom had warned me about, so I tried to straighten it discreetly, aware my every move could be scrutinized.

When the hearing concluded, press accounts described me as cool, calm, and collected. A *Washington Post* columnist wrote that I "had a preternatural poise." And in truth, once the hearing began, my nerves quickly settled as Liz Cheney, whom I had come to trust and admire, began to question me. But before the gavel came down and Liz began her inquiry, I had felt debilitated by my nervousness.

I was an ambitious twenty-five-year-old conservative Trump White House staffer, who had occupied a position in proximity to power. I had worked myself to near exhaustion to prove worthy of it. Now I was about to provide testimony in a high-stakes congressional hearing that I knew could damage, and potentially incriminate, the former president of the United States. I was also going to alienate friends and former colleagues.

How had I gotten here? Shortly before I graduated from college, with several congressional and White House internships on my résumé, I had shared my aspirations for the future with a reporter for a student newspaper. I wanted to "be an effective leader in the fight to secure the American dream for future generations," I volunteered, "so they too will have the bountiful opportunities and freedoms that make the United States great." Corny? Maybe. Presumptuous? Certainly. But I meant it, and I would work my tail off in service to that aspiration, to be useful to my country.

Before retaining my new lawyers, at times I had told less than the whole truth to a congressional committee charged with investigating a matter of the highest national importance, a matter that posed a threat to America's future greatness. I had withheld information about events that I had witnessed or that had been recounted to me by witnesses. Those events had precipitated the shocking assault on the United States Congress, an institution I cherish, and threatened the continued success of American democracy. My conscience was bothering me, and I came to the decision, in parliamentary language, to clarify and extend my testimony. That's the short answer. That's *why* I was there.

The long answer, the story of *how* I got there, is a little more complicated than that, and takes a little longer to tell.

PART I

GROW

CHAPTER 1

Early Days

ONCE THE SUN WAS LEVEL with the treetops, I knew it was time to wait in my spot. I never waited alone, though. I waited with Abby, our chocolate springer spaniel. Sometimes Abby and I did not have to wait very long, but most of the time, the glow of summer fireflies was flickering across our front lawn when we heard the first rumblings of Dad's landscaping company trucks. Once we were certain it was indeed Dad making his way toward our house on Reed Road in Pennington, New Jersey, Abby and I burst with excitement. It was officially our favorite part of the day: time to welcome Dad home.

Barefooted, I sprinted down our long gravel driveway alongside Abby as the trucks came into sight. Dad led the caravan in his white 1992 Ford pickup truck. Slowing down, but not coming to a complete stop, he would open the passenger door for Abby and me to hop in. We would belt "Black Water" by the Doobie Brothers and Glenn Miller's "Chattanooga Choo Choo" at the top of our lungs as we drove to the back of the property, where Dad rested the equipment for the evening.

Dad, Mom, and I had moved to Reed Road when I was three and a half years old. It was the third house we had lived in as a family of three, and so far, it was my favorite. My second favorite was our town house on Hilton Court, just a few miles across town, where we had lived for six months. That house was special to me because it was where Mom gave birth to me.

Recently, I had learned that while we were to appreciate some of the miracles of modern medicine, we also were skeptical of doctors in hospitals. And doctors and hospitals in general. Since a home birth did not involve any medication, it was the safest and most responsible option for Mom and me. The privacy of home births was a bonus for Dad, who always said privacy is power. They found the perfect holistic midwife, who delivered me in the early morning hours of December 12, 1996.

Though Dad was born and raised in Pennington, he never shared stories from his childhood. Before my paternal grandfather, Dick, passed away in 1995, he made Mom promise to share as many stories as possible about his life with his future grandchildren. But Dad did always tell me that our family had a long history of cultivating the land and building businesses in Pennington. Dad claimed his relatives made such important sacrifices so he would have the perfect place to raise his family.

Mom's family was the only extended family I knew. The eldest of seven children, she was close to her siblings. My grandmother's heart was soft and her spirit was free. Mom's family moved all over the United States before settling in New Jersey for a few years.

After Dad, Grandma was the hardest worker I had ever met. Sometimes while Mom cooked dinner, Grandma and I would stash a handful of chocolate chip cookies from the kitchen cupboard, and we would tiptoe out the back door together. After we set aside two cookies for ourselves, we would smash the rest into tiny crumbs to sprinkle on the ground. Grandma and I did this so we could "witness one of nature's miracles." Right when I began to fidget with impatience, the miracle began: a single ant would appear from a crack in the dirt and navigate its way to the crumbs. Before we knew it, hundreds of ants marched across the earth to collect and carry the cookie crumbs back through the dirt.

Grandma told me that ants were some of the hardest-working insects in nature. They worked for their community and their family. We were able to see one of their daily tasks, Grandma said, but some of the ants' most important work happens underground.

Though we would never be able to see it ourselves, there was a whole world being built beneath our feet. Grandma promised that if I learned to be curious and attentive, I could help others see what's often overlooked.

———

Once a week while Dad was at work, Mom and I went to her favorite nail salon on the Pennington Circle for manicures. One morning when I was four years old, Mom said that we had to go to her doctor's office after our manicures so she could pick up important paperwork. Later that night, she and Dad gave me the best news—we would soon be a family of four. We didn't yet know if I would have a brother or a sister, so I named the baby Cake, after my favorite treat. Baby Cake was due in April 2001.

I never wanted to leave Mom's side when she was pregnant, and I think she always wanted me by her side. Though I was supposed to attend preschool a few mornings a week, Mom let me start skipping days so I could be with her, and we would do my schoolwork together at home. As my sibling grew, I would read it books and sing it lullabies while rubbing my hand around Mom's tummy, anxious to feel a fluttering movement. Mom and I prepared the baby's nursery together, and she started teaching me how to cook.

Because our family was growing, Dad had to work more. His landscaping hours were pretty much the same, but Dad tinkered with the equipment out back long after the sun went down. Sometimes Dad was still outside working when Mom tucked me into bed.

One night that winter, Mom and I were snuggled in my bed when she asked if I could keep a secret. I nodded eagerly, and we wrapped our pinky fingers together. Mom told me that the baby was a boy, and that she decided that his name would be Jack Henry. Dad had wanted to name the baby Hunter Henry. Henry was a family name on Dad's side, she told me. But she loved the name Jack. I loved it, too.

I realized that I didn't know my own middle name. Mom laughed. "Your middle name is Jacqueline. Cassidy Jacqueline Hutchinson." We practiced saying it together—it was what she called a tongue twister. I asked if Jacqueline was also a family name, like my baby brother's middle name. She shook her head. Many years ago, Mom told me, there was a United States president named John F. Kennedy. His wife, Jacqueline Kennedy, was one of the most intelligent, elegant, and generous souls Mom knew of. Mom told me that your name can determine your entire future, and she hoped I would look to Jacqueline Kennedy as a role model.

I felt special that Mom had chosen such an important middle name for me. I asked her how she had come up with my first name. Mom said that her very first doll, a Cabbage Patch Kid, had been named Cassidy, and ever since she had wanted to name a daughter Cassidy.

———

When I woke up on April 15, 2001, I found a giant Easter basket in my bedroom doorway. I grabbed a gold-foil-wrapped chocolate egg from the basket and bolted downstairs in my nightgown, only to find out Mom was in labor. I took Abby into our backyard and piddled around, trying to distract myself from all the excitement I was missing inside. Before long, a midwife appeared at the back door and extended her hand. I wrapped my hand around hers, and she squeezed mine tight as we climbed the stairs. I found Mom in her bed looking a bit sweaty and red-faced, and I caught a glimpse of Dad in the bathroom with another midwife, cleaning my baby brother. I climbed in bed next to Mom, and Dad handed the baby to her.

His face was chubby and so squished it was hard to identify his features. I noticed his head was covered in bright red fuzz. Mom looked at Dad and cried. She didn't know that there were redheads on his side of the family. Dad made one last effort to name the baby Hunter, but Mom repeated that his name was Jack Henry.

None of their bickering mattered to me. I ran my hand over the red peach fuzz and told Baby Cake how much I loved him already.

———

After a long summer at home with Mom and a screaming newborn, I was excited to return to preschool—my final year before kindergarten. One morning in September, Mom picked me up unexpectedly. With Jack balanced on her hip, Mom hurried me into the school parking lot. Frightened, I kept asking Mom what was going on. Once Jack and I were buckled into our booster and car seats, Mom began driving and explained that something bad had happened in New York City, and she wanted me at home with her. I pressed her for more information. She said that men the news reporters were calling "terrorists" had flown airplanes into the World Trade Center towers.

When we arrived home, she turned on the TV and immediately called to check on our next-door neighbor. Just as they connected, we watched one of the towers collapse. Mom shrieked and slammed down the phone receiver before picking it back up to try to get ahold of Dad.

Dad did not answer her calls for a long time, though. He came home later that day and told us how he had driven to the top of Baldpate Mountain, where he claimed he could see the Manhattan skyline, and a column of smoke rising from the disaster. As we listened to Dad describe his adventure of the day, Mom pulled Jack and me close.

Soon, our phone rang again. Mom jumped up to answer the call and started crying when she heard the voice of her closest sister, my aunt Steph. Mom stretched its long cord from the kitchen into the living room to sit with me on the couch. Aunt Steph lived in Indiana but promised she would drive to New Jersey to see us soon.

When photos of the aftermath appeared on TV the following day, I could not understand why anyone would attack the United States and kill thousands of Americans. All I knew was that I loved my country, and those men had hurt us. I felt my first surge of national pride as Mom, Jack, and I rushed with our neighbors to local stores in search of American flags. Several stores were sold out of flags, but we finally found some at Home Depot and bought dozens. I planted the flags all over the yard, wearing an American flag T-shirt I found in Dad's drawer as a dress.

———

Dad went hunting every winter. He had taken me turtle trapping and fishing before, but he would not take me hunting until I turned five. But in the fall of 2001, Dad promised he would take me, even though Mom told him I was too young. Dad reminded her I was starting kindergarten next year and that it was better to learn to be a hunter than to be the one hunted.

Early one Sunday morning, Dad and I woke up before the sun for a long day of hunting preparation. We started the day with our usual tradition: hot chocolates from 7-Eleven and a bagel with olive cream cheese. We then drove around town to the local ponds Dad set his snapping turtle traps in. We found a massive turtle at our first stop. Dad yanked the turtle out of the trap by its tail and chucked it into the bed of his pickup. I was giddy with excitement as he drove us to the Clubhouse.

The Clubhouse was a tiny shack in the middle of the woods. There were a few pens outside for pigs, chickens, and sheep. All the club members were men Dad hunted with, which is why I did not get to go very often. When Dad and I drove down the packed-dirt road, a few guys were standing outside. Dad stopped me from getting out of the truck with him, instead handing me a pair of safety earmuffs.

I stretched my neck to look over the dashboard to see Dad hurl the turtle onto a tree stump. One man handed Dad a gun.

All the men walked a few steps behind Dad as he fired the first shot. The turtle's shell shattered, pieces flying in the air. Dad tossed the gun to the next man. When he took his shot, the turtle split.

I opened the truck door and screamed, begging them to stop. The turtle was dead. Dad stormed back to the truck and shoved me inside as he scolded me to stay in the truck. I buried my face between my legs and hugged the safety earmuffs closer to my head with my elbows.

On our drive home, I told Dad I never wanted to go hunting again. Dad nodded. "That's fine, Sissy Hutch," he said. "But just so you know, warriors are not afraid to hunt. If you want to be a warrior just like Daddy, you must learn to hunt, Sissy. What you saw today is the circle of life."

Dad always talked about how he was a warrior, and I wanted to be one, too. I knew how important it was to be a warrior. But I didn't want to be a hunter, at least not yet. I decided to become a vegetarian.

———

Later that year, Aunt Steph visited us, this time with her boyfriend, Joe. At dinner, Mom dug her elbow into my ribs and whispered harshly to quit staring, but I couldn't help it. From the time Joe arrived with Aunt Steph, I couldn't *not* stare at him. Joe was taller and thinner than any man I had ever seen in my life. He almost looked like a character from a storybook. I thought maybe he was related to Jack, since they both had bright red hair, but I decided that Jack was too chunky and talkative for that to be true. Joe was polite and soft-spoken in a way that was very different from Aunt Steph's other boyfriends. Steph told me that midwestern men tend to be a bit more reserved than Jersey men.

After dinner, Joe and I sat on the back steps where Grandma and I usually fed the ants. He lit a cigarette and began to tell me all about his job as a police officer and a member of the Indiana

National Guard. I had only seen police officers around Pennington before, but Dad would bristle when they encroached on our space. Other than the few New Jersey state troopers who Dad was friends with, Dad frequently reminded me that I should never trust anyone with a government badge.

I knew about soldiers, too, but only from the morning news shows. Joe nodded confidently when I asked him if being a soldier meant he could go to war and die. Joe explained that he loved America and its freedom so deeply he was willing to sacrifice his life to make sure our country stayed safe.

I decided Joe was the tallest, thinnest, bravest man I had ever met in my life.

———

When I started kindergarten in September the following year, the idea of taking the school bus for the first time made me nervous weeks in advance. I had been complaining to Mom that my tummy hurt whenever I thought about it. She told me one story after another, painting the bus ride as a fun adventure in an effort to convince me I would be okay. Still, on the morning of my first day, my stomach was twisted in knots, and my hands and feet were damp with sweat.

Mom ran upstairs, promising to be right back with a magic trick. The trick turned out to be baby powder, which she sprinkled in my shoes, claiming it was fairy dust. "This will take all your worries away," she promised. "Now your feet won't be sweaty."

When Mom turned her attention to Jack, I dumped piles of the baby powder into my sneakers and slipped my feet into the shoes before Mom could notice. At the bottom of the driveway, clutching her hand, I watched the yellow school bus pull to a stop. Mom walked me onto the bus and buckled me in and kissed my head, with the bus driver at her side. "You're going to have a great day," she assured me.

The driver stayed by my side until Mom had stepped off and stood in the driveway. As I peered through the window at her, my eyes welled with tears, and I quietly unbuckled my seat belt. When the driver had settled into her seat and was preparing to pull the door shut, I bolted off the bus, sprinting past Mom and Jack. Clouds of baby powder puffed from my sneakers as I screamed, "I am not riding the school bus!"

From that day forward, from kindergarten through fifth grade, Mom drove me to school.

———

I had heard Mom and Dad start to bicker a few months back. I was frightened when Dad's screams rattled the walls at night. I couldn't block out the sound with my pillow over my ears. I sometimes left my bedroom and sat at the top of the staircase to get a better listen. I only confronted Mom about it one time, later. She looked a little heartbroken when I brought it up, and told me I was probably just mishearing things—I was probably hearing the movies they watched at night.

That explanation may have worked a year ago, but I was a wise kindergartener now. I knew that I was not mistaken.

Dad was disconnecting from our family and focusing too much on work, Mom said. She loved how close I felt to him, but he was letting that start to slip away, too. Recently, I had been injured while I was in the yard with Dad and his employees. The yard was junked up with machines that Dad had taken apart to fix, but he had not gotten around to finishing the projects yet. I was out back with Abby and tripped over a machine part and fell on an old lawn mower blade.

Mom had begged Dad to take me to the hospital for stitches, which I probably needed. The cut was deep and bled more than I thought I had blood. Dad thought Mom was being ridiculous. Working with Dad made me stronger, and warriors don't get stitches for little cuts and bruises. I was just happy that Dad still thought there was a chance I could be a warrior, even though I had decided to become a vegetarian after the turtle incident.

———

They kept bickering through Christmas, and eventually we all sat down for a family discussion. Mom looked so happy, I could not wait to hear what they had to say. I thought maybe we were getting another pet or, even better, another baby sibling.

The news was much different than I had anticipated. They informed me that we were soon moving to Spencer, Indiana. We would buy a house there and live very close to Aunt Steph and soon-to-be Uncle Joe. Dad was selling his landscaping business, so it would take a little extra time for him to join us in Indiana, maybe six months. Dad promised to come visit us every weekend, and he said that he would call us most nights before bedtime.

I loved our house on Reed Road and didn't want to leave it behind, but Dad told me that even if we didn't move to Indiana, we would probably move to a new house in Pennington soon. Trees are meant to stay in one place until they die, Dad said, not people. Mom rolled her eyes at this, and said that moving around Pennington didn't quite count.

Mom packed up the house quickly. Dad brought a moving truck to the house, but he had to work the day Mom began to load boxes in it. At one point, I saw Mom muscling our baby grand piano through the house on her own. I scolded Mom to stop—she was going to hurt herself, and that was a project Dad should do, since he was the strongest person in our family. Mom lowered the piano onto the ground and calmly walked over to me. She was slightly winded as she told me that the biggest mistake a woman could make was to think she couldn't do the same thing as a man.

Mom walked back to the piano before I could respond. I

watched her maneuver that piano right out of the house and hoist it into the moving truck by herself. Mom repeated this process with every large piece of furniture we were bringing to Indiana.

Dad wasn't the strongest person in our family after all.

———

Life in Spencer was carefree and fun. In many ways, I enjoyed when it was just me, Mom, and Jack. I missed Dad, but I saw Uncle Joe almost every day. And I liked being around Uncle Joe and Aunt Steph—their love was unlike love I'd seen before. They spoke to each other with so much kindness, and he looked at her with tenderness in his eyes.

After Mom picked me up from school, we would drive to the police station with fountain Cokes and hang out with Joe for a while. Sometimes he would take me around in his police car and show me how to protect the community. We would drive past the farm where he grew up, which prompted Joe to tell my favorite story about his dad. Joe's family did not have a lot of money while he was growing up, but his dad knew there were people less fortunate than they were. He designated part of his field to grow crops for the poorest people in Owen County, Indiana. Joe would tag along with his dad to distribute the food every week. "A true countryman gives," Joe told me, "even when he doesn't have much for himself."

After six months, Dad finally sold the landscaping company and the house on Reed Road, which meant it was time to join us in Spencer. I wanted to run out to greet him when he pulled up in his truck, just like old times. But Mom looked concerned and told me to wait inside with Jack. Through the window, I watched Dad wringing his hands and sobbing. He walked over to the pool and laid flat on the diving board as he continued to cry. My heart hurt so much, I could not wait a moment longer to be with him, so I ran outside. I asked him what was wrong, but I could not understand what he said. Mom was frozen, like a statue, and did not say a word herself.

Eventually I understood enough of Dad's words. He could not do it, he said. He could not leave Pennington, the only place he had ever called home, to move to Indiana. Dad's chest was heaving as he tried to calm himself down. Mom went to tend to Jack, since I had irresponsibly left him alone inside to console Dad.

I sat on the edge of the pool next to Dad and dangled my feet in the water. I rubbed his leg and tried to reassure him that everything would be okay. We would never leave him behind in New Jersey.

By the end of that weekend, Mom and Dad had put our house in Spencer on the market. We paid one last visit to Aunt Steph and Uncle Joe. Knowing my love of animals, Uncle Joe walked with me to the barn to show me a litter of kittens and told me to pick one out. I looked at him with awe. I had been heartbroken when Mom and Dad rehomed Abby before we moved to Indiana. Dad said that Abby would have been too much for Mom to handle in Spencer, but Mom disagreed. She asserted we had to give Abby away before we moved to Spencer because Abby had massacred all of Dad's guinea hens at our house on Reed Road. Abby was one of many pets I had loved dearly that I had to give up, despite my protests.

I found a perfect black-and-white kitten and carried her to the front yard, where Mom and Dad were hanging out with Aunt Steph. Dad was smiling as Mom scolded Uncle Joe for giving me a feral stray that was not meant to live indoors. Uncle Joe laughed and assured Mom that while you cannot tame the wild, a loving home will help it grow.

———

We made a fresh start at a new house in Pennington borough. I was now an independent first grader and insisted that I could walk to my new school on my own. Dad agreed with me. He believed that my survival skills were sharper than those of any other child my age. Mom rolled her eyes, so I preemptively began to debate her, and did so until I was out of breath. Mom would not budge. I compromised with Mom after a long-winded negotiation: she could walk with me to school, but only if she walked far behind me. Mom and I shook on our deal.

I loved the predictable routine of school, and I loved learning even more. But I felt out of place in a classroom and with the other students. I always finished my schoolwork before my classmates, and instead of playing with them during recess, I often stayed back in the classroom with my teacher to eat lunch and tidy up. It did not bother me that some of my classmates called me the teacher's pet.

When I talked to Mom and Dad about this, Mom encouraged me to remain patient; my studies would become more challenging soon enough. Dad, on the other hand, lectured me and Mom on how it was critical that I get a good "edu-muh-cay-tion."

Dad had already decided that I would be the first person in our family to go to college, even though it would cost him a fortune. But Dad thought of everything; he started my college savings account before I was born. Privately, Mom told me that I was way too young to even think about college. But she was too late—my mind was made up: I would go to college, just like Dad said I would.

While I liked my new school, Dad was unhappy in Pennington borough. We had no privacy, Dad said, and he needed privacy to protect his family. Dad and Mom found a house in a more rural part of Pennington, on Poor Farm Road. It had a large pond in the front yard with a dock and a rowboat, and a creek off to the side, with acres of wilderness to explore. I was in love with the house on Poor Farm Road from the first moment I saw it. Dad was right—living in privacy was better.

CHAPTER 2

Changes

MY RIGHT PINKY FINGER wound around Dad's to show him how loyal I was to our promise. If Mom knew what we were about to do together, she would have a conniption. I fully trusted Dad's judgment—he would never put me in danger—and Mom tended to rain on our fun-parades.

For my eighth birthday, Dad surprised me with my very own four-wheeler, a miniature version of his own four-wheeler. Dad surprised Mom and Jack with the four-wheeler, too. For months, Mom made it clear that I was far too young for my own four-wheeler, so if Dad had consulted her on the purchase, she would have put an immediate stop to it. I was glad he made the purchase by himself. The four-wheeler was, by far, my favorite birthday gift.

Dad wanted to wait for a special occasion for us to ride our matching four-wheelers for the first time together. School had been canceled due to an incoming snowstorm. While Dad would normally plow when there were snowstorms, this day was different.

Dad and I waited until Mom brought Jack down to the basement playroom before we made our break. We still hadn't bought my proper helmet but decided my bike helmet would do. Dad showed me how to operate the four-wheeler; the lesson didn't last very long, since the gears were nearly identical to his.

When I mounted my four-wheeler for the first time, Dad's hands squeezed my shoulders. Then Dad released his grip and used his free hand to pinch my nose—almost too hard—then he tightened his grip on my nose to pull my face toward his. The flecks of orange in his hazel eyes danced like fire. I knew something exciting was about to happen.

"Let's rock and roll, Sissy," he exclaimed, and we broke out in laughter. Dad hopped on his four-wheeler, and then we were off.

The ground was still blanketed with snow from the last storm, but the snow was more wet than powdery. At first, Dad and I rode our four-wheelers cautiously around our backyard so I could get accustomed to steering. I trailed close behind him as he wove in and out of the trees. After I felt comfortable, Dad beelined to the front of our property. Stopping at the end of the driveway, Dad told me to follow him to the field down the street.

When we made it safely to the field, Dad took off at full speed. I pushed my throttle until it wouldn't budge as I sped after Dad. We drove figure eights in the snow with our tire tracks, chased a few deer, and laughed until our lungs burned. I had never felt so wild and free.

Until I hit a patch of ice.

Once I hit the ice, every emergency safety lesson that had been taught to me was pushed out of my memory. I felt my four-wheeler skip sideways across the snow, like the flat skipping stones we Frisbee'd across the pond when it was thawed. The weight of my vehicle favored one side, and I tried to balance it by leaning in the opposite direction, like Dad had told me to do.

But it was too late. I screamed as the four-wheeler gave in under the force and began to roll across the snow. Then I made my second mistake—I forgot to let go. I heard Dad shout at me to release, but his direction was frightening, and made me tighten my grip on the handlebars and tuck my head in close to my tummy.

The ordeal felt like it lasted for several minutes, but I only rolled two or three times. When I finally stopped, the four-wheeler was upside down, and my thighs were pinned under the seat. I heard Dad's steel-toed boots crunch in the snow as he jogged toward me.

He twisted my key out of the ignition, then stood near my feet so he could look me in the eye.

He asked if I was hurt. I screamed and tried to push the four-wheeler off my body with my arms, but it was too heavy. I screamed more. "Sissy, stop!" he shouted. "Answer my question! Are you hurt?" I screamed and thrashed—I was pinned down and needed his help. Dad instructed me to stand up, and I felt him kick the bottom of each of my snow boots. Now I was mad, and, still pinned, I tried to wiggle my hips down enough to kick him back. I kicked and kicked but couldn't find his legs.

"See, Sissy. You're not hurt, you can move perfectly fine. Now, get up," he ordered, as he kicked the bottoms of my snow boots again. I screamed that I hated him, and that surge of anger gave me the strength to get out from under the four-wheeler. As I staggered to my feet, Dad effortlessly flipped my four-wheeler upright.

I screamed again that I hated him. Dad did not say a word as he twisted my key back in the ignition, roaring the vehicle back to life. He told me to sit down. I was trying not to cry, but my face was so numb, I did not know how successful my efforts were. I sat down, and Dad started walking back to his four-wheeler. I screamed a third time that I hated him.

Dad turned around. There were two deep lines etched between his eyebrows, and I saw his jaw clench. Almost immediately, his expression softened, and a smile grew across his cheeks. "Sissy, I helped you. What would you have done if I wasn't here?" he asked, in a syrupy tone. "Warriors are self-sufficient, Sissy."

"I would not have been on this stupid thing if you were out plowing, where you should have been anyway!" I screamed. Dad spun around and stormed toward me. In one swift movement, Dad ripped my key out of the ignition and chucked it overhand across the field. "You better find that key before it gets dark, or you will not find it until spring," he instructed. Then he stomped back to his four-wheeler and sped away.

Fortunately for me, Dad did not think that one through too

well. The key landed in a tire track of packed snow, so I didn't have to spend much time searching for it. Still, I waited a few extra minutes, so he thought I had to search for it. I did not want to set Dad off again, or even worse, spark a fight between him and Mom.

———

Uncle Joe left for the war in Afghanistan at the beginning of my second-grade school year. Before Joe deployed, he promised to email as often as he could. I did not expect to hear from him often because Dad said Afghanistan's technology was a couple centuries behind us—if they were lucky to have any technology at all. But, true to his word, Uncle Joe emailed as soon as his plane landed.

Mom had the idea for my school to sponsor Uncle Joe's unit, and my elementary school principal agreed. Mr. Friedrich, a third-grade teacher, volunteered to organize the effort. We sent care packages to the soldiers and conducted drives to collect toys for Afghan children. Each student was assigned a soldier as their pen pal to send snail mail and holiday cards to. We held fundraisers and donated the proceeds to a charity of the soldiers' choice. Our effort inspired other classrooms and local schools to sponsor donation drives for the courageous men and women fighting for our country. Our community began to recognize Aunt Steph, Mom, and Mr. Friedrich as local heroes.

A few months after Uncle Joe deployed, a beat-up package arrived on our front porch. Inside were gifts and letters Uncle Joe had been collecting for us. At the very bottom of the package was a long, flat box with my name on it. I ripped off the duct tape that sealed the box shut and found an American flag in the traditional trifold. In a note, Uncle Joe explained that he had saluted the flag every morning and had sent it all the way from Afghanistan just for me. I had never received such a meaningful gift before. Mom helped me thumbtack the flag above my bed so that it was the first thing I saw when I opened my eyes every morning, and the last thing I saw before I closed my eyes at night.

Mom, Jack, and I took a road trip to Indiana that summer and spent a few days decorating Aunt Steph's house to welcome Uncle Joe home from Afghanistan. We had to be at the airplane hangar early on the morning of his arrival to secure good seats. The heat was unforgiving the day he returned. Aunt Steph and I had made T-shirts with Uncle Joe's name on them, and I decided to match mine with a navy blue skirt and American flag nails. We filled our shirts and skirts with frozen water bottles to ensure we would not lose consciousness like others around us.

The hangar door slowly began to lift, and for a while, only the soldiers' boots were visible. Inch by inch, the door rose, revealing more of the soldiers' uniforms. I wrapped my arms around my stomach to suppress the butterflies as I searched desperately for a sign of Uncle Joe. When the soldiers were fully visible, the hangar erupted in cheers.

I stood on my metal chair quietly as I scanned the crowd for Uncle Joe. Once I saw him, I thought my lungs were going to explode from my screams. In that moment, I began to understand what Uncle Joe had meant when he talked about making a sacrifice for your country. The thought of that alone made my belly burn—a feeling I had never experienced before. When I explained this to Mom later that evening, she told me that burning feeling meant that my passions were coming alive.

———

The tree maintenance company Dad started when we moved back to New Jersey from Indiana began to take up a lot of his time. On top of that, Dad got a second job with a local animal control department. Many days I did not see Dad at all, since he got home so late. On the scarce days that Dad did arrive home at a normal hour, he was much quieter than he used to be. He would take his dinner into the living room and watch TV while he ate so he could have time to "rest and relax" before he went upstairs to bed.

He used to hate TV, warning us that it was the government's tactic to rot our brains with new technology, and that they were being dishonest about its long-term effects. Dad had limited the TV programs he watched to NASCAR races, *60 Minutes*, and the morning news. But now Dad had found a show he loved: *The Apprentice*. Dad boasted about Donald Trump's accomplishments—he was a warrior, just like us, and he had built a global multibillion-dollar business from the ground up.

Dad fixated so much on Donald Trump. I wished he would pay attention to us like he did to *The Apprentice*. When I told Dad this, his dinner fork clamored across his plate and he said that Donald Trump was teaching him how to become a better businessman so he did not have to work as much. The other option, Dad said, was that he could stop working altogether. Dad didn't think his family would like how suffering felt, and since he had worked so hard, we had no idea what it meant to suffer.

In a way, Dad was right. I did not know what it felt like to suffer—to worry about not having food in the house, or a warm home to sleep in. But I felt like we were suffering as a result of his absence. I wanted Dad to be at home with us—with his family. And I wanted Dad to acknowledge how hard Mom was working, too.

Dad was gone so much, and as Jack and I got older, it was clear to me how essential Mom was to our family. In my opinion, Mom's work was far more important than his. But Dad was growing more sharp-tongued with Mom, and I did not want to spark an argument. When I was not at school, I tried to help Mom with household chores and caring for Jack to take any load off her that I could.

———

Around this time, Steph and Joe learned that the army was moving them to Washington, DC. Soon after their big move, Mom took Jack and me to their new apartment in Arlington to help them unpack, just as they had helped us when we moved to Indiana. We arrived late at night, and when we woke up the next morning, Steph brought Jack and me out onto their balcony, and I saw the Washington skyline for the first time. It took my breath away in a way that the familiar New York City skyline never had.

After Uncle Joe finished his workday at the Pentagon, he met us across the Potomac River in Washington to sightsee. After Joe parked his pickup truck near the Tidal Basin, we began to walk on the Mall. We walked along the river toward the Lincoln Memorial, then planned to walk all the way to the US Capitol. Joe and I were the history buffs in the group, and we stopped to inspect every monument and plaque, passing the memorials to the Vietnam War, the Korean War, and World War II. We stood near the Reflecting Pool and drank in the view that stretched to the majestic, white-domed Capitol.

We stopped at a food truck selling hot dogs and Cokes for a quick bite to eat, and chose the benches near the Washington Monument as our impromptu picnic spot. Mom and Aunt Steph were discussing our shopping trip to Pentagon City mall the next day. But I was too mesmerized to pay attention—my eyes were fixed on the blinking red lights atop the Washington Monument.

While I had spent less than forty-eight hours in Washington, DC, during that first trip, I was inexplicably, physically, emotionally, and spiritually tethered to the city. I felt a magnetic bond—a sense of premonition—that Washington was my home.

———

As if Dad didn't have enough work, he decided that the community needed an authentic Italian gelato store. Mom supported the idea, knowing it would give her a measure of freedom. Dad had assured her that he would cut back his hours at the tree company and animal control to offer his hand at the store, since she would need to spend most of her time building that business. Instead,

Dad spent more time at both the tree company and animal control. Mom was often left to build the new business alone.

Mom empowered me as her trusted sidekick in the new endeavor. Our mornings started hours before the store opened for business and ended long after it had closed. Mom, Jack, and I went to Sam's Club every morning to purchase gallons of milk and industrial-sized bags of sugar. Later, it was usually just Mom and me who closed up at night, often staying well past midnight if we were making gelato for the next day. I struggled to stay awake despite wanting to help, and Mom would make a bed for me out of kitchen rags when she saw my eyelids begin to droop. She would apologize that Dad or an employee wasn't there to help. But I didn't mind—I loved spending the time with Mom.

I watched in awe as Mom built the business from the ground up, all while juggling bookkeeping for Dad's tree maintenance company, managing our household, and raising me and Jack. The gelato store would only last a year or so before Dad told Mom we had to sell it, but while it was ours, I loved helping Mom there—especially engaging with our customers. I was good at it. One day, I was chatting with a man who started asking me questions about my parents' business. "I've got some questions," he announced. I listened intently.

After twenty minutes or so, Mom came out from the back and diplomatically ended the conversation. When I asked Mom why that customer had so many questions for me, she explained, "You're an approachable person, Cass. People like talking to you. It's a good thing."

I internalized what Mom had said. Suddenly I began noticing that adults did seem to enjoy talking to me, and I realized that I'd rather talk to them than to children my own age.

———

Dad stopped by the shop one afternoon unexpectedly in the animal control van with a bunch of feral cats in the back. He opened the doors to show our customers the cats and tried to auction them off for adoption. Mom politely asked Dad to step into the store so they could have a private discussion. Dad pulled one of the cats out of its crate, and as it thrashed and screeched, Dad pushed it toward Mom's face and asked if she wanted to hold it. Mom shook her head and again asked Dad to come inside.

He flung the cat back into the van and told me to get in the front seat. "Come on, Sissy. Let's get out of here. We're going for a ride," he said. I looked at Mom, unsure whose side I should take. She smiled and nodded, my signal to go with him.

Dad told me that we were going to the place that would make us wealthy—that we wouldn't need to play the lottery anymore. I had almost forgotten that he and I had once been in the habit of buying lottery tickets together. When we pulled into a big yard, he triumphantly exclaimed, "Welcome to paradise, Sissy." I was confused. The place looked nothing like what I had pictured paradise might look like. It looked like a dump.

He let the feral cats go. Then he handed me a long-handled wooden poker and told me to "start looting." I asked him what I was looking for. "Anything that looks like treasure."

We found a splintered jewelry box with a few earrings.

When he dropped me back off at the shop, I bragged to Mom about our treasure hunt at the dump.

"He took you where?" Mom blinked.

"To the dump. We found jewels!"

Dad began taking his new hobby more seriously than he had taken his hobbies in the past. His treasure hunt went from junkyards to dumpsters, with no treasure too small or cheap. Dad was certain he would eventually find a treasure that would make us rich.

Mom's patience with Dad was stretched thin. With my well-developed eavesdropping skills, I would listen to their intense conversations whenever Dad decided to come home at night. Sometimes Dad would storm out of the house, shouting that he would never come back because Mom, Jack, and I were all too ungrateful to have a man like him as head of our household. I would run after him, begging him to stay.

I wished for things to go back to how they had been when we lived on Reed Road, when Dad still thought of me as his best friend.

Mom did her best to fix things herself, but she was running on fumes physically and emotionally. I started feeling more and more anxious, so Mom began to research homeopathic remedies for anxiety. She made concoctions of essential oils and herbs and found ways to incorporate them into my daily routines, spritzing me with the essential oils before I went to school, and restuffing plush toys with lavender stems for me to cuddle when I started to get the jitters.

I loved that Mom went to such lengths to keep her promise to always protect me. But what I wanted most was for Dad to give her the support she needed to keep our family together.

But it wasn't meant to be. When I was in fifth grade, around Christmas, they sat me down after Jack went to bed, and Mom explained that we were starting a new adventure. We were going to move into a town house just down the street from where I was born.

From the look on Dad's face, I knew he was not moving with us. Mom said that they were going to temporarily separate while they worked on making their marriage stronger. I think all three of us wanted that to be true, but none of us believed it.

———

Our first night in the town house, our first home as a family of three, felt more unfamiliar and frightening than the immediate aftermath of past moves. I struggled to fall asleep, tossing and turning until I heard Mom rustling in the hallway and saw the silhouette of her body at the top of the staircase. I crept out of bed and startled her when I sat down next to her. She began rubbing her eyes, and I asked her if everything was okay. Mom told me that she wanted to call the landlord because the air filters were bad, and that her allergies were bothering her. But I knew she was sad. I was sad, too. Sensing that she didn't want to talk about what was on her mind, I told her that my allergies were acting up, too. I wrapped my arms around Mom and we sat there for a long while.

A few days later, Jack and I were scheduled to spend our first night with Dad. He didn't want to see Mom, instructing her to drop us in a pizza parlor parking lot with our overnight bags. He expected us to be sitting on a bench waiting for him. Since it was winter and we were young, Mom kept us in her car. When he saw her car idling in the parking lot, he drove past and angrily called her, telling her she had to leave. They eventually got to a compromise—Mom drove to the other side of the parking lot, letting us out of the car, and waited until Dad picked us up.

The three of us ate dinner at the pizza parlor. Dad was not very talkative. I did my best to entertain little Jack. When Dad drove us back to the house on Poor Farm Road, he asked if I cared if he went back to work for a couple of hours. I did mind, I told him. It was a school night, and we were still a family. Dad seemed agitated, and asked when Mom was picking us up for school in the morning. I told him it was his responsibility to take us to school. He broke down—it was Mom's fault that our family was getting torn apart, so it was her responsibility to take us to school, he said.

Dad yelled that Mom had already turned me against him. I could not figure out how to calm him down on my own, so I called Mom and asked her what I should do, and she said she was on her way. By the time Mom arrived, Jack and I were waiting in the driveway with our overnight bags. Dad would not let her in the house, and Jack and I would never spend another night there.

As Mom, Jack, and I adjusted to our new life, we found support in a community of friends who became family to us. My two best friends since elementary school became more like my sisters during those years. But when the three of us entered eighth grade together, both girls abruptly had to move out of state. I felt the world shift beneath me again, and poured myself into school.

My eighth-grade history teacher took notice that I was especially interested in his US history class, and asked if I had thought about running for student government. I shook my head. He told me about the mayor's program, the Youth Advisory Board. My teacher served on the board alongside the mayor, and each year he was tasked to select three students who would serve as board members for each high school class. The student representatives were to go to town council meetings to represent our high school, and then relay meeting minutes to the senior administrative school staff.

I was not sure whether I would fit into a role like that, even though the opportunity piqued my interest. I did not know much about government other than what Dad told me about not trusting people who worked for it. I was apprehensive and was not sure if local government was something I should be part of.

But after I thought about it, I decided it might look good on a college application. I was already planning to leave Pennington for college in five short years. I accepted the opportunity, believing I had nothing to lose.

CHAPTER 3

High School

I WAS SOUND ASLEEP when Mom came into my bedroom and stood over me to see if I was awake. I had not been, but was now. Mom sat down on the edge of my bed and told me that she had just returned from the doctor, who had taken a tissue sample from the growing bump on her arm to biopsy. I sat up. Mom said it was cancer. Sarcoma cancer. The doctor thought they had caught it in time.

Was she going to be okay? Mom said she would spend the summer going to Sloan Kettering for surgery, followed by weeks of radiation treatments, if they were necessary. She ran her fingers through my hair and promised me that my summer wouldn't be affected. I did not care about my summer; I told her she had to survive. Mom smiled and told me that everything would be fine.

Until that point, Mom had seemed invincible. We had never encountered any hardship she could not overcome. In my heart, I knew that even if something happened to her, we would never return to Dad's. In the years since their divorce, I had learned that blood alone does not determine who family is. Home is a feeling, a sense of security and belonging. If you have people who love and care about you, you have a home.

———

"Hutch!" seemed to echo through the high school hallways. I learned quickly that I had inherited the nickname the teachers had used for Dad when he had studied at my high school. Dad had

spent the whole summer bragging around town that I was starting high school and had reached out to his former teachers and
school staff he had known to "keep an eye" on me. I was a good
student, responsible and independent, but I also valued my privacy, just as he had. But Dad was becoming a bit of a town gossip.
I did my best to keep my head down and distance myself from the
chaos Dad thrived in.

When Jack decided that he wanted to try to repair his relationship
with Dad, I was supportive but privately skeptical. Jack wanted
the three of us to go deer hunting, and I encouraged him to ask
Dad, who surprisingly agreed. But the plan was abruptly cut short
after Dad took Jack to purchase his hunting gear. When Dad unexpectedly dropped Jack off at home, Jack said that he had wronged
Dad, and felt responsible for upsetting him. I told Jack that if Dad
was upset, he could be sure it wasn't his fault.

Dad texted me a few days later to tell me that he had left a surprise for Jack and me in the mailbox. I pulled out a gallon-sized
Ziploc bag with something weighty wrapped in aluminum foil. As
I brought it inside, Mom and I exchanged a look, and she told me
to take it to the kitchen sink. We opened it on the counter and
unwrapped the foil to discover two deer hearts, still warm and
dripping with blood.

I was tempted to text Dad but stopped myself. He responded
to my silence by asking if I had opened the gift. I said yes, and
thanked him. He didn't respond.

———

The first election I genuinely paid attention to was in 2012.
Despite my family never speaking much about politics and the
fact that I was still too young to vote, I took it upon myself to
study both parties' platforms and the nominees for president,
and watched the presidential debates. Assigned to watch the

debate between Republican candidate Mitt Romney and President Barack Obama for school, I turned the project into a case study of both candidates. I spent an extensive amount of time researching each party's policy platforms, and found myself relating to the Republican Party. I decided that if I could vote, I would cast my ballot for Mitt Romney.

During this campaign season, something inside of me clicked. I felt a gravitational pull toward politics—the notion that politics were central to history and had a profound impact on the everyday lives of Americans. I felt a shift in me, that politics were part of my life's purpose.

I told Mom and Steph about my newfound passion. Politics was an unfamiliar business to Mom, but what she knew about it she didn't like—she had appropriated some of Dad's hostility to government. Aunt Steph was more encouraging. But, Mom and Steph both had seen my patriotism grow over the years and told me that since the time I was little, they knew I had a higher calling.

I embraced the uncertainty, knowing this would be a journey shaped by every choice I made. Soon, I would discover that politics was not just my passion, but a pathway—one that would lead me to heights I could not yet fathom.

———

When Mom was declared cancer-free in the middle of my sophomore year of high school, she decided it was time for a fresh start and began looking for a house to move Jack and me into. We found one listed on Craigslist and drove over one evening after the sun went down.

Mom and I peered through the back window and could see peeling paint in a few of the rooms, and holes in the baseboards. But I noticed there was a gas oven, which I knew Mom preferred to electric, and there were ceiling fans—a plus since the house didn't have air-conditioning. "I think it's cute," Mom declared. "What do you think?"

I heard cars roaring down the highway next to the house. I hesitated, but I knew Mom was proud to be able to move Jack and me into a house. "Let's do it, Mom." She smiled.

―――――

We went to the house one night to drop off some boxes, and a truck was in the driveway. For years Mom had spoken highly of a man named Paul, who she had met at work. While she had not yet admitted she might have some interest in Paul, I had a sense of it by the way she spoke about him.

I looked at Mom and gasped. "Is Paul here?" I asked, excited at the possibility that I would finally meet him. Her face turned pink and I bolted into the house so fast I forgot to close the car door. I startled Paul when I rushed through the back door, and Mom quickly followed. Without preamble or introduction, I launched in, speaking admiringly of how much Paul's craftmanship had transformed the inside of our new house. Mom apologized for my rudeness and the first impression I'd made. Paul and I exchanged a look—it was all we had to go on so far, but I sensed a camaraderie.

Paul joked with Mom, saying he wished she had been as excited to see him as I had been. I turned to Mom and crossed my arms. "Are you just going to stand there, or are you going to introduce us?" She looked mortified and swatted at me. "Behave yourself, Cassidy Jacqueline!" Paul broke in. "Hey, now, I'm with Cassidy on this one. You're being very awkward." From that moment on, I knew they were a match. He quickly became our nucleus: Mom's soulmate, Jack's role model, and my best friend. He made our new house a home.

―――――

Since our home was practically on Dad's drive to Poor Farm Road, he began keeping tabs on us. Earlier that spring, he told me to meet him for breakfast at the Ewing Diner every Sunday. He had been withholding child support off and on since the divorce when I was in fifth grade, always paying eventually but usually after substantial machinations. Mom never asked for alimony, though we relied on his payments, since Jack and I never stayed at his house. Dad refused to speak with Mom under any circumstances, so I was the designated recipient to collect the checks. The once-a-week meet-ups were ideal for Dad, allowing him to retain minimal responsibility as a caregiver. Admittedly, I also looked forward to spending a little time with Dad.

One afternoon when I was walking home from school, Dad texted me to check the front door. I texted back and thanked him. In my mind, our weekly engagement was helping to repair our relationship. Clearly he had left the check without my needing to beg for it.

I hurried up the front porch steps and didn't see a check taped to the door. Out of the corner of my eye, I caught a glimpse of what Dad had actually wanted me to find: two snapping turtles making their way across the porch.

I spun and instantly spotted Dad's pickup idling in the parking lot across the street. I was spitting mad. Without a second thought, I snatched the turtles by their tails and stormed toward him. I chucked the turtles into the bed of his truck and immediately began walking back to the house.

"Sissy Hutch! Did you like my present?" he called out the window. I raised my arm into the air and flashed him the middle finger without turning back around.

———

Mom and Paul went away for a night to the Jersey Shore. My stomach had been bothering me for a few days, but I decided to have a few of my girlfriends over for the night anyway, since I didn't have the house to myself often.

I awoke the next morning in soaking-wet sheets and with an acute pain in my gut. I dialed Mom a few times before she finally answered, irked that I had woken her up so early on her first vacation in years. I explained my symptoms, expecting her to tell me the ailment I had. "Call your dad," she advised. It wasn't quite the answer I had hoped for, but since she was a few hours away, it would have to do.

I reluctantly called Dad. When I explained what was happening, he told me to come straight to his house. "I'll have the operating table ready for you, Sissy," he said. "You get to pick out your own pocketknife for the surgery." I was lying in the fetal position on the bathroom floor and told him I wasn't in the mood for his games. He urged me again to come to his house, promising that he would take better care of me than any doctor at the hospital would.

I hung up on him and shook one of my friends awake. She agreed to stay at the house with Jack until Mom and Paul got home from the Shore. I drove myself to the hospital and parked at the entrance to the emergency room.

Not much time had passed when the doctors determined that I needed an emergency appendectomy. The next thing I remember is waking up in a hospital room with Mom and Paul standing over me. Mom was sympathetic at first, apologizing profusely for not listening to me sooner. But then her temper flared. She said that I had been reckless for driving myself to the hospital in my condition and that I should have called Dad. I needed to be less stubborn, she said.

I wanted to tell her that I had called him, but there was no point. It wouldn't change what had already transpired, and I didn't want Mom to feel bad. Plus my story was much more fun to tell because of it.

———

I arrived at the high school with just minutes to spare before the SAT exam began. Most students had formed study groups to comb through their flash cards from the preparatory classes they had taken all summer. That was great for them, if cramming for a standardized test increased their confidence that the expensive classes would pay off. I wasn't envious of friends who spent their days locked in sterile classrooms, but I was chastened when they ridiculed me for not taking the test as seriously as they had. I promised myself I wouldn't study a lick. And other than watching a YouTube video on test-taking strategies, I didn't.

Mom had been worried sick about my going to college. The financial burden of paying for college was heavy, especially since Dad was unreliable. I reminded her that he had opened a college fund account when I was a toddler. Mom didn't have a response, which I took as a bad sign. Still, I knew how Dad had stressed the importance of college to me since I was a child. I was confident that he would help pay for some of my education or at least help me figure out how I could pay for a portion of it myself.

Deep down, I suspected Mom was afraid I would leave and never come back, which was a valid fear. I didn't intend to move back to Pennington. But Mom and I knew how to do life together, and even though we didn't always arrive at the life she had envisioned for us at each stage, I was grateful for every moment of what we built together. The only thing I wanted was to feel that Mom was excited for me to go to college.

I visited Gettysburg College, fell in love with it, and decided not to tour other universities. From my first moment on campus, I felt that Gettysburg was where the next chapter of my life was meant to unfold. And then I received a small envelope, not the big one. I had been wait-listed, and my future crashed before my eyes.

Mom tried to convince me to take a year off and work. That's what she had done, she reminded me, and then it turned out she did not need to go to college anyway. I reminded her that times were different then—I needed a college degree, especially to pursue my dream of working in politics. I began to think that maybe a gap year might not be such a bad idea—it would give me an opportunity to build my savings account so I would not have to worry about college finances as much. But in my heart, I knew I needed to leave for college now. It would only get more difficult to leave Pennington if I waited.

Late one night when we were visiting Joe and Steph in Stuttgart, Germany, Joe crept into the bedroom that Mom, Jack, and I shared and motioned for me to follow him outside. He asked if I was considering a gap year because it was what *I* wanted, not Mom. I considered his question before shaking my head no. He nodded, and then asked if I had heard where his next duty station was: "Williamsburg, Virginia. Fort Eustis. Didn't you apply to a school near there?"

I had. Christopher Newport University.

———

Two days before high school graduation, I drove to Dad's shop. Thankfully, his trucks weren't there, so I quickly scurried to the back door to tape an envelope to it, with tickets to the ceremony. I had texted Dad for several weeks asking if he wanted to come, but he never texted back. I had decided to make one last good-faith effort to connect before I left town for good.

Grandma flew to New Jersey for my graduation. We all took photos in the front yard before heading to the high school. When I walked across the stage, I saw Mom, Paul, Jack, and Grandma stand up. The people who mattered most had shown up.

We were mingling on the field waiting for the traffic to clear before we left the school when I saw Grandma's wide-eyed stare. I looked over my shoulder.

Dad was standing outside the fence with a few of his buddies. "Sissy Hutch graduated high school!" he shouted, and whistled loudly to summon me in his direction. I cringed, and with a glance appealed to the rest of my family.

And then I walked over to Dad.

PART II

BECOME

CHAPTER 4

The Washington Start

B EING THE FIRST PERSON in my family to go to college, I did not know what to expect.

Mom, Paul, and Jack drove me to Newport News in Virginia. When we arrived at the college, I realized that for most of my life, it was us against the world. "Mom, I don't think I can do this. I think I want to come home," I said, hoping she would remind me how much I had wanted to go to college.

"Oh, Cassidy, just come home then," she said. "We can leave tomorrow."

I found her response strangely reassuring. *I'll always be welcome home.* I knew I had to leave Pennington to start afresh and begin my own life. A piece of my heart would always remain there, but it was time to move on.

Thankfully, Aunt Steph and Uncle Joe's house was only fifteen minutes from campus, which helped ease the transition. Still, as I waved goodbye to my family the next day, I experienced my first pangs of homesickness. But as much as I would miss them, I was proud that I was hitting a generational family milestone and claiming a future I had dreamed of. It felt liberating.

During my first week at CNU, in the lobby of my dorm, a six-foot-tall lacrosse player with piercing blue eyes caught my eye. He was filling a water bottle. We made eye contact, and before he noticed how flustered I was, he purposely squirted water at me. I was hooked. William and I started dating right away and became each other's rock. What social life I had involved him, and I was a calming influence on him. We were both majoring in political science, and we shared an ambition to enter public service.

College was a means to an end for me, so I wanted to do well in my studies in order to get a good job in Washington. I needed to work as soon as I could because I had to earn money to pay school costs. My parents helped some, but I also had loans, state financial assistance, and savings from various jobs throughout high school.

By sophomore year, the 2016 election was approaching. Neither candidate, Hillary Clinton nor Donald Trump, jumped out at me at the time, but the moderate policies that Trump embraced were appealing to me. As a Republican, I decided I would vote for him, though I did not think he would win the election.

It was still dark outside as I drove to my polling location the morning of November 8, 2016. I convinced Aunt Steph to come early with me, warning her the lines would probably be wrapped around the building. We met in the parking lot and, to my surprise, were among the first people there. We had been texting Mom and Paul, who had also woken up early to vote. I was proud to cast my first ballot, aware that only a hundred years before, women hadn't had the right. My family shared my enthusiasm for voting for Donald J. Trump.

Until I attended the Trump 100th-day rally in April 2017, I had been interested from afar. Out of curiosity, I checked out the rally, with William, who came begrudgingly, given his reservations about Trump. I was transfixed once Trump came onstage. His magnetism electrified the crowd. Suddenly, some of his more controversial viewpoints seemed to fade away as the energy buzzed around the arena, sweeping me up in the fervor.

That January, I had applied to every House and Senate Republican office internship, determined to land at least one interview. I managed to get four, one in the Senate and three in the House. As I was about to accept an offer, I received an email for an interview in the office of majority whip Rep. Steve Scalise, of Louisiana. I prepared relentlessly for the phone interview, making flash cards with biographical information about Steve and other members in leadership and historical facts about the Capitol. Dennis, Steve's internship coordinator, quickly put me at ease on that first call. We engaged in more of a conversation than an interview, and I was impressed by his relaxed yet professional demeanor. At the end of our conversation, he told me how outgoing and personable I was, and that he would be in touch soon.

A few weeks later, I received an email from Dennis welcoming me to the summer 2017 internship class. Although Steve held more conservative viewpoints than I did, I recognized how competitive it was to get an internship in the leadership office, especially without connections.

Before I could accept, I knew that I had to find an affordable place to live. When William's family learned about my internship offer, they quickly invited us to live in their home. I couldn't wait to start this new chapter with William in DC, acknowledging that his family's generosity opened the door.

———

Leading up to my start date, I was anxious about entering the unfamiliar world of politics. On my first day, I met Dennis at the right time and place—the south Capitol steps. Because the House was in recess, the Capitol was quiet. Dennis gave me a quick tour of the whip's office, and on our way, we walked onto the House floor through Statuary Hall. We stopped in the Rotunda, and an unexpected feeling of belonging swept over me as I admired its grandiosity and the eight enormous oil paintings lining its walls. The whip's office was less grand: it was made up of three floors connected via a spiral staircase, with staffers and interns working in every nook and cranny, flying from office to office.

I ate lunch by myself on the Capitol steps that first day, remembering that as a child I had dreamed of working here. I took a selfie and sent it to Mom, who posted it on Facebook, along with a photo at the same spot of me as a child: "Cassidy then and now." That was the only time I had lunch away from my desk for the rest of the internship.

Leadership offices serve a separate purpose from typical congressional offices, which focus on a representative's district. As the majority party, Republicans controlled what legislation was brought to the floor for a vote, but that didn't guarantee a particular bill would pass. That's where the majority whip came in—Steve's job was to make sure that House Republicans were unified on how they were going to vote, and to persuade skeptical members to acquiesce to the majority position. To accomplish this, the whip needs a staff who knows the representatives and the pressing needs of their districts.

That first week, senior aides on the team encouraged me to use the recess period to study so I would be able to identify each member. I made flash cards with faces, names, states, districts, and basic biographical details. I used the information to help establish a camaraderie with them and build relationships.

I was immediately captivated by the job and realized I wanted to stay on Capitol Hill for the rest of the summer, though my internship in the whip's office was slated to end mid-June. I worried my decision to stay on the Hill would be financially irresponsible, so I sought advice from a senior staffer, who encouraged me to apply for a second unpaid internship in the Senate. If I could land an internship in the Senate, I would gain valuable experience and connections in both chambers, which would pay off in a few years when I began to apply for jobs post-graduation. I took his advice, printed one hundred copies of my résumé to drop one off at every Senate office, and planned to take on a second job during the school year. Within a few weeks, I accepted an internship in the office of Senator Ted Cruz, of Texas, agreeing to forgo my vacation with William and his family to the Jersey Shore. William cautioned me that I was working more than in any normal internship and had been reserving no time for our relationship. I loved him and my job, and was unsure how to have time and energy for both.

When the House reconvened the following week, I quickly learned that Steve Scalise was a skilled whip who made himself completely accessible to the House Republican Conference. I was in proximity to members, who were in and out of our office all day, a level of access priceless to an intern. I built a rapport with them by using the information from my flash cards that I had memorized effortlessly. Before long I was on a first-name basis with many of the members and began to understand that I might have an aptitude for making people feel comfortable.

On a hot, muggy mid-June morning, I got off the Metro and walked to the Capitol when a police officer swept me inside, bypassing the magnetometers. "You need to get up to your office. Your boss was shot."

I went into Steve's office with other staffers and turned on the news. We saw images of Eugene Simpson Stadium Park, in Alexandria, where Steve and his Republican teammates had been practicing for the annual congressional charity baseball game. A gunman had opened fire, spraying the field with sixty rounds and hitting six people, including Steve, and two members of his security detail, David Bailey and Crystal Griner. Had Capitol Police not been there, it would have been a massacre. Steve had dragged himself across the baseball field after being shot in the hip while David and Crystal were still engaged with the shooter.

We watched as Steve was helicoptered to MedStar Washington Hospital Center for emergency surgery. He was in very bad shape, with internal injuries and uncontrolled bleeding. For the next eighteen hours, he was in and out of surgery.

The staff went together to the congressional baseball game the next evening, all wearing Team Scalise T-shirts. An intense bipartisan swell of concern and care washed over the stadium when Steve's name was announced with an update on his current condition. Everyone in the stadium stood and applauded. It made me realize how devoted I was to Steve and how bonded his staffers were as a team.

On my last day, I participated in a venerable tradition of departing leadership staffers. Steve's office had access to an underground bunker that members had used to flee the Capitol in August 1814, during the War of 1812, when British troops set fire to the building. As of June 2017, it was the worst attack on the Capitol in our nation's history. That bunker is sealed now, but it was a long-standing ritual for staffers to climb down to the entrance and sign the door. I left my name on the door with a heavy heart, not wanting to leave. Steve, still recovering, didn't return to his post until the end of September, when both sides of the House gave him a standing ovation.

———

I moved to Cruz's office at the beginning of July 2017 and realized within a day that I preferred the House. The Senate was intentionally designed for the wheels of government to turn more slowly there, making it harder to get things done. This was a necessary check on the House's more fast-paced environment. And senators were much less approachable than House members, including Cruz, whose politics I disagreed with.

I had only one memorable interaction with Cruz in the time I worked in his office, at an intern lunch where the food was as bland as the conversation. Cruz had gone to Princeton as an undergraduate, and when I was introduced to him, I mentioned that I was from nearby Pennington.

"What do you order at Hoagie Haven?" he asked, referring to a beloved sandwich shop in Princeton.

"A Sanchez, extra dirty," I replied: chicken cutlet, American cheese, mozzarella sticks, fries, and Sanchez sauce.

He said, "I like the Phat Lady." Cheesesteak, mozzarella sticks, fries, ketchup, and hot sauce.

"Oh, you're one of *those* people," I joked.

He said flatly, "It's the best." He didn't seem to get my humor.

Toward the end of my time working for Cruz, the Senate voted against repealing Obamacare. John McCain, terminally ill with brain cancer, dramatically cast a late-night vote, giving the bill a thumbs-down on the Senate floor. Cruz, a proponent of repealing Obamacare, was livid. I had long admired McCain, and found his action an inspiring example of an American patriot putting his country before his party.

The night before my final day on the Hill, I delivered thank-you notes to several House offices. My last stop was the office of Speaker Paul Ryan, of Wisconsin, where I stepped out onto the Speaker's Balcony a final time before returning to college. With its stunning views of the Mall, it was one of my favorite places to visit for a moment of peace. When I had visited Washington as a child, I'd looked up in awe at the Washington Monument and beyond it to the Capitol. Now I was standing at the other end of that vista, in a place that I had once dreamed of being part of.

I would leave the Hill having learned more about government during my summer with Scalise and Cruz, and in the upcoming internship at the White House, than in four years of college. I valued the experience I gained to be able to discern the subtleties and needs of various personalities. And I learned that my ambitions weren't outside my reach.

———

When I started my third year at CNU, I knew that I would apply for a White House internship the following summer. With experience on both sides of the Capitol, I believed that the White House internship would strengthen my résumé when I applied for jobs on the Hill after graduation.

One available internship jumped out at me: in the Office of Legislative Affairs (OLA). OLA was the liaison between the executive and legislative branches of government. The office was tasked with harmonizing the president's legislative agenda with Capitol Hill—or, in the Trump administration, finding ways to reinvent tradition and decorum between the two branches. In OLA I would be able to observe the intricacies of policymaking while continuing to develop my understanding of Congress. I sent in my application, identifying OLA as my first choice for placement, and emailed a copy of my application to several Hill staffers I kept in touch with.

A few months later, I accepted a White House summer internship in OLA, set to begin in May. I was ecstatic. William accepted an internship in Washington, too, and his family graciously let us stay with them again that summer.

———

On my first day at the White House, Grace, an OLA staffer on the House team, met me on West Executive Avenue, greeting me warmly. Before walking to OLA's House and Senate team offices in the East Wing, Grace gave me a quick tour of the West Wing. As we passed quietly by the Oval Office, where a Secret Service agent was posted outside the closed door, she whispered, "The president's in there." But I already knew, having heard his unmistakable voice. We passed through the Rose Garden, a place that I would come to view as a safe haven.

My internship granted me an invaluable perch in the East

Wing. OLA was divided into two teams, one for the House and one for the Senate. I had been assigned to the House team. With the 2018 midterm elections approaching, the president's schedule was crowded with congressional events. I interacted frequently with House members when they came to the White House and accompanied them to meetings or events with the president.

I also spent a lot of time on the Hill, where lawmakers were busy in advance of the August recess. Congress typically adjourns early in the fall in election years, so the best chance to pass bills presents itself in July.

The OLA internship ended in August, and on my final day, I signed my intern desk and left the way I first entered—through the Rose Garden. My heart broke a little walking out of the north gate for the final time, but I had a feeling I would be back in some capacity.

———

Back in Newport News, William and I adjusted to our final year of college. We were relaxing on our front porch on a balmy summer evening, the crickets making the only sound, when my phone started buzzing with a stream of texts from Dad.

I had recently heard from his girlfriend at the time, who'd found my number on his phone and called to congratulate me for starting my senior year; she was looking forward to attending graduation, she told me. When he found out about the call, he considered it a betrayal. It led to a barrage of hateful messages. He said he no longer considered me his daughter.

In the past when things like that had happened, I had managed to go numb. This time his words were meant to leave a wound too deep to ignore. I felt it as a physical pain that hurt all weekend, until William convinced me to leave the house with him.

We were buying gardening supplies at Home Depot when the hurt overtook me again. William pulled me close to his chest. "It's okay to cry. But you've always found a way to heal yourself. You're going to be okay." For years I had clung to the hope that my love for my dad would make him a better man—make him the father I wanted him to be.

I would soon have a college degree, which meant independence from my past.

———

With spring came graduation. Mom, Paul, and Jack were waiting on my front porch following the graduation ceremony.

"Remember when I tried to convince you to come home the night before freshman move-in?" Mom asked. "I'm proud you stayed."

Mom and I stayed up all night cleaning the house and packing. We would drive to New Jersey the next day, after making a stop in Washington for an official interview I had for a job at OLA. William and I had planned to move in with his parents in DC until we found a place of our own in the city.

I met with Ben Howard, the director of the OLA House team, whose calm demeanor disarmed me. I smoothed my light pink dress and adjusted my necklace as I walked toward him. "Hey," he called out, "I hear you're finally eligible for a paid job."

"Yep," I answered. "Only took me four years."

Ben had been in the White House when I was interning on the Hill and had returned when I interned at the White House. He had deep roots in the House leadership, having worked for both Kevin McCarthy and Steve Scalise. As we sat on sofas in his office, I handed him my résumé, neatly packaged in a leather portfolio. We chatted about our mutual affection for the House, and our passion for legislative affairs, which we both considered one of the most important offices in the White House. He seemed like a moderate conservative, and his father had also worked in legislative affairs, in both Bush administrations.

He asked what my immediate plans were, and I told him that William and I were going to Europe for two weeks. I pulled up an

Excel sheet on my phone, handing it to him to show our itinerary. With a quick laugh, he shook his head. "Wow, you're really organized, aren't you."

"Yes, I am," I replied. "I track everything in my life on Excel and Microsoft Outlook." I tapped my head and smiled. "It's what keeps me sharp."

He handed my phone back. "Well, I'm not organized, and I know for sure the president isn't organized." He paused. "So when do you get back from Europe?"

CHAPTER 5

Legislative Affairs

"BACK FOR GOOD?" the uniformed Secret Service officer asked as I passed him my driver's license. "Back for good," I replied with a smile. I went straight to get my White House identification badge. Eric Ueland, the director of OLA, had received permission to cut my onboarding short so that I could be on staff in time for the congressional picnic at the White House, on June 21.

After picking up my ID, I walked to the East Wing, cutting through the Rose Garden. There was no breeze, and the humidity kept the scent of the blooms hanging in the air.

Reaching the office, I was surprised to discover that I was the first staffer to arrive. Ben Howard walked in moments later. "You beat me on your first day," he observed. "I knew I made a good choice." The rest of the House team arrived shortly after. My new colleagues, all male, escorted me to my first senior staff meeting in Eric Ueland's West Wing office. It was Eric's first official day, too. I introduced myself to him, and he asked that I stand next to him as he ran through the week ahead for Congress. Before he turned the floor over to colleagues, he reintroduced me to the OLA staff, reminding everyone that I was now the point person for all House member inquiries.

Back in the East Wing, I went into Ben's office with a list I had prepared: I needed access to his email and calendar, to make sure his schedule was organized and ran smoothly. My second priority was anything related to member services. He took a long look at my list and started laughing, placing it on top of a stack of papers on his chronically messy desk. "This is all great," Ben said. "I wasn't expecting to hit the ground running this fast, but it's great." I started to respond as he stood up. "I actually have to be up on the Hill right now," he said, cutting me off. "Why don't you come. As you know, the best way to learn about the place is on your feet."

We walked outside and got into a black SUV idling on East Executive Avenue waiting to take us up to Capitol Hill. "The first day of every week Congress is in session, I meet with Kevin McCarthy, Speaker Nancy Pelosi, occasionally Liz Cheney, and their chiefs of staff—all separate meetings," he explained, as he scrolled through hundreds of unread emails. I made a mental note to learn who the contacts were for his meetings, and to get access to his email as soon as possible. "We'll head back to the White House after these meetings," he told me, "and then come back to the Hill for whip team meetings, Republican Conference meetings, and when the House is voting."

We got out at the south Capitol entrance, walking straight to House minority leader Kevin McCarthy's office. Ben had worked for Kevin for many years and developed a professional relationship and friendship with him, as well as his chief of staff, Dan Meyer. Ben introduced me.

"Leader McCarthy," I said, extending my hand.

"Kevin, please," he replied. "We're all friends here."

Pelosi's staff canceled our meeting that morning, so we headed to Liz Cheney's office, in the Cannon House Office Building. Liz was Republican Conference chair then, in charge of forming a unified Republican message on issues. Her position was third in House Republican leadership, behind minority whip Steve Scalise and minority leader Kevin McCarthy. On the way, Ben advised me not to address Liz informally. "She takes her job very seriously," he explained. "Not that Kevin and Steve don't. But Liz is all business until you really get to know her . . . if she lets you."

When we reached her office, an aide whisked Ben into her personal office while I waited in the lobby. I don't know if it was because Ben suggested it, but I did sense an air of formality in Liz's office that felt more traditional, old-school Republican, where staff operated by the book, people were addressed as "Mr." or "Ms.," and you were expected to observe certain courtesies.

Back in the White House that morning, I began digging into my new assignments, starting with an email to all House members and their chiefs of staff, introducing myself as their new point of contact in OLA. Over the next few weeks, I scheduled meetings with the heads of various White House offices instrumental in the care of members. I brought homemade baked goods to each meeting, and before I left, I had collected biographical information— birthdays, kids' names, that kind of thing—for future use when I might send a card or schedule a Capitol tour. As the forward-facing staffer for the House OLA, I wanted to be on good terms with everyone in the White House who could help us advance the president's agenda on the Hill.

After votes the next night, we hosted a dinner at Trattoria Alberto for about twenty members. Former speaker John Boehner was standing under the awning, smoking a Camel, when we arrived. "You're new." Ben answered for me. "Yeah, second day." About an hour into the dinner, Boehner came over to our table to address the members. He looked down at my cranberry vodka and whispered, "Dark liquor or red wine from now on." Then he tugged on the ends of my hair, saying, "And lose the ponytail."

Ben and I were usually of the same mind. He seldom had to tell me what to do. We both appreciated how being personable helped you with members and their chiefs of staff, so we would come up with ideas for fostering those bonds, like retreats, and White House tours for friends, family, and donors. I gave tours a handful of times a week. I also checked in on every member every two weeks. I spent as much time as I could on the Hill, sitting in the cloakroom or standing on the floor during votes, where I kept a running tally, noting where members stood on bills being voted on that day, and what concerns they needed addressed and by whom before we secured their vote.

By the middle of July, Eric had noticed my close relationships with members and my growing network of Hill and administration staffers. After negotiating a two-year budget deal, he asked me to work with acting chief of staff Mick Mulvaney's office to assemble a list of members to include on a call with the president about the budget. From then on, Mick and his staff viewed me as a conduit for House outreach on behalf of the president.

Trump was late joining the members' budget call, because he was on the other line with Ukrainian president Volodymyr Zelenskyy, a whistleblower would later report.

———

In early August, I stopped by the office of Rep. Mark Meadows, of North Carolina, to drop off a few gifts from the president for his birthday. Since Mark and the president were close, no one in OLA, including me, had much of a relationship with him. Mark also had a reputation for preferring to work directly with Trump, circumventing our office. "He'll never work with us," Ben told me, "and it's useless trying to read him. He's a solo operator."

But that one word, "operator," gave me enough of a reason to try to establish a relationship with him. A leading figure in the House Freedom Caucus, he was influential, and, more importantly, he had the president's ear.

Mark was in his office lobby on his phone when I walked in, and he held up a finger to indicate that I should wait for him to finish his call. When he hung up, I was prepared to introduce myself, and extended my hand to shake his. He pulled me in for a hug. "Sir, sorry to disrupt your day. I just came by to drop off a few things for you from POTUS," I said. "And here's your birthday gift," I added, handing him a gift bag. Mustering the faux surprise of a veteran politician, he beamed, "Oh my gosh, how'd you know it's my birthday soon?"

I replied, "Nothing gets past me."

Studying my face for a moment, he then welcomed me into the office suite to introduce me to his staff. He asked me to give each of them my contact information. He stopped me as I turned to leave his office and handed me his phone. "Can you make sure all of your information is correct in my contacts?" I was taken aback to see that he had it. I handed the phone back to him. "Yes, sir, it's all there."

"Alright, then, you have a good August," he said. "I'm sure I'll be talking to you soon."

We would, in fact, be talking soon, almost every day.

While my colleagues rotated taking time off during the recess, I volunteered to stay at the White House the full five weeks. William and I had rented an apartment together earlier that summer, but we had grown apart. I was focused on building my career, knowing we were headed into the busiest time of the year on the Hill. William didn't support Trump, questioning his policies as well as how much time I devoted to work. When we broke up at the end of the summer, he cut ties quickly. We went from four years by each other's side to there being a gaping hole where my best friend used to be. The change was jarring, but while I grieved the loss, I didn't process it much and escaped into work. After all, this was the first time in my life I was on my own. Renting an apartment in the Navy Yard neighborhood, I embraced my new independence, free to do what I wanted.

———

On Tuesday, September 24, 2019, I was at Tortilla Coast with my colleagues when Eric called and asked me to hurry back to the White House. Speaker Pelosi had just formalized the impeachment inquiry against Trump over his call with President Zelenskyy. The president directed White House staff to launch a media campaign against the impeachment inquiry, which he called a "witch hunt." We were to rely on his most vocal allies, many of whom were members of Congress, and begin to personally assemble messages they were to amplify. The president also recognized how critical it was to ensure that no Republicans turned their back on him as we neared the midterm elections.

On the call, Eric informed me that until the House formally voted on the articles of impeachment, I was to send hourly emails to every House Republican with messages from the president, flooding people's inboxes with talking points, rebuttals, and pointed criticism meant to rally the troops like when Trump ripped out an article from the *New York Times* and wrote over it, in black Sharpie, "House Rs must have PERFECT VOTE." I didn't stop to think more about it at the time, other than doing what the president asked of me.

I ran through the East Wing doors, holding my dress in place, and raced to my desk. Catching my breath for a moment, I had the distinct sense that this was how my life would be from this day forward.

CHAPTER 6

Impeachment

"HEY, BY THE WAY, Happy Halloween," Ben said, laughing, as we climbed into the SUV on East Executive Avenue and sped to Capitol Hill. I suppressed a groan. I'd always hated that holiday, thanks to a lifelong phobia of people in costumes.

It was a gray, still day, and the House was set to vote to establish procedures for public impeachment hearings. I'd stayed up late the night before to watch the Washington Nationals win their first World Series, and I was tired. I held a nitro coffee in one hand and a sugar-free Red Bull in the other. Ben and I had spent so much of the morning planning which members to invite to the president's event on the South Lawn to celebrate the Nationals' win that we nearly missed the vote.

Before the impeachment inquiry, we had planned a busy fall legislative calendar, with votes on major bills the president wanted to campaign on in 2020. Then questions of quid pro quo emerged from Trump's call with President Zelenskyy, during which he allegedly promised military assistance to Ukraine in exchange for his investigating Democratic presidential candidate Joe Biden.

The final vote to formalize the inquiry went as expected. There were no Republican defections, but the Democrats had enough votes to proceed with hearings, which we perceived as the Democrats having a political advantage heading into the election year. Ben and I returned to the White House with the news we had anticipated but would have preferred not to have had to deliver.

When Pelosi had begun counting votes in late September, the president had instructed his staff to give the impression that we were unfazed by the impeachment inquiry. From members and senior staff, I heard that the president was uneasy about the optics of an impeachment as we neared the election year and worried how it might impact his reputation and legacy. It was with those considerations in mind that he continued to rally his base with his signature us-versus-them rhetoric.

I was confident that the Senate would never have the votes to remove him from office, but I feared ramifications if Republicans began to turn their back on the president. I felt that impeachment should be reserved for an offense so egregious that it was certain a president should be removed from office. I worried that the 2019 inquiry would establish precedent for presidents to face any politically motivated impeachment.

Trump invited a select few of his fiercest Capitol Hill defenders to the welcoming ceremony for Australian prime minister Scott Morrison on the White House South Lawn. Mark Meadows and I stood side by side as the United States Marine Band played the national anthems of both countries. A nineteen-gun salute was fired, a fife and drum corps marched, the two leaders made brief remarks, and hundreds of spectators waved tiny Australian and American flags.

When the ceremony ended, I was preparing to escort Mark and the other members out through the East Wing when Mark made a last-minute request to visit Mick Mulvaney. As I cleared a path through the crowd, I quickly picked up on the fact that he was in no rush, eager to socialize and take photographs with lingering guests. I slowed my gait. Once we were clear of the crowd and alone at the Rose Garden colonnade, he turned to me and said,

"You're pretty good at this. I think you're going to end up working for me someday." I told him he would need to ask the president's permission. "I serve at his pleasure," I said, laughing, and then we both fell silent.

From that day forward, I became Mark's main White House contact. Sometimes he called me to escort him to the West Wing, sometimes to ask me to send his tweet ideas to Trump. Sometimes he called just to check in. "What's the president doing today? Do you think I can stop by and see him?"

As Mark emerged as a key surrogate for Trump during the impeachment inquiry, he met more and more with POTUS, often at night, after Mick Mulvaney had left. There was a lot of secrecy around those meetings, and rumors circulated that Mick was on thin ice with Trump after a White House press briefing at which he'd referred to withholding aid to Ukraine in exchange for investigating the Bidens. Trump and various surrogates had been saying for weeks that this was not a quid pro quo. When a reporter asked Mick how it wasn't, he answered, "We do that all the time with foreign policy . . . Get over it."

While trying to defend Trump's actions, he had accidentally undermined himself and thus the president. The sound bite "Get over it" caused a lot of grief for the communications department, and for Mick. If Mark were angling to take over as chief of staff, Mick had inadvertently helped him.

As the inquiry proceeded, OLA strategized to come up with a plan to meet the president's directive that no Republicans defect in the course of the final impeachment vote. We invited groups of members with specific backgrounds in common—former law enforcement, military, prosecutors—to come to the Oval Office to meet with the president. We ensured we had a good mix of moderate Republicans and staunch Trump allies. Our goal was to build a united Republican front.

I prepared the briefing materials for the president, members, and staff, and would sit at the back of the meetings to make sure everything went as planned. After several meetings, I could sense that the president was aware that I was in the room. I was a new, unfamiliar presence to him. I noticed that his eyes often wandered the room when the meetings outlasted his attention span. A few times, his gaze rested on me, as if he were trying to remember whether we had met.

We were never formally introduced, but someone had told him my name. In the wake of the president's decision to withdraw US troops from northern Syria, he convened a meeting in the Cabinet Room with a bicameral, bipartisan congressional delegation. The meeting would produce a notorious photograph of Speaker Pelosi standing and dressing down the president. She had stormed out right after that, cutting the meeting short. I had been waiting outside the Cabinet Room to escort members out of the West Wing when she emerged and demanded her cell phones, which had been stored in a secure lockbox, as had everyone else's in the meeting. "I assume you stripped my phone for data to spy on me," she said accusingly. "That's what you people do." I assured her we hadn't, and rushed to retrieve her phones. When I met her again in the West Wing lobby, she protested that there were no umbrellas for departing guests and that it was raining heavily outside. She and the rest of the House Democratic leadership intended to hold an impromptu news conference outside the press briefing room.

"Where are all the umbrellas?" she asked peremptorily. I stuttered a response before racing to the chief of staff's office, where I borrowed several staffers' umbrellas. "Four umbrellas, only four? You're incompetent, just like the president," she snapped, before marching outside sans umbrella. The rest of the leadership took that as their cue to also decline the umbrellas. Rep. Steny Hoyer, of Maryland, patted my shoulder sympathetically. "I know you're trying. You're doing a good job."

I laughed about the incident with Ben and Eric. At the next

Republican House meeting, Eric pointed to me and informed the president that I was the staffer who had been berated by the Speaker. The president drew a sharp breath through clenched teeth. "She's a nasty, nasty woman, isn't she, Cassidy?" he declared, in the first time I remember him calling me by name. I lacked the confidence to tell him that I had found the matter funny rather than upsetting.

Ben had the idea of hosting Camp David retreats with Republican members to discuss legislative issues, then finishing by focusing on the impeachment near the end of each one. We considered Rep. Elise Stefanik, of New York, a moderate. She was usually reluctant to engage with the White House, and would always decline when invited to meetings and trips on Air Force One with the president. Elise did accept an invitation to a Camp David retreat, until she found out that impeachment—which she was still on the fence about—would be a topic of discussion. She was furious, and accused Ben and OLA of being "as deceitful as Trump." A few weeks later, Elise would become one of the president's most vocal defenders against the impeachment inquiry.

We held twelve retreats in total that year. The president would dial in to discussions on Saturday, and he would always compliment Ben for coming up with the plan to host at Camp David. Members loved being at Camp David, and they loved hearing from the president, even if only by phone. And the president loved that he otherwise had his weekend free to spend at his northern Virginia golf club.

As the impeachment hearings commenced in November, Mark and the president moved their secret meetings to the White House residence. Mark would confide in me to keep the meetings confidential to avoid leaks. I would keep Ben informed nevertheless. Ben seemed skeptical of Mark's intentions but didn't voice an objection. The meetings often ended late in the evening, and Mark would stop by my office on his way out to share some of the discussions he'd had with the president and recommend ideas for the next day's talking points.

Mark began to grow on me. We built a relationship rooted in mutual dedication to the success of the president's agenda.

As senior administration officials began to recognize my role as the conduit to House members, Eric and Ben entrusted me to communicate with them on the president's behalf rather than just for OLA. Members now knew to reach out to me if they wanted to speak with the president, the White House counsel's office, or senior staff. And I would still convey Trump's messages to members, most of whom came to depend on my talking points. But a handful didn't appreciate that I clogged their inboxes, like when Rep. Adam Kinzinger, of Illinois, wrote, "Please for the love of Jesus and America, stop. I do not want to block these."

My last email alert of the day usually went out at around nine. Afterward, I prepared a daily summary for White House senior staff that included an Excel spreadsheet with members' most recent comments on impeachment. I detailed any movement of votes that day, marking members as yes, no, or undecided. I paid closest attention to Democrats in districts Trump had won, and those who had flipped their seats in the 2018 midterm elections. I relied on Twitter and official press releases, and I called in to members' town halls, sometimes listening to three simultaneously. I seldom left the office before midnight. When I finally made it to bed, I'd keep my phone right next to my pillow at full volume, ready to respond if someone texted or called me in the middle of the night.

As we neared the holidays, the days grew longer and our workload intensified. We were in the final stretch of passing significant legislation to boost the president's chance to win a second term. It's the responsibility of OLA to remain fairly politically neutral in order to preserve relationships with members on both sides of the aisle and pass meaningful legislation that impacts everyday Americans. Many people don't realize that the majority of bills that pass through Congress are overwhelmingly bipartisan. In a hyperpartisan political environment, the ability to cultivate diverse relationships is one of the most sought-after skills.

———

"Thank you, Grace, I really appreciate you staying to help me get ready," I said over my shoulder to my former colleague as she zipped up my black gown. "Of course," she said. "I knew the guys wouldn't help you." I touched up my mascara and gave her a quick hug before hustling out of the office and through the east colonnade, careful not to bump into any of the Christmas decorations adorning the halls. I was headed to the State Room, where members were gathered for the annual congressional ball.

As I was searching through the crowd for my OLA colleagues, I turned with a start when I felt a tap on my shoulder, and was relieved to see that it was only Mark. "I heard today's your twenty-third birthday," he said with a smile. I hadn't told anyone, a fact my perplexed expression obviously conveyed.

"I know everything," he said, still grinning. "Does POTUS know it's your birthday?" I shook my head and pleaded with him not to tell anyone. He ignored me. "Hey, guys, make sure you all wish Cassidy here a happy birthday. We couldn't do any of this without her." My face burned as members gathered around. Ben pushed his way through the swarm, pulling me away to spare me further embarrassment. "You didn't tell me today is your birthday," he said kindly.

"I know," I said, my eyes on the president and First Lady as they descended the staircase. Ben and I retreated to the back of the room, helping ourselves to champagne. "Well," Ben said, raising his glass, "cheers to twenty-three." We clinked glasses and drank. "I'm a little pissed Mark wished you a happy birthday before I did," he noted.

Ben had been urging me to take a few days off, worried I would burn out. I had rebuffed him repeatedly. We had a lot of work to finish before the holidays, when we would all have a week off. And he was wrong, or at least I thought he was.

The Ukrainian affair caused some initial embarrassment and concern on the Hill, but Republicans would come to see the whole thing as partisan gamesmanship. In the final days before the vote, a Republican representative was still undecided. I had heard that he was attending a Kevin McCarthy fundraiser at a restaurant, Mission Navy Yard, right across from my apartment. I left the office early to track him down.

I spotted him immediately, talking with three other members near the bar. I ordered four shots of tequila and carried them over to the group. After a second drink, I began talking with the other members about our mutual disdain for the Democrats' impeachment case. My target member stood quietly to the side. "Don't you agree?" I asked, trying to draw him out. He didn't respond.

But he texted me the next morning. "Yes, I agree. Move me to no." I smiled and screenshotted his text and sent it to Ben: "We're gold."

December 18, 2019, was impeachment vote day. I got into another SUV with Ben and we were taken to Capitol Hill, where we spent the whole day standing post between the House floor, the cloakroom, and Kevin McCarthy's office. The president had scheduled a rally in Michigan that night at the same time the House was scheduled to vote.

We were in the cloakroom fielding calls from staff traveling with the president, updating them on the count as the vote was underway. We weren't certain how many House Democrats would join Republicans to vote against the articles of impeachment, but we were confident we had met the president's demand that no Republican member would vote to impeach. Still, it was satisfying when the last votes were recorded with zero Republican defections, and three Democrats voting no. I felt in control, with a purpose, happy to have achieved the goal the president tasked us with. That goal coincided with my belief that impeachment wasn't the appropriate response to his inappropriate Zelenskyy call.

Exhausted, I hadn't had much time to think about what I had been asked to do. I hadn't thought how it might be a loyalty test of any kind, or how my hourly barrage of messages contributed to anything beyond achieving the mission, or anything more about the whistleblower. I had landed my dream job and was a loyal foot soldier.

As members filed off the floor, exchanging congratulations, Mark Meadows and Rep. Matt Gaetz, of Florida, asked me to walk with them to a Fox News interview. On the way, Mark guided us to a quiet corner in Statuary Hall. "I wanted you to hear this from me," Mark said. His expression was more serious than usual; there was no trace of his signature jovial smile. "Tomorrow, I'm going to announce that I'll be retiring at the end of this term." I shifted my glance between Mark and Matt, whose hands were shoved deep in his pockets. "Is everything okay?" I asked Mark. He assured me that it was. "We work really well together, don't we?" Mark continued.

I masked my surprise by resorting to practiced glad-handing. "We do, sir." He nodded. "That's not going to stop anytime soon. Let me know how things are at the White House tomorrow, what people are saying about my announcement," he said, then handed me his red impeachment vote card. "I want you to have this. No one worked harder for it than you." I studied the card and turned it over in my hand.

"No one except for you," I said with a wink.

As the last members trickled out of the Capitol, I walked to Capitol Lounge, a local bar, with several of Kevin's and Steve's staffers. Matt Gaetz had asked what my plans were, and I had sarcastically invited him to join us, thinking he would rather be caught dead than be spotted with leadership aides.

When Matt walked into the bar a while later, I could have sworn I was hallucinating. A few of my friends jabbed me with their elbows as he waltzed in our direction, and I wished I had more than one drink to deal with the incoming charade.

"How are you taking the big news?" Matt said by way of greeting. I yanked him away from my friends. "Shut up, Matt. Mark doesn't want anyone to know yet. You heard him." I scowled. A tight smile crept across his face as he nodded. "Mark has big things in store for you. He's not going anywhere, don't worry," he said. "Just let it all play out. He truly adores you."

Suddenly I felt claustrophobic, but I was torn between running outside into the frigid winter air and pressing Matt for more information. I did not understand what he meant or why he was sharing this information in the middle of a crowded Washington bar after one of the most consequential votes in US history.

"Okay," I said, shifting my weight from one leg to another. "So, do you want a drink?"

He chuckled and brushed his thumb across my chin. "Has anyone ever told you that you're a national treasure?"

CHAPTER 7

Winter 2020

F ROM THE BACK OF THE FLOOR, Ben and I watched the
House pass the United States-Mexico-Canada Agreement
(USMCA), historic legislation that replaced NAFTA as the pact
governing commerce with America's largest trading partners. It
had been a complicated treaty to negotiate, and securing its passage in the House had been a significant challenge, but it would
prove to be one of the Trump administration's most significant
legislative accomplishments. Ben had risen to the occasion and
had helped to push the bill through the House with overwhelming bipartisan support, and I expected that he would be elated by
the success.

But he was silent on our drive back to the White House. He
had been quiet for several weeks, and I had begun to worry about
him. I tried to convince myself that his subdued demeanor was
the result of fatigue from the chaotic fall months, but I knew that
there was more to it.

"Well, we only have eleven more months until we know all our
hard work paid off," I said, trying to lighten the mood. "The boss
will probably promote you when he's reelected, you know." He
was silent. "Ben, you're not leaving the administration, are you?"
I stunned myself when I said this—I had meant for that thought
to remain in my mind. Ben also seemed roused by my question.
"Why, what are you hearing? Am I getting fired or something?"
he asked.

That wasn't an answer to my question, and he knew it. His

evasiveness fed my anxiety, which I tried to fend off with half-hearted rationalizations and delusions that I was overthinking again.

In our first team meeting after the holidays, Ben still seemed checked out and offered little or no commentary. We hadn't finished discussing the business at hand when he abruptly dismissed everyone. It was nearly time to go home when he finally broke his silence. "Cassidy, is everyone gone yet?" he asked me. When I confirmed that we were alone, he asked me to come into his office and shut the door.

Ever since that unsettling car ride back from the USMCA vote, I had been able to think of little other than Ben's status in the White House. Near the end of the holiday break, I had been sorting through his emails to prepare his schedule for our first week back. I'd finished reading his incoming emails, and my cursor hovered over his sent file. Normally I did not look at what Ben had sent, even though I was the author of many of those emails. I considered it an unnecessary intrusion to read emails he had sent on his own. I dispensed with my discretion this time, worried about what was going on. I found what I expected, off-boarding emails.

When I'd closed the door and taken a seat, he broke the news. He had received a job offer in the private sector that he would be foolish to turn down. I tried to act surprised, and the tears welling in my eyes were authentic to my grief over his news. I begged him to stay. "The boss needs you. The House team needs you. We can't do this without you," I implored him. But despite the "we" I invoked, I knew I was the one who needed him most. Ben had taught me the ropes, and we did this job so well together, I had really come to rely on him as a mentor and friend, besides a boss. I worried about how I would function without him.

He smiled understandingly but didn't say more. I begged him to take me with him. He was sympathetic, but he didn't think it was in my best interests. Echoing my plea to him, he told me, "You're doing an amazing job here. The president needs you to stay. OLA needs you." He wasn't going far, he reassured me. He'd always be there for me. *It won't be the same, Ben.*

———

On January 3, 2020, a US drone strike at Baghdad International Airport killed Qassim Suleimani, the head of Iran's Quds Force, who was responsible for the murder of hundreds of Americans. The administration cited the 2002 Authorization for Use of Military Force Against Iraq Resolution as legal authorization for the strike. The Democratic-controlled House disagreed and scheduled a vote to invoke the War Powers Resolution. If the Senate were to do the same, which no one worried it would, the president's ability to use force against Iran in the future would be severely restricted. The vote was scheduled for January 9.

A handful of Republicans were known to be leaning toward supporting the motion, including Matt Gaetz. Eric put me in charge of whipping Matt's vote. I tried my best, to no avail. He wouldn't even take a call from the president. Later that night, after the rest of the House team had gone home, Eric, who rarely visited the East Wing, dropped by with a specific directive from POTUS: no one in OLA was to communicate with Matt until Trump said otherwise. Eric asked me if he could rely on me to enforce the "ice-out." I said I would try.

I was disappointed in myself for having failed to persuade Matt to vote with us. But Eric hadn't found fault with my effort. On the contrary, he quickly changed the subject to my position in OLA, offering to promote me to Special Assistant to the President. The promotion would put me on the same level with the rest of my House OLA colleagues and recognize my growing influence in the White House and on the Hill.

I'm pretty good at reading people, but I'd had few personal conversations with Eric, and I was finding it hard to discern his intentions. I was taken aback by the offer of a promotion. I didn't think I had the requisite policy experience for the position. I asked him directly why he was offering it to me, and he gave me a direct answer—he was worried I would leave, too, and he didn't want to lose me.

We had held the signing ceremony for the USMCA on the South Lawn on January 29, just two days before Ben left. After the ceremony, Trump met with Ben in the Oval for a goodbye photograph and made an effort to convince him to stay, which Ben laughed off. I was standing in the outer Oval listening when Trump shouted, "Cassidy, if Ben is going to be disloyal and leave me, make sure he goes out with a bang!"

I walked straight to Mick's office and asked his deputy chief of staff if there was space for Ben to fly on Marine One for the president's trip to promote USMCA the next day. She quickly added Ben to the manifest, which required that we boot Mick from the helicopter.

Ben was elated when he learned he would fly on Marine One, and I saw a glimpse of the man who had hired me less than one year ago. I understood that my pleas for him to stay were selfish. He had served the administration, Kevin McCarthy, and Steve Scalise with an honorable dedication that was rare for Washington in the Trump years.

On January 31, 2020, as Ben packed the last of his belongings, our colleague David rushed into his office. David explained that he had just returned from a senior staff meeting about the coronavirus. I wondered who thought it was wise to name an infection after a Mexican beer. David rolled his eyes and asked me to call Terri McCullough, Speaker Pelosi's chief of staff. The president would soon announce a travel ban from China, where the virus had originated, and David thought that the news would be received better if it came from OLA directly.

I asked David why I had to call Terri. We had worked together throughout my tenure in OLA, but still, I did not want to bear the burden of informing the Speaker or her chief of staff about a travel ban I felt confident Democrats would perceive as racist. David explained that Eric had thought Ben had already left, and that I should be doing his job until his replacement was hired. Ben and I exchanged a look. He set down a banker's box of documents he had packed for delivery to the National Archives. "I literally have one foot out of the door," he moaned, and I dialed Terri.

Terri answered in good spirits. "Hey, Terri, I have Ben here. Do you mind if I put you on speakerphone?"

She paused, then said, "I should get the Speaker." When they joined us, Ben delivered the news that David had just shared with us. The Speaker was grateful that we had told her office promptly, but I knew that it was only a matter of time before Democrats began publicly shaming the president for his decision.

The president's statement read, in part: "Given the importance of protecting persons within the United States from the threat of this harmful communicable disease, I have determined that it is in the interests of the United States to take action to restrict and suspend the entry into the United States, as immigrants or non-immigrants, of all aliens who were physically present within the People's Republic of China."

Pelosi responded that same day with a statement of her own: "The Trump Administration's expansion of its outrageous, un-American travel ban threatens our security, our values and the rule of law. . . . [It is] discrimination disguised as policy."

When the call ended, in good OLA tradition, Ben added his signature to his desk. We walked together down the east colonnade, through the Rose Garden, and out of the West Wing. It was pouring rain as we exited the north gate of the White House. We found a bench sheltered by tree limbs, and sat down. I had done a decent job of keeping my emotions in check all day, but the thought of his absence made me anxious, given how much I relied on him.

Ben broke the silence first. "I couldn't have survived the last nine months without you. I mean that, Cassidy. I really couldn't have."

"Me neither," I said. "You don't have to go. You can have Eric's job."

The rain continued to fall and Ben forced a smile. "It's my time to leave. And you have to stay. This is part of your journey. I'm not going far. You know I'll always be your biggest cheerleader."

I watched Ben walk north toward the Metro station, and realized in that moment that I would have to change something about my job in OLA if I was going to survive without Ben.

———

The Senate was scheduled to vote on the articles of impeachment in early February. I was still sending out daily email blasts to House Republicans but not at the volume that had annoyed Adam Kinzinger. Matt Gaetz regularly called and texted me in response, but I adhered to the presidential edict and ignored them. I called Mark to explain that I had been given strict instructions from Eric to ice Matt out, but that it was becoming difficult because Matt would not stop texting me. Mark laughed and promised that he would handle it. I didn't hear from Matt again until he was "unfrozen."

OLA convened impeachment briefings with the White House counsel's office every morning in the Roosevelt Room. Those present included deputy chief of staff for communications Dan Scavino; the president's daughter Ivanka and her husband, Jared Kushner; attorney Eric Herschmann; strategy advisor Tony Sayegh; and former Florida attorney general and Trump impeachment defense lawyer Pam Bondi. Eric Ueland asked me to help lead the meetings. That's when I started to form personal relationships with senior principals, especially Pam Bondi, whom I talked to several times a day. She was on the Senate floor for the impeachment trial, and she had me brief her before and after each day's proceedings. She also had me accompany her to meetings with members of both chambers.

On February 5, the Senate voted to acquit, with Senator Mitt Romney the lone Republican voting to convict—a defection that made Trump seethe with anger. The president's approval ratings actually rose after the impeachment vote, as Trump and most Republicans celebrated the outcome as vindication. We were looking forward to the Democratic nominating contest, pleased that former vice president Biden was polling poorly in the first two early states, Iowa and New Hampshire, and rooting for social democrat Bernie Sanders to win the nomination.

No one anticipated, of course, that 2020 would be one of the strangest years in peacetime history, bringing social and economic upheavals that could've sprung from the imagination of dystopian fiction writers. The virus soon dominated headlines. I asked the staffer who managed the administration's public health portfolio on the Hill if we were going to have a vaccine before the 2020 election, a mere ten months away. "No way," he answered.

I doubt any politician could have led the country through the deadliest pandemic in a hundred years without making errors of judgment and execution. But of all the people in the world, President Trump was uniquely unsuited to the challenge. He lacked empathy and was stubborn and impatient. For all but the MAGA base, his aggressive personality made his leadership appear more erratic than inspirational. Still, with the general alarm that the pandemic created in Congress and in the country, the administration would manage to push massive spending legislation through Congress, including the $2.2 trillion Coronavirus Aid, Relief, and Economic Security Act (CARES). It was initially imagined as enough to see the country through the crisis in those early days. No one knew what COVID-19 really had in store for us all.

Eric asked to have lunch with me the day after the president's acquittal, in Ben's old office, which was out of character. When Eric arrived, his first question was how the team was holding up in Ben's absence.

"Great. We're all great," I assured him. Then he asked if I had decided about the promotion he had offered, and I told him that I needed a couple more days.

I called Dan Meyer, Kevin's chief of staff, who had worked in OLA in the George W. Bush White House. Dan is a talented Washington operator with sharp instincts. I had grown to trust him over the last several months. I spent considerable time with Dan and Ben while I was on the Hill, and he routinely checked on me after Ben decided to leave the White House. Dan spent over an hour explaining why accepting Eric's promotion would be a good career move for me.

Next I called Steve Scalise's policy director, Bill Hughes, for his take. Bill is a quiet, knowledgeable policy wonk who was one of the smartest people I had ever met. I trusted his judgment. Like Dan, Bill advised me to accept the job. I called Eric that night and told him I'd do it. He said that he would talk to Mick in the morning to get the process moving.

Part of me was not confident with the decision, a feeling that would grow more pronounced in the weeks ahead as I started getting nervous about the November election. I didn't enjoy my job as much as I had enjoyed working with Ben. I now directly reported to Eric and Mike McKenna, his deputy, whom I was not fond of. Mike had a tendency to publicly single out women with crude and demeaning comments.

———

My relationship with Mark Meadows grew more familiar in the weeks following the Senate acquittal. Mark and his wife, Debbie, contacted me almost every day with a series of requests: a belated birthday card for a constituent signed by the president, a retweet by the president of one of Mark's tweets—those kinds of things. Mark frequently asked me to ask White House staff secretary Derek Lyons to issue presidential proclamations for various interests, and to review Air Force One manifests for the president's upcoming travel. He began advising me which members he thought deserved to fly with the president and which didn't.

I got the sense that Derek suspected that there were underlying reasons for the sudden surge in Mark's requests that he would not share. Other colleagues speculated that Mark was going to replace Mick as chief of staff, but I did not believe those rumors. Mark would have told me if it were the case. As far as I could see, Mick seemed to be in good standing with the president after the acquittal vote. Both Ben and I had ventured that if Trump really wanted Mark to be chief of staff, he would wait to make the change after the election. Reinforcing my certainty was my knowledge that while the president had asked Kevin McCarthy repeatedly to make Mark ranking member on the Oversight Committee, Kevin had done so only after Trump had assured him that he had no intention of recruiting Mark for Mick's job.

I also suspected that Eric had his sights set on the White House chief of staff job, and that he saw Mark Meadows as his biggest competitor. Eric knew that Mark and I were close. At a Camp David staff retreat, Eric had invited me to ride in his golf cart after dinner. We were both a little worse for drink, and we ended up crashing the cart. Eric had found out that he was no longer included in a trip the president was taking to India. He asked if I thought Mark would get the chief of staff job.

I told him that I thought it was just a rumor, and that even if Mark were offered the job, he would decline. "He told me he serves the president best in Congress and once he retires, he will serve him best from the outside," I explained.

"I've heard otherwise," Eric said.

In the following days, I stopped by members' offices, including Mark's, to put out soft feelers for a job in their offices or on their committees. My stated reasoning for coming to Mark's office was to drop off a letter Debbie had requested from the president. He called me into his office to catch up with Ben Williamson, his communications director. I debated whether to mention my interest in leaving the White House for the Hill with Ben in the room, and I worried that Mark would think I was disloyal to the president. But I asked anyway.

I didn't explain my reasoning to Mark—I just asked him to keep his ears open. Mark looked at Ben. They both seemed surprised. "Listen," Mark began, primed to deliver a lecture. "I know it's been a tough few months, but the president really needs you." He told me to give it more thought. Later, if I still wanted to leave, "we'll look for a job on the Oversight Committee for you. I'll make sure you're taken care of."

I didn't push back and thought maybe Mark was right.

Later that day, Ben Howard and I were catching up on the phone and I told him about my conversation with Mark. Ben paused, then told me that he had heard that Mark was going to be named chief of staff soon. I told Ben it was impossible—Mark would have told me, and he had literally just reaffirmed his intention to serve out his term. I added that he had urged me to stay at the White House.

Ben was quiet for a few seconds before he launched in. "Cassidy, listen to me. The fact that he told you to stay—which is the correct advice, regardless of how I feel about him—says a lot about the accuracy of what I've heard. Keep your guard up. Mark may ask you to work for him."

I was packing my car to drive to New Jersey for the weekend on the evening of Friday, March 6. Paul's birthday had just passed, and I wanted to take him to breakfast at our usual diner, our favorite thing to do together. I wanted to go home for another reason as well. COVID was starting to dominate the news, and if it was as bad as health experts were warning, I was not sure when I would be able to see my parents again.

As I put my overnight bag in the back seat of my car, my Apple Watch buzzed three times, the notification I assigned presidential tweet alerts. I stopped to read it: "I am pleased to announce that Congressman Mark Meadows will become White . . ." My fingers fumbled as I tried to open the rest of the tweet, but it wouldn't load because of the poor cell reception in my apartment building's parking garage.

I jumped in the driver's seat, made it quickly to street level, and read the rest of the tweet: ". . . House Chief of Staff. I have long known and worked with Mark, and the relationship is a very good one. . . ."

I was stunned, but I knew I should not have been. People had been warning me about this for weeks. I wondered why I had not believed them. I wondered why Mark did not tell me himself.

I turned right on M Street and headed for the I-395 extension. Mark called a minute later, and I hesitated before answering, not sure how to address him now that he was chief of staff. He had always been "Mark" to me.

I answered the call and thought about joking, *Calling on a Friday night? What if I was out partying?* But Mark jumped in right away, his southern drawl a bit more rushed than usual. "Hey, sorry to bother you on a Friday night," he said. He sounded genuinely apologetic. "POTUS just officially made me his chief. I don't want to hold you up too long, but my life is about to get real crazy for a few days. I would really like for you to come work for me in the chief's office. Will you give it some thought for me?"

I pulled over. "Uh, sure, yes, sir . . . and—"

"Thanks so much. I'll talk to you next week."

I finished my sentence—"congratulations"—but he had already hung up.

CHAPTER 8

Chief of Staff

A T THE END OF a fifteen-hour workday, I was locked in a trance at my computer, about to email every House member announcing my departure from the Office of Legislative Affairs. I had bumped into Mark Meadows the previous day—his first, unofficially, as chief of staff—and he had asked if I could move to his office immediately. "I talked to Eric Ueland and got his blessing," Mark informed me. I asked Mark for a little time to close out my job on the House team. "Yes, you have a big job there," he agreed. "Make sure they're able to function without you. I'll see you in a couple days."

I swallowed the lump in my throat and sent the email. Then, I walked into Ben's empty office to finish organizing the informational binders I was preparing for my successor. With the House deputy position and my job vacant, I was not sure how long it would be until someone read them. My heart ached thinking about leaving that office.

As I packed the last of my belongings, I thumbtacked a goodbye letter to my colleagues on the bulletin board mounted above my desk. And then I honored the same OLA tradition Ben had observed: I signed my desk. I put my name in the middle drawer and, breaking with tradition, added one of the president's favorite rally lines: "The best is yet to come."

———

After Mark's move had been announced, he went into a weeklong quarantine, having come in close contact with someone at the

Conservative Political Action Conference (CPAC) who had tested positive for COVID. During this time, Trump had declared a national emergency, sending states into lockdowns. The president issued another travel ban to noncitizens flying in from Europe. Confusion and fear gripped the country.

At that time, I still was not sure if leaving OLA was a wise decision. Although speculation was growing that I was moving to the chief of staff's office, I had not yet made a final decision.

I called Ben, who carefully considered my situation from various angles. We both believed that there was an opportunity for tremendous professional and personal growth in that job. He advised that I should be clear with Mark: if I were to accept the job offer, I would be working for the White House chief of staff, not Mark Meadows personally.

Ben also insisted that my role needed to have a clear title and specified duties. He was concerned that my responsibilities would be left deliberately vague and open to differing interpretations if I did not make my expectations explicit. I agreed.

I felt that the president needed a strong White House team if he was going to be reelected in the middle of a pandemic. Even if I did not entirely trust Mark, I believed we could serve the president well together.

Mark was Trump's fourth chief of staff in four years. If he failed to deliver, it was entirely possible there would be a fifth. If Trump won in November, I figured Mark would probably stay on as chief of staff for six to eight months to set up the second-term administration, and then leave while he was still in Trump's good graces. If I lasted that long, I could ask Mark to place me somewhere else internally, ideally in a more senior OLA position.

I thought I could help Mark transition from ultraconservative rabble-rouser—his profile then—to statesman. And I could help improve morale among White House staff who had concerns about Mark's leadership and that he would push his Freedom Caucus agenda in the West Wing, trying to make it more mainstream.

I made the call to take the job. My transfer from OLA to the chief of staff's office was a rushed process, without an opportunity to discuss my specific role with Mark before my first day. I tried to convince myself that the conversation would not have mattered, that Mark trusted me enough to know that I would define my own role. It did not take long before I began to wish I had cut out the time to have had a thorough conversation with Mark about my role, as Ben suggested.

———

I shifted uncomfortably in my chair while Mark caught up on text messages and emails. The office was quiet except for Fox News playing at low volume on Mark's TV and the ticking clock mounted above his door.

I started to stand up. "I can come back in a few minutes if you're busy." Mark immediately put down his cell phone, placing it next to mine in the office lockbox. "Sorry to keep you waiting. How was your day?" I gave him a quick rundown before opening the binder of notes on subjects I had prepared to discuss with him. First was my job description. But he preempted me. "Who do you think are the worst leakers around here?"

I stiffened, and planted both feet on the floor. Trying to buy time, I replied, "Leakers? Could you be a little more clear, sir? What do you want to know?"

"Oh, please," he said with a laugh. "Keep calling me Mark."

"Okay."

Returning to his subject, he explained, "We're going to start working on people we need to get rid of who are disloyal to the president, starting with the people who leak to the press."

He passed me a binder. Relieved to have something else to turn my attention to, I thumbed through the pages quickly and realized that the binder was filled with organizational charts for every executive branch office, including the White House. "I'll have you sit down with Johnny McEntee soon," he promised, referring to the president's former body man, who was now the director of the Presidential Personnel Office. "But I wanted to get your immediate thoughts about changes we can make in the White House."

"I'll take a look at this and get back to you," I replied, still hoping to have time to call Ben for advice. But Mark kept pressing me. "Can you name anyone off the top of your head, even if it's obvious?"

I continued thumbing through the pages of the binder. I prayed Mark would sense how uncomfortable I was and drop the subject. I saw him take off his glasses as he cleared his throat. I lifted my eyes. "How about Eric Ueland?" he asked. "Is Eric a leaker?"

I closed the binder and straightened my posture. "It would not be smart to fire Eric. That is not a decision I would advise you to make," I offered. I held Mark's gaze for a moment before flipping to the OLA organizational chart and circled Mike McKenna's name in black Sharpie. "If you want to fire someone," I said as I passed him the binder, "this is the guy." Mark put his glasses back on and read the name.

"Mike McKenna. Is he a leaker?"

"I have heard rumors, none of which I could personally confirm. Leaking is not my primary concern about Mike, though," I replied. Mike's cocky and sexist attitude had rankled more than just me. Staffers on the House and Senate OLA teams also seemed to resent his abrasiveness. I knew that some House members and staff thought him brash and condescending as well.

Mark nodded. "Alright, tell me what you think you're going to do for me."

"I thought you would be telling me," I countered. Mark laughed and told me that he wanted to hear what I had in mind.

"Well," I started, choking back a cough, worried Mark would think I had COVID. I tried to be diplomatic. "I serve at the pleasure of the president, Mark. I will do whatever you or the president ask of me. But I think it's important for all of us that I have a title that reflects the authority you're giving me, with clearly specified duties."

"We'll worry about your title later," he said. "Just tell me what title you want and we'll make it happen. Now, about your responsibilities . . ." He leaned forward. "You're going to be my eyes and ears."

I wasn't sure how exactly to interpret that instruction. It was just the sort of amorphous job description Ben and I had worried about, subject to wildly differing interpretations. "My eyes and ears here in the White House, on the Hill, everywhere," Mark added.

He explained that my role included being his gatekeeper, which I was confident I could do, but that it would be more than that. "You'll be my person," he added, "and I want you with me all the time. You'll be my shadow. I want everyone to see you with me, that you speak and act for me."

The job was both ill- and very well-defined. I sensed I could be good at it, as long as I self-imposed limitations not to become Mark's henchman. Instead of viewing my role as Mark's "eyes and ears" as feeding into the general paranoia of the administration, I was emboldened by how he was empowering the position to speak and act on behalf of the chief of staff. And the chief of staff would rise to the occasion of the job, and not be willing to watch his own back by taking others down. Right?

Then I asked him a question of my own. "Why did you take the job?"

"Well, I wanted to finish out my term in Congress," he said. "But with everything going on, I felt that the president could be better served by someone else."

"By you."

"Yes."

I did not think Mark was the kind of political sycophant who woke up every morning wondering how he could wrest personal advantage from every situation. I felt he was an ideologue, but a sincere one, someone who got into politics to make changes he thought would benefit the country. That said, if the president were reelected, Mark would enjoy the reputation of being the chief of staff who led the mercurial Trump White House through the economic and social upheavals of the pandemic and into a second term. And he would enjoy the influence that came with it.

"Just to be clear, sir," I said, as we wound up our conversation, "my job would be to serve the White House chief of staff, who serves the president, correct?"

He smiled as if expecting the question, and I used the split-second break in conversation to add, "It isn't to serve Mark Meadows." The distinction was important to me, and he nodded. "That's why I chose you, Cass."

He indicated that our conversation was over. "Alright, you go get a good night's sleep. You and I are going to the Hill tomorrow to help negotiate the final terms of the COVID relief package. But before you leave, see if Tony is still in his office. I want you two to get to know each other better."

I had met Tony Ornato, the current deputy chief of staff and former special agent in charge of the president's Secret Service detail, for the first time that morning. I had been unpacking a few personal items at my desk outside Mark's office when the senior staff meeting, already underway inside, wrapped up and staff funneled out. I already knew most of them—press secretaries Stephanie Grisham and Hogan Gidley, Jared Kushner and Ivanka Trump, and Larry Kudlow, director of the National Economic Council—except the last person who walked out, a slim, middle-aged man.

"Hey. Cassidy, right?" Tony asked. I nodded as he added, "I'm Tony, the deputy chief of staff. I have a feeling we'll be working closely together." I knew Tony by name, if not by face. "It's great to finally meet you, Tony." I smiled.

He smiled and asked where I was from. "Jersey," I responded.

"Sort of near Princeton." Tony patted his chest and said, "I'm from Connecticut, but I lived in New York for a while. I'm one of your people. I think we're going to get along well. Stop by my office later and we'll talk more." He gestured to his office across the hall, with the Oval Office and dining room just a few paces down the hall, the vice president next door, and the press secretary a little farther. I said, "Sure, thanks."

Following Mark's instructions, I found Tony wrapping up his work for the day. He invited me in and told me to close the door and sit down. "I'm sorry we didn't have a chance to talk more this morning. It's been a day."

We soon fell into a warm, friendly conversation as we shared stories about our lives and careers. We were alike in many ways, both fast talkers, personable, and passionate in our enthusiasms. He's a hard worker, and extremely dedicated to his job, loyal to the president, but he didn't consider his work to be partisan—a careerist Secret Service agent who had served under several Democrat and Republican presidents. He was always respectful, and would run most decisions by Mark or, in his absence, me. But he also wasn't afraid to tell us hard truths. I left his office that night certain we would work well together, and pretty sure we'd become close friends.

Mark might not have appeared nervous, but I could tell he was unsure of himself. In just forty-eight hours, Mark went from being a conservative bomb-thrower who had never participated in a successful bipartisan negotiation to being a key representative of the president as the executive and legislative branches flushed out the final details of critical COVID relief legislation. This was his first true test as the president's chief of staff. I felt it was important he establish that he could set his partisan history aside when the stakes for the country were this high. It could set the tone for how history would view his tenure.

After we wrapped our first few meetings of the day, Mark asked how I thought he had been received. Wanting to build his confidence, I complimented his demeanor and openness to compromise. I encouraged him to lean on the policy experts who accompanied us whenever he felt out of his depth debating policy nuances. "Nobody expects you to know everything, Mark. Not even the president. They expect you to lead."

Mark fell into a rhythm as the day progressed, getting more comfortable with Treasury Secretary Steve Mnuchin and the OLA team—with one exception. Eric was trying to prove his value to Mark, but Mark did not appear to be impressed. He had mostly ignored Eric.

During a break later that afternoon, I spotted Eric abruptly leaving the room to take a call. He returned minutes later, slack-jawed, and went back to his seat in a trance. He slowly lowered himself into the chair and brought his forehead to the palm of his hand.

I was trying to decipher Eric's expression when my cell phone vibrated with a message from Tony, informing me Mike McKenna had been fired and escorted off the White House grounds.

I fought to mask my shock and slowly glanced over at Mark, who was already staring at me. We locked eyes, and the corners of his mouth twitched upward as he winked. I locked my cell phone and tipped my chin once.

"We make a great team, you and I, don't we?" Mark whispered as we walked to Senate majority leader Mitch McConnell's office for our next scheduled meeting. I looked over my shoulder and stole a glance at Eric, who was trailing far behind us, then turned to Mark. "We do," I replied with a smile.

I was pleased Mark trusted my judgment to help him make better decisions. At the time, I hadn't considered how little Mark had seemed to look into the matter before firing McKenna, neither aware of the hit I might have just ordered nor viewing it as a potential initiation.

———

A few days later, on Saturday, I was seated at my desk, the first of many weekends spent in the West Wing. As Mark was leaving the office for the Situation Room to attend a classified COVID briefing, I saw him cross paths with his predecessor, Mick Mulvaney, who had come to retrieve the last of his personal belongings. I could not tell if they said anything to each other, but Mick graciously offered me encouragement and advice as he left the chief of staff suite for the last time. "No matter who occupies the Oval Office and chief of staff's office," he observed, "it's never an easy role to assume . . . But we got through it, and you all will get through it. I know it. . . ."

He slowly rapped three times on the wooden doorframe for emphasis as he continued. "This is a special office. Many people would kill for the opportunity to be here as chief of staff or to serve the chief of staff. You've got this. I know you do. Don't ever hesitate to call me, and please make sure Mark knows he can always call me." And he walked away.

I was momentarily speechless, but when he reached the West Wing staircase, I stood up and called out his name. He turned back to face me, and I realized I had not thought about what to say. "Thank you, Mick," I said. "Thank you for everything. I think you did a great job, and I really hope you heard that enough."

Mick nodded and flashed a quick, closed-mouthed smile before shouldering the door open and disappearing down the staircase one final time.

For the first time, I was completely alone in the chief of staff's office, and felt weighted by the honor to serve in my role, yet naive to its depth and possible historic impact.

———

Mark had brought Ben Williamson to the White House with him to serve as a top communications aide for himself and the president.

Ben and I had grown close in recent months, and I was grateful to have an ally in the West Wing. Mark also moved the president's scheduler, Michael Haidet, into our office.

Another of Mark's hires was Eliza, a former staffer of his who had since taken a job as Vice President Mike Pence's scheduler. Our personalities were completely opposite—formal and reticent, Eliza was a quiet force who, through her sheer presence, commanded every room she entered. She was enormously competent and highly respected. And she put my organizational skills and Excel spreadsheets to shame with her uncanny ability to jigsaw Mark's schedule in perfect fifteen-minute segments each day, while fielding dozens of requests for meetings and phone calls from CEOs, cabinet secretaries, national security officials, lobbyists, and friends and allies of the Trump White House.

Meeting with the directors of every White House office and their closest staff, I came to understand that people were palpably apprehensive about job security. That was normal in the Trump White House, and it might not have been out of the ordinary in previous administrations. But people were more on edge than usual when Mark arrived because of rumors of ideological purges. I wanted them to see that I intended to work with them and would advocate for them with the chief.

One person I made a point to build a relationship with was Tim Pataki, who led the Office of Public Liaison (OPL), which is responsible for outreach and communication to various public interests and communities. A Kevin McCarthy protégé, Tim was known by colleagues, Hill staff and members, and the president as an exceptional leader and for his innovative mind. He was quiet and unassuming, and we forged a professional but candid camaraderie. From mentors and close friends, I knew OPL was in need of a morale boost. I also learned OPL was understaffed, overworked, and assigned inadequate office space in the Eisenhower Executive Office Building (EEOB).

I spoke with Mark, who gave me permission to work with Tony so OPL could increase the number of staffers and amount of space allocated to the office. Mark also began checking in with Tim every week, making clear he wanted an open and trusting relationship. We signaled the same to other offices that were seriously overworked and too often ignored by senior staff. I proposed to Mark that we convene thirty-minute individual meetings with each office in the White House. He eagerly agreed with the proposal.

People streamed in and out of Mark's office all day. I ordered a daily supply of bagels and donuts for the mornings, and pastries and other snacks for the afternoons. I also kept a sizable stash of candy in my desk, learning the preferences of my colleagues— Hershey's bars for the president, Tootsie Rolls for Hope, peach rings for Jared, and mints or Skittles for Tony. Dr. Anthony Fauci, an advisor to Trump on the coronavirus and the director of the National Institute of Allergy and Infectious Diseases, liked manuka honey cough drops. The vice president was seldom selective, but usually preferred chocolate of some sort.

One night before leaving the office, Mark opened my desk drawer and looked at the heap of candy it contained.

"Too much?" I asked.

"No." He smiled and shook his head. "No, not at all. I want you to keep doing more."

———

I became fixated on Mark's desire to restaff OLA. He did little to hide his dislike of Eric, which only exacerbated OLA's fears that he viewed them as tools of congressional leadership and the bureaucracy who would undermine his authority. To calm the growing anxiety and uncertainty, I encouraged Mark to meet separately with the House and Senate teams in their respective East Wing offices. Afterward, I learned that it was the first time any Trump White House chief of staff had paid a visit to the East Wing.

Mark had asked me to attend the OLA meetings with him, an invitation I declined. I wanted Mark to assure OLA that he would empower them to use their experience and independent judgment to advance the president's legislative agenda. He seemed pleased with how he had been received when he returned from the second of the two meetings, admitting that he had initially been hesitant. "But you were right," he said, adding that everything I was doing had reinforced his confidence in me.

The last week of March, Mark asked if Ben Howard would be willing to meet with him. I was taken aback by his request, but asked Ben anyway. He accepted the meeting request.

Ben signaled for me to follow him out when he emerged from Mark's office. On West Executive Avenue, he stopped and looked at me and took a few contemplative moments before he said anything. I asked him if everything was okay, worried that he would tell me I had made a mistake working for Mark.

"I never thought I would say this," he told me, "but I actually think Mark may be the best person for that job." I begged him for more details, but he would only tell me that Mark had been very complimentary of me. He thought that Mark genuinely appreciated me and would look after me. "He thanked me repeatedly for giving him the opportunity to work with you," he said.

Before he turned to leave, Ben gave me some advice. "Keep your guard up still, but you're in a powerful position, Cassidy. You can bring some needed changes to this place. You have his ear." Ben's approval and his sincerity boosted my morale, and his report of Mark's sentiments was the encouragement I needed. I was on my way to using my opportunity not just to advance my career but to do right by the White House and the country. I walked back into the West Wing vowing to work even harder.

Because of our proximity to the president, Mark and I were required to test for COVID daily. We had to come to the White House early to test when we were going to travel with the president for the first time. We were going to Norfolk, Virginia, near where I had gone to college, to see off the USNS *Comfort*, which was deploying to New York Harbor to help out hospitals overwhelmed by the pandemic.

I had prepared two travel pocket cards for Mark, a routine I continued for every trip we took together. On the front of the first card was the day's travel schedule, and on the back was a list of the White House reporters traveling with us on Air Force One. On the front of the second card were the purpose of and the facts concerning the event we were attending, with a list of special guests and their basic biographical details, so that Mark would always be prepared for the people he would meet on-site.

"You know, you're really something else," he said, when I gave him the cards that morning. He motioned for me to sit down. "Where did you learn all this?"

I asked what he meant, but he didn't clarify. Instead Mark looked at me and asked, "Did you have a good childhood? A happy one?"

No one had ever asked me that question. My expression must have conveyed my surprise, because he quickly followed up. "I mean, your parents must be really proud of you, right? Of how successful you already are."

"Of course they're proud of me. But they would be proud of me if I were a teacher or a nurse and felt fulfilled by my work."

My answer didn't seem to satisfy him. He was quiet for a moment before he continued. "Well, you sure are making me proud. It's clear you love your work. I love to work, too. Especially this job. Is that how you feel, too?" I agreed it was, and he emphasized again how much he loved his job. "I think I can do a lot of good for the president."

I wanted to be supportive, so I told Mark that the president would not have chosen him if he was not confident in Mark's ability to succeed. I didn't fully absorb the moment, finding it easier to focus on him than myself.

He smiled. "Well, you better get going. Thanks for the cards. I wouldn't have known what time we were leaving."

Whenever the smaller C-32 Air Force One was designated for travel, my assigned seat was next to Bobby Engel, head of the president's Secret Service detail. That trip was the first time I would meet Bobby, and I was delighted it gave me a chance to start building a relationship with him. Bobby is reserved and soft-spoken—shy, even—and I had to keep our conversation going on both legs of the trip. But he warmed to me and was considerate and welcoming. He often dropped by our office to say hi. "You must have done something to break Bobby," Tony Ornato noted one day. They had worked with each other for decades and were very close. When I asked him to explain, he said he'd never seen Bobby this happy or personable at work.

By the end of March, COVID was consuming the White House and the country's attention. Although Mark continued to maintain that the pandemic would be under control by summer, I could see that his spirits were down. COVID was preventing us from turning to the policy initiatives we hoped the president could run for reelection on in the fall campaign. I decided to prepare a plan for once COVID was under control.

It seemed to me that the Trump administration usually reacted to events or played defense when it was beset by troubles or attacked by adversaries. Compounding our lack of offense was the administration's fixation on pushing huge policies like tax reform, comprehensive immigration reform, and a big higher education bill that stood little if any chance of attracting even modest bipartisan support. I thought they were a waste of our political resources.

I had made a quick study of President Clinton's reelection, and admired how he had brilliantly capitalized on scoring smaller, bipartisan legislative victories and used his travel and splashy White House events to portray them as massive accomplishments. I recommended that we follow a similar plan, identifying several issues where we might be able to make bipartisan progress, such as modernizing areas of the government where COVID had exposed cracks, addressing the opioid abuse epidemic and human trafficking, and strengthening workforce development programs. The president couldn't always be relied on to stay on message, so I proposed using senior surrogates to promote the achievements at carefully staged White House events and on the road.

I was confident in what I had prepared, but Mark barely looked at it when I handed him the binder. He dismissed me with a brief "thanks for doing this." I asked him if I had overstepped, and he assured me I had not. "We just want bigger legislative wins for the election, not bipartisan wins," Mark said. "We need to use our conservative base."

I felt deflated yet did not push back, worried that if I pressed my ideas, advocating for bipartisan wins, Mark would consider me disloyal to the president's agenda. Still, I had worked in legislative affairs long enough to know that the chances for big conservative victories when the Democrats controlled the House were negligible. Yet I remained committed to the cause, determined to make a difference within the parameters set by those in power.

———

As lockdowns swept the country, the president could not travel, we were not hosting many events at the White House, and we restricted the number of people he could interact with in person. The president was bored and idle, not the ideal state of mind for someone with his restless, impulsive personality. I brought Mark an idea: Could we invite some of the president's favorite members to lunch the following Saturday? When I suggested that we include Kevin Mc-Carthy, Mark hesitated a moment before agreeing. "Yeah, that's probably the right thing to do. The president does like him, and I don't want him to think Kevin and I can't get along."

When I arrived at the White House that morning, Ben Howard called to suggest I use this day as an opportunity to develop a closer relationship with Kevin. Ben emphasized that I should be discreet about it, to avoid irritating people who thought I already had too much influence, and to be particularly cautious around Mark. But Ben stressed that a good relationship with Kevin would be extremely important to my career. "You could be Kevin's new Ben Howard," he joked.

Ben and I were still on the phone when Kevin called me. I answered his call, and he asked if Mark had come in yet. I told him he was on his way. Kevin explained that he wanted to talk with me before the lunch and was hoping to catch me alone. Mark arrived before Kevin, and I suggested he go up to the residence to see the president before lunch. He had left by the time Kevin showed up. We talked for thirty or forty minutes, mostly about COVID, but also he wanted to know how I thought the White House was doing under Mark's leadership.

Then Kevin brought up Chris Cox, a Republican lobbyist who was in the running to fill the House deputy position. Ben, who had worked with Chris in the George W. Bush White House, had recommended Chris as his replacement. Mark had been suspicious of Chris's Bush White House pedigree and had put the brakes on the appointment. I had been trying to persuade Mark to let him come on board, but without much success. Kevin told me that he was going to raise the subject at lunch with the president, and suggested I follow up with Mark afterward. Neither of us knew Chris that well, but we trusted Ben's judgment.

Halfway through lunch, Mark returned to the office looking a little disgruntled and explained that Kevin had brought Chris up to the president. Mark asked if I thought Chris would be a good fit for the job. I told him I thought he would, though I barely knew Chris. "Well, alright, get me his number and I'll call him this afternoon."

After lunch, Kevin asked me to walk him to his car. When we left the office, I told him that he should call Ben and let him know that Chris would come on board in a few days. Kevin smiled. "You're even better than everyone says you are," he said. From that day forward, Kevin and I spoke almost every day.

———

I had my first one-on-one interaction with the president on Wednesday, April 15, 2020. Mark had asked me to convene weekly calls between the president, senior administration officials, and bipartisan members and senators to discuss the latest coronavirus developments. The first was scheduled for the next day, Thursday, and we had yet to issue the invitations because we had been going back and forth on whom to include. I had recommended including several centrist Republicans and left-leaning Democrats, and Mark had struck them from the list. I thought that was a mistake and said so.

As Mark was leaving Wednesday night, he instructed me to take the remaining names to the president for his sign-off. I didn't think it was appropriate for me to barge into the Oval dining room without Mark. "Can you stay and come with me?" I pleaded. "I've never talked to him alone." Mark just smiled and said, "I trust you. Go talk to him. He's expecting you." And then he left the office. I printed out the list, and called Kevin for advice. I told him the names of the members Mark had rejected, and Kevin told me to put their names back on the list and to tell the president that he had asked me to do it. I added them with a Sharpie and walked to the Oval.

The valet was in the butler's pantry, and I asked him if the president was in the dining room. "Yes, he's just started his dinner," he responded. I explained my business and said that the chief had sent me. He told me to go on in but cautioned that the president usually liked to be left alone when he was eating. That made me even more nervous, but I had no other option. I opened the door and found the president eating a hamburger and watching Fox News.

"Sir, Mark asked me to bring this list of members for your approval. I'm sorry he's not with me. He went home." I set the list on the table and added, "I'll leave you alone, but if you have any questions or edits, I'll connect with Molly." I turned to leave, but he stopped me. "What are these Sharpie names?" My stomach churned as I turned around, self-conscious of my sloppy handwriting, and nervous to breach the Mark-versus-Kevin stalemate.

I explained that they were last-minute additions—people I thought would be good to have on the call. He said nothing for a moment and then asked, "Are you sure they're good people?" I said, "Good for you? Not all the time. But good to have on the call, yes, I'm confident they are." He nodded and stared at the list again as I started to walk out.

Before I opened the door, I turned back around and added, "If you want more insight, you should call Kevin McCarthy. I'm sure he would approve of these members, too."

"You and Kevin are close?" he asked.

"Yes, sir," I answered. "I know him well because of Ben Howard. I worked for Ben before I worked for Mark." He nodded and smiled at the mention of Ben's name. "I don't need to call Kevin. List looks good to me. Good job."

After the president went up to the residence, the valet stopped by my office to tell me that the president had asked how well he knew me. It was still early in my time in the West Wing, and the valet and I had not yet gotten to know each other well. The valet had said as much to the president, to which Trump had replied,

"Well, get to know her. She's good. I like that girl. Mark was smart to hire her." The valet told me that he had never known the president to compliment someone so quickly. But from that point on, the president often asked for my insights on matters that concerned House members.

The president's cabin fever grew with each passing week of the pandemic. I proposed another lunch with Kevin, and two other members in leadership—Steve Scalise and Liz Cheney. Mark pushed back on Liz but gave in when I assured him it was the proper decision. The morning of the lunch, he laughingly warned me that I was "going to realize inviting her was a bad idea."

"Good thing I can admit a mistake, then," I shot back.

Kevin was the last guest to leave after the lunch ended. He asked me to walk him to his car. When we were outside, he told me that the president had seemed annoyed at lunch and not his usual self. I explained that he had not been himself for a while—that COVID was getting to him, and he wasn't getting enough human interaction. Kevin insisted that something else was wrong. He thought maybe Liz had irritated him. She had pushed back on a few points the president had made, which we knew he didn't like.

Later that same day, Molly called and informed us that the president wanted to see Mark and me. He was still in the dining room, she added. I was prepared to be reprimanded for having invited Liz, ready to take the blame and a told-you-so from Mark. The president was eating a second (his real) lunch and looked cross. Mark asked if everything had gone okay, and the president immediately started to complain—not about Liz, but about Steve, who he said had tried to dominate the conversation. Steve had been acting like an "obsessed fan" with no concept of personal space. "He kept bringing his chair closer to me, and getting too close to my face when he spoke, like he doesn't know I can hear him fine," the president said. He stressed several times that he did not want to be put in that situation again.

I burst out laughing when Mark and I left the dining room. "What's so funny?" he asked. "Nothing," I said. "I'm just relieved he isn't pissed about Liz!" Mark gave a quick forced laugh. I called Kevin a few minutes later and got a real laugh when I told him what had happened.

———

We planned a weekend at Camp David at the end of April to get the agitated president out of the White House. The president wanted to go to Mar-a-Lago, his Palm Beach, Florida, resort, or to his golf club in Bedminster, New Jersey, though Tony and Hope persuaded him that the optics of a golfing holiday while so many Americans were dying in a pandemic were less than optimal. They argued that the media could not criticize him for traveling to Camp David. Besides, Tony reminded him, he could play golf there. "It's only one hole, Tony," he replied. "One is better than none," Tony said.

I drove to Camp David early that morning. This would be Mark's first time—and the president's first trip in a while. I had arranged to meet with the navy commander, Jeremy Ramberg, and his staff—I wanted to make sure that everything went smoothly and that we had done everything we could to avoid irritating the president. We spent a few hours finalizing meal plans and seating arrangements and making sure that the movies the president wanted to watch were queued up.

Hope arrived on Marine One with the president. We had a drink together in our cabin as we freshened up for dinner, and drove our golf carts a little tipsy to Laurel Lodge, the main cabin, where meals are served.

At dinner, I was seated between Ivanka and Mike Pence's wife,

Karen, and across from Mark and Debbie, Dan Scavino, and the president. The president looked directly at me as he announced, "I see some new faces," and then turned to Dan to ask if everyone there was "in the circle of trust."

I looked at Mark and Dan, and back at Mark, as Dan answered, "Don't worry, sir. Everyone here is in the family."

PART III

TRANSFORM

CHAPTER 9

Empowered

I FROZE WHEN ELISE STEFANIK's name flashed across my phone screen. I had come to deeply admire her, but we had not yet formed a relationship. I thought perhaps she was calling me by mistake, but I answered anyway. Elise immediately began pleading for help—she needed to find someone at the Justice Department who could assist with an urgent issue at the Federal Bureau of Prisons. She and her staff had tried every contact they had at Justice, with no luck. I told her I would call her back in thirty minutes with a name and contact information. I had no idea where to turn, so I called Attorney General Bill Barr. He had been in our office several times, though I doubted he remembered me. Nevertheless, I got permission to give Elise his office number.

Elise texted me later that night to thank me and sent a picture of herself sitting at my desk in the chief's office. She had worked for Josh Bolten, President George W. Bush's chief of staff. She explained that she was a little older than me when her photo was taken, and though she was tasked with mail, it was an important job that shaped her career trajectory. She reminded me how special my desk was, and joked that I had big shoes to fill.

The president had actually enjoyed himself at Camp David that weekend, so much so that he wanted to schedule a visit a few weekends later with a group of House members. Knowing it was not an occasion to lobby for a balanced mix of members, I assembled a group I knew the president got along with.

Mark instructed me not to inform anyone in OLA about the trip and to issue the invitations myself, "to avoid leaks," he explained. By this point, his lack of relationship with Eric Ueland was beyond repair, and plans were taking shape to move Eric out of the White House. I had lobbied Mark repeatedly not to fire him. I advised Mark that if he did not trust Eric in that job, we should find another position for him in the administration—one where Eric was not likely to fuel Mark's paranoia about leaks. Mark remained convinced that Eric was helping Republican leadership undermine him.

I met with the House OLA team despite Mark's wishes—I felt that it was important to tell them what we were doing. They were upset that they weren't involved in planning the trip or invited to attend. I reassured them that the decision to bypass them reflected Mark's distrust of Eric, not them, as well as the president's concern about leaks. I wished that they could have come, but they weren't my main responsibility, Mark was—and at that time I still operated on the belief he had good reasons for his concerns.

A few days after we returned from the first Camp David visit, the president was scheduled for a roundtable with members of Congress that I had scheduled a few weeks before. Just as the members were set to arrive, Tony notified Mark that Katie Miller, the vice president's press secretary and Stephen Miller's wife, had tested positive for COVID. She had been at Camp David with us the weekend before, and was the second person in the president's inner circle to test positive that week. Earlier in the week, one of the president's valets had tested positive, which had privately infuriated Trump. Irrationally, he banished the valet from further duties of that kind when he returned from quarantine.

As soon as Mark got the news, he pulled me, Eliza, and Michael into his office and told us to put on masks. We were anxious, but I felt obliged to point out that if we suddenly wore masks now, the entire White House staff would assume that someone in proximity to us had contracted COVID, and the news would almost certainly get out. Mark told us to wear them anyway. As if to prove my point, Robert O'Brien, the president's national security advisor, came down the hall minutes later and asked, "Who tested positive?" Mark mumbled a confusing non-answer, and after O'Brien left, he told us to "forget about the masks."

At the start of the roundtable, the president made a few remarks. He turned to reporters who were invited for the first minutes of the event, all of them grouped behind Mark and Matt Gaetz. They immediately asked who had tested positive, and Trump blurted out Katie Miller's name. Kevin shot me a look as if to say, *My God, did no one prepare him for this?* I looked at Mark, who was scribbling on a sheet of paper—he waved it at me to indicate that I should approach, and I noticed reporters straining to read what he had written. Matt and I made eye contact as I made my way over; reading my concern about the reporters craning their necks behind them, he snatched the paper out of Mark's hand to shield it from their view. On the paper, Mark instructed me to alert Tony and the communications team so they could begin damage control.

The roundtable lasted longer than expected, well after the press pool had departed, and members competed for the president's attention. The president was relishing the time and asked the ushers to bring pigs in a blanket for the members. They passed the snacks around on a large silver platter, and the famished members picked at them, unconcerned with pandemic protocols in the COVID-infected White House.

Mark and I discussed the chaotic meeting as we walked back to the West Wing. "Make sure we coordinate better with the Usher's Office next time," he warned me. I needed to make Mark more confident in the OLA team's ability and loyalty, and I was failing.

I made members the focus of our second Camp David retreat and invited the president's closest friends in the House, which included Kevin McCarthy; Rep. Elise Stefanik and her husband, Matt Manda; Rep. Dan and Tara Crenshaw, of Texas; Rep. Lee and Diana Zeldin, of New York; Rep. Devin and Elizabeth Nunes, of California; Rep. Jim and Polly Jordan, of Ohio; and Matt Gaetz. Mark and Debbie were attending, as were Robert O'Brien and his wife, Lo-Mari, and acting national intelligence director Ric Grenell and his partner, Matt Lashey. Dan Scavino, Johnny Mc-Entee, and I were the only staffers there.

On Friday, May 15, I drove to Camp David early to meet with staff, as I had the last visit, with Mark and Debbie arriving next. The members were stuck on the Hill voting on the Democrats' $3 trillion COVID bill and wouldn't arrive until after dinner. The president was in a foul mood when he emerged from dinner, because someone had leaked the guest list for the weekend to *Politico*. Looking directly at me, he said, "I need you to figure out who it was." I already knew it was a communications aide who had shared the list of members with *Politico*, but I also knew that their intentions were harmless, and that they had shared the list with Mark's permission.

The president announced that he was going to skip the movie and return to his cabin. After he left, I reminded Mark that the members would arrive in a few hours for dinner and drinks. I offered to notify him when they arrived, but he and Debbie decided to head to bed early.

Kevin was unbothered by the president's and Mark's absence when he arrived. He ordered a few bottles of bourbon and wine from the bar and invited some of the members to his cabin. We hung out at Kevin's for a while, drinking quite a bit before people drifted off to their quarters. A few of us were left when, at one o'clock or so, Dan Crenshaw, who had lost an eye in Afghanistan, brought out a display case of variously designed glass eyes he always carried with him, and began popping in one after another and asking us which we liked best.

There was a knock on the door. I thought it was Camp David staff coming to warn us to quiet down—Kevin's cabin was across from the president's. But when Kevin opened the door, we discovered Matt Gaetz leaning against the doorframe. Matt straightened his posture when Kevin asked him what he wanted, and he explained that he had seen my golf cart parked outside and thought that this was my cabin. Embarrassed, I got up and asked Matt what he needed. He explained that he was lost and asked me to escort him to his cabin. I told him to proceed around the circle drive—all the cabins were clearly marked and it was impossible to get lost. He asked me one more time to leave with him. "Get a life, Matt," Kevin said, then shut the door.

The president was in a great mood the next night and genuinely enjoyed himself at dinner, talking about the election and other things with people he felt he could trust. Everyone watched a movie together after dinner. I rode with Kevin to the movie theater and we arrived at the same time as the president. The three of us walked in together, and Kevin said to the president, "You know, Cassidy's your secret weapon." The president looked at Kevin with a smug grin and turned to me. "Not so secret, Kevin," he replied. "Not so secret."

After the movie, many of us returned to Kevin's cabin for drinks again. It was equipped with a woodstove, and Dan kept the fire going all night. Kevin asked if I heard Mark talk to the president about election messaging. I was clearly confused, so Kevin elaborated that during the movie, the president had showed him a draft tweet he wanted to send that included the phrase "stop the steal." I had heard the phrase before, but not in a serious context. He suggested I keep my ears open, but it would be incredibly irresponsible messaging to promote. We agreed to keep each other in the loop.

As the sun began to rise, I decided to head back to my cabin for a power nap and to sleep off the wine. As I crawled into bed, I heard fire trucks and wondered if it was a drill, which seemed unlikely at that hour. Just before I fell asleep, Kevin texted me a photo of firefighters outside his cabin. Undetected by any of us, it had filled with smoke from the woodstove, setting off alarms. "We had too much to drink," he wrote. "We almost burned the place to the ground."

Before we left Camp David that morning, Mark pulled me aside to compliment me for "cozying up to Kevin," which he thought would prove useful to the White House. He seemed to believe that there was some acting on my part, but I genuinely enjoyed Kevin's company and valued our growing friendship. I did not realize then that I would become caught up in one of the most complicated three-way relationships in contemporary Republican politics.

———

The president tried on several N95 masks at the Honeywell plant in Phoenix, Arizona, which manufactured all manner of personal protective equipment (PPE). He was not thrilled that staff urged him to wear a mask, believing it would make him look weak and afraid of the virus. He decided on a white mask and strapped it to his face before asking each staffer whether or not he should wear it in front of the press pool.

I was standing behind Mark and had not expected the president to ask for my opinion. But he did, making a thumbs-up/thumbs-down gesture. I could feel Mark glare at me as I slowly shook my head. The president pulled the mask off and asked why I thought he should not wear it.

I pointed at the straps of the N95 I was holding. When he looked at the straps of his mask, he saw that they were covered in bronzer. "Why did no one else tell me that," he snapped. "I'm not wearing this thing." He wore safety goggles on the tour. The press would criticize him for not wearing a mask, not knowing that the depth of his vanity had caused him to reject masks—and then millions of his fans followed suit.

Unaware of the larger repercussions or even the humor of the moment, I instead worried that he might have resented my presumptuousness. He always checks himself in a mirror his valet carries before starting any public event, so he would have probably seen the bronzer-smeared mask before stepping in front of the cameras. I also worried that Mark would be angry with me, but when the president began the tour, Mark assured me, "I don't know what you're doing, but keep doing it—he really likes you," followed by an elbow bump.

———

The president was scheduled to attend a NASA SpaceX rocket launch in Cape Canaveral on Wednesday, May 27. But weather conditions forced a postponement until Saturday, when Mark couldn't accompany him because his daughter was getting married in Atlanta. Mark asked me to go in his stead. I had not had a day off since I started in Mark's office and had been looking forward to a quiet weekend alone. I suggested sending Tony instead, but Mark insisted I go and keep him "in the loop," since several members of Congress were flying with the president. I agreed, knowing I could spend time with Kevin, Elise, and Alyssa Farah, whom Mark had hired to be White House communications director. Alyssa and I were instantly close friends.

The president was cheerful from the moment we started out, and his mood lightened further on the flight as the members gathered in the conference room on Air Force One complimented him incessantly. Mark repeatedly asked for updates, and at one point I excused myself to call him. When I returned, I learned Matt had been lobbying the president to pardon Roger Stone. Kevin and Elise were looking to me almost desperately to put an end to the conversation. I didn't know what to do. Fortunately, the president returned to his personal office at the front of the airplane. I glared at Matt, who responded with a flip remark: "No guardrails when the chief is gone."

A little while later, Michael Waltz, another member from Florida and an Afghanistan war veteran, excused himself. I found him in the president's office, asking for a campaign donation. Appalled, I told him I needed him back in the conference room. The president smiled and told Michael, "You better listen to her. She's tough. You don't want to be on her bad side."

Alyssa and I had driven together to Joint Base Andrews that morning, but when we landed back there, Kevin insisted that we ride home with him in his motorcade so I would not have to drive through the Black Lives Matter protests in Washington. A white Minneapolis police officer had murdered George Floyd, a Black man, earlier that week, and protests had broken out in the Twin Cities and quickly spread around the country, including Washington. On the flight back, the president had expressed his desire that Lafayette Park, across from the White House, the epicenter of the Washington protests, be cleared of the protesters, even the majority of whom were exercising their First Amendment right to free speech, calling attention to social injustices the Black community faces on a daily basis.

The night before the Cape Canaveral trip, protesters had swarmed over temporary barricades in front of the Treasury building, next to the White House, and hurled objects at Secret Service agents, striking dozens of them. The Secret Service, following established protocol, had ordered that the White House be put on temporary lockdown, and had moved the president to the underground Emergency Operations Center. This news broke in the *New York Times* on Sunday, and the president was immediately criticized for moving to the bunker. The movement had been mandated by Secret Service security protocols. Trump's predecessors would have done the same in similar circumstances.

I had been in constant phone contact with the Secret Service over the weekend. They had moved Mark to a secure room in Atlanta for private calls. I'd tried to convince him to take an earlier flight back to Washington, but he had refused, explaining that he thought everything was under control. It wasn't.

The president was incensed by the *Times* story. The protests fueled his anger and supplied him with reasons for ordering a crackdown. Among the acts of violence and vandalism that had occurred Sunday night was a fire set in the basement of the parish house of historic St. John's Church on Lafayette Square. He demanded that Mark return to the White House, find the person who had leaked the story, and have the Justice Department indict them. Tony arranged for the military to fly Mark back Monday afternoon.

By Monday morning, the protests in Washington were surging, and reports of vandalism and violence proliferated. The White House was in chaos. Elise texted me to say that she was getting menacing text messages from Roger Stone. He had heard that she had pushed back when Matt had suggested on Air Force One that the president issue Roger a pardon. I told Mark about Matt's and Roger's inappropriate behavior with Elise when he returned from Atlanta that afternoon, but we never discussed the matter further.

When Mark arrived, the president had already seized on the idea of making an appearance at St. John's Church. Mark, Tony, Bobby Engel, and I checked out the site that afternoon. The Secret Service cleared a path for us, as the scene was crowded, chaotic, and tense.

Around six thirty that evening, riot police and police on horseback began clearing the park, using tear gas and pepper spray. The president planned to make brief remarks in the Rose Garden before walking to the church. Minutes before he was to speak, I heard him yell from the Oval Office, "Someone bring me a Bible. I need to hold a Bible. Bring me a Bible." I was confused—the president kept a Bible in the Oval Office, but I thought maybe he had forgotten. Staff scrambled and collected every Bible they could quickly locate in the West Wing, bringing him a dozen or more to choose from. He picked the Bible he thought was "best looking."

The president began his speech that evening by describing himself as "your president of law and order and an ally of all peaceful protesters." He declared that he was "ending the riots and lawlessness," which he denounced as "domestic terror." He promised to strictly enforce, using "thousands and thousands of heavily armed soldiers," a 7:00 p.m. curfew in Washington. He closed his remarks by announcing, "Now I'm going to pay my respects to a very, very special place."

With that, we began to make our way across the North Lawn to Lafayette Park. Mark stopped to talk to some of the National Guard soldiers and Secret Service, and I started coughing. He glared at me, but I couldn't stop. That's when an agent told me that the police had used tear gas to clear the area. I was horrified. The president stood in front of St. John's Church, posing for photographs, holding upside down the Bible that had been procured for him. Then he gathered around him administration officials who had accompanied him there, including Mark, for more pictures.

Kevin called me while we were still at St. John's and asked plaintively, "Did someone not even give him a simple Bible verse to remember? The country is on fire and he's holding a Bible upside down." I filled him in on the frantic treasure hunt for Bibles that afternoon.

———

Eric Ueland was preparing to leave the White House for a senior position at the State Department. He emailed OLA staff, directing them not to come to the White House that week because of COVID. But his email had been somewhat cryptic, so I went to his office to check in, and found him packing his belongings. I casually asked if I could help, and he told me that he would rather be left in peace. I didn't know what to say. I was both sad he was leaving and relieved he was going—in the false hope it would placate Mark's concerns with OLA.

I knew I had done my part to make sure Eric was given another compelling job opportunity within the executive branch, but I felt sorry his tenure at the White House was ending this way. I knew how deeply Eric cared about his job, and he never had a fair opportunity to succeed under Mark's leadership. But I reminded myself that my role was to support Mark—relying on my belief that he had the president's best interests in mind. I was not entrusted with my job and its responsibilities to get hung up on emotions, I reminded myself. Emotions were unwelcome in the Trump White House. It was imperative to turn them off as a means to survive.

Amy Swonger, the director of the Senate OLA team, had been emailing Mark requesting a meeting ever since she heard the news of Eric's imminent departure. Mark would have preferred not to take the meeting—he knew that she was going to ask to be promoted to Eric's job. I had advised him to give Amy the job or at least make her acting director until after the election. He was worked up minutes before the three of us met, pressing me again about whether I was sure he should promote her. The reason I gave Mark for supporting the move was simple: I was worried that if we brought in someone new, we would likely lose a lot of the rest of the OLA staff and would not have time before the election to replace them or train their replacements. I was also concerned—though I did not say it—that Mark would have me do the job if he denied it to Amy, and I had enough on my plate as it was. Mark was still questioning my advice when Eliza let us know that Amy was outside, and I opened his door to let her in.

I was seated to Mark's left on his couch as Amy made her pitch for the job of OLA director. Mark responded sympathetically but said he could not promote her. What he could offer was the position of acting director—until after the election, at which point he would reevaluate staffing decisions and consider making her appointment permanent.

His offer seemed to satisfy Amy, and I felt relieved. As Amy stood up to leave, Mark said, "Oh, by the way, Amy, I'm going to make Cassidy my legislative advisor. I know you two are real close from her time in OLA. Make sure whatever you do, you work with Cassidy. It's going to be a very busy election season, and I just need her to help keep me on track."

Judging by the smile still plastered across her face, Amy was unbothered by Mark's comment. But I did not expect Mark to throw that curve ball, and I struggled to keep my composure. I knew exactly what Mark was doing. He was making me Amy's supervisor, and the de facto director of legislative affairs.

"See?" Mark said after Amy left. "I told you I would take care of you."

I could barely muster a response. "If that's what you need me to do," I said. "I serve at the pleasure of the president."

The next afternoon, flying back to Andrews on Air Force One from the president's trip to a PPE factory in Maine, I was copied on an email from the White House press office that had been sent to their entire distribution list—White House staff, Hill staff, reporters, lobbyists, and others. It was an announcement: Amy Swonger was now acting director of OLA, and I had been appointed special assistant to the president and legislative advisor to the chief of staff. The press office typically did not widely disseminate news of staff changes, especially when there was a contentious departure like Eric's. Mark ordered this press release to signal to OLA and anyone familiar with normal White House protocol that I had as much authority over OLA as its new acting director.

Rep. Greg Walden, of Oregon, was traveling with us. I had gotten to know Greg, a Republican, through Kevin, and I liked him.

I showed him the release, and he congratulated me. "No, Greg," I said, "this is going to tick off a lot of people." He understood, but tried to reassure me that I had a good head on my shoulders and would do just fine. I did my best to avoid Mark on the flight back. As we were getting off the plane, he asked, "Did you see the press release?" Without looking at him, I answered, "Yep."

Before I went to sleep that night, I mapped out a plan that I thought could work for all involved. I would convene weekly meetings with Amy so she could fill me in on what was happening on the Hill that week. I would attend OLA staff meetings once a week as an observer. I would not reach out to any OLA staffers directly without letting Amy know. We met that Monday, and I assured her that I wouldn't step on her toes, but that she needed to keep me in the loop to avoid creating problems with Mark.

It would not take long for my plan to fall apart, and I would begin to question how much longer I'd be able to sustain my "Mark knows best" rationale, given how often I was beginning to find myself in contentious predicaments.

———

I was late for work on June 4, and before I had time to check the president's morning tweets or my emails, Kevin called, inflamed about Mark meddling in the Republican primary for North Carolina's Eleventh Congressional District—Mark's former district. Kevin had endorsed Madison Cawthorn and was caught off guard when the president tweeted that morning endorsing Cawthorn's Republican opponent, Lynda Bennett, who happened to be friendly with Mark and Debbie.

Kevin had never raised his voice with me, so I, too, was caught off guard. I admitted that I had not been tracking the race, and when I asked him to walk me through the issue again, he erroneously thought I was defending Mark and hung up.

When I arrived at work, Mark was in the Oval Office with the president. I scrolled through the president's Twitter feed and found the dreaded offending tweet. Mark returned and went directly into his office, shutting the door behind him. Moments later, my phone vibrated with a text from him, asking me to come in.

Mark was on his sofa and appeared distraught when I entered. The president was furious that his endorsement of Lynda Bennett had sparked a conflict with Kevin, and he had ordered Mark to fix it. Mark said it was Debbie who had suggested the endorsement, and assured me he had no personal involvement with it. He begged me to smooth things over with Kevin. I told him I would call Kevin, but asked him to promise that he had no role in Lynda's endorsement. I explained that I would not disclose the information to Kevin if Mark did not want me to, but that I was trying to cover myself from fanning the flames and worsening the conflict. Mark assured me that he had no role in the endorsement, and I believed him.

I walked outside and called Kevin from West Executive Avenue. I explained what Mark had told me. Kevin did not interrupt, and when I finished, he said calmly, "Cassidy, Mark is playing you. Call me back when you realize that."

Irritated with Kevin, I stormed back into the West Wing and went straight to Mark's office. I told Mark that I had spoken with Kevin and that things were going to be fine. He brought me to see the president, who, still infuriated, just glared at me and demanded, "Fix it with Kevin!"

It did not take long or many sources for me to figure out that both Mark and Debbie were behind Lynda Bennett's endorsement. When I learned of this, I immediately texted Kevin and apologized. I was mortified—and irritated with myself for having trusted Mark so easily. Kevin chuckled and said he knew I would figure it out eventually.

To do my job well, Mark and I needed to have a close working relationship that included a high degree of trust. Over the past several months, I had begun to let my guard down with him. I was enforcing what Mark wanted across the administration and had done so effectively. But finding out he had lied to me with such convincing confidence made me realize that my guard should have always been up, at least partway.

Kevin had been right all along. I needed to watch out for myself.

Mark's relationship with OLA did not improve after Eric's departure. It seemed to me that Mark wanted to continue keeping Amy and the rest of the team in the dark about our interactions with members of Congress, or only inform them after the fact. But Mark expected OLA to run everything they did by us. Mark did not invite Amy to a meeting we had with Jared and Senator Tim Scott, of South Carolina. He ordered me not to tell her or anyone at OLA when he and I went up to the Hill on another occasion. I felt terrible about it, and some of the OLA staff texted me to say how upset they were that I hadn't told them; they had found out from congressional staff. They rightly complained that I had made them look unprofessional.

A few days later, Amy and Chris Cox emailed Jared and asked for his help in whipping a bill in the House. Amy neglected to include me on the email, and Jared had asked for my permission, which was embarrassing for both of us. Mark was furious when he found out, and I had to talk him down from firing not only Amy but also Chris. He scheduled a meeting for the four of us.

I sat in a chair across from Mark's couch as we waited for Amy and Chris to arrive. He told me to sit next to him, explaining, "I want them to understand who is in control here." Mark told Amy and Chris that they were on thin ice, and stressed again that they must report to me. It was hard for me to maintain eye contact with my two colleagues, but I did. I said nothing during the meeting, even when Mark invited me to.

———

Presidential ire was becoming more of an occupational hazard every day in the pandemic-constrained White House. Stories of

Trump's eruptions circulated daily. Mark returned from the Oval late one night after the president had gone up to the residence and shut our main office door, looking defeated. The president was on a firing spree that day, so Mark and the White House counsel's office had their hands full, trying to offer the president sound advice that would not stir unnecessary controversy. The president had demanded that Attorney General Bill Barr fire Geoffrey Berman, the US Attorney for the Southern District of New York.

Mark leaned against the door and rubbed his temples. "Cass, if I can get through this job and manage to keep him out of jail"— referring to our boss, the president—"I'll have done a good job. Can you call my detail and tell them I'm ready to go home?"

———

What little patience the president possessed had been exhausted. He wanted to be out on the campaign trail. "We have to start doing rallies again," he stressed to anyone within earshot.

The consensus among senior staff was that rallies were a bad idea both for reasons of public health and because it wasn't the time to wade into politics. Clearly indoor rallies were off-limits, for the former reason.

"Antifa is having rallies every day on the streets," countered Trump, referring to the Black Lives Matter protests. "We are going to plan a big rally, and it's going to happen as soon as possible."

Brad Parscale, the campaign director, and other senior campaign aides selected an indoor arena with a seating capacity of nineteen thousand in Tulsa, Oklahoma, for the first pandemic-era campaign rally. It was scheduled for June 19, Juneteenth, the federal holiday commemorating the day Texan enslaved Black people learned of their emancipation, honoring the end of slavery in the US. It would occur the same month as the ninety-ninth anniversary of the Tulsa Race Massacre, when hordes of white rioters burned Black Wall Street to the ground, injuring and killing over a thousand Black people. Tony and I agreed it was such a bad idea. Wiser minds prevailed, and the date was changed to June 20.

Trusting his campaign aides, the president was under the impression that the arena was going to be packed, with an additional hundred thousand supporters in the overflow area outside. No one of sane mind in the White House believed this, though. Tony had been tracking ticket distribution all week. "They're all nuts if they think that many people are coming," he told me in his office. "But people are flocking online to get tickets," I said, parroting what we had heard from the campaign.

"Antifa is getting the tickets. Kids on TikTok are getting the tickets. Trust me, it's not our people. We've never had tickets go this fast," he observed.

Mark pulled out of the Tulsa trip at the last minute. By now, when Mark did not want to go on a trip, he was comfortable sending me alone, reminding me, "Eyes and ears, Cass." As a general rule, Mark only wanted to hear from me if I had news that could affect the outcome of the election or knew something consequential about the president's state of mind. If Trump was angry or if he said something that might hurt the campaign, Mark needed to know right away. I exercised my own judgment about when to contact him.

So, on Saturday, June 20, I flew without Mark on Air Force One to Tulsa. The president was still in a horrible mood on the flight, and he kept asking anyone in his vicinity for an update on the number of rally attendees who passed through the magnetometers in an effort to judge how full the space was.

Alyssa was in the conference room with the president for a while. She came back to sit with me. "He thinks the arena is full," she said. "But we have pictures from inside the arena, and it's definitely not full." I looked at her, concerned. "Maybe it will be full by the time we arrive," I suggested. We both knew that was not going to happen. As we landed, I texted Mark that we might have a problem on our hands. He told me to get everything figured out.

I asked the OLA staffers who had traveled with us to help the House members find their seats, and then I ran into the arena to see with my own eyes how bad it was.

Very bad. There were more seats open than there were seats filled.

I saw Herman Cain, former presidential candidate, Tea Party activist, and friend of the president's, in the VIP section. I went over to say hello. He gave me a hug over the railing.

"How do you think this is going?" I asked.

"It looks great in here," he said. "You don't think it looks great?"

"It looks like . . . something."

I kept walking around the VIP section and found Elise, and we exchanged a concerned look. "How is he right now?" she asked. I shook my head.

I went backstage and called Mark with an update. "We're maybe halfway full. The entire upper level is empty. The boss is going to be so mad."

Behind me, the president was giving an interview to a local media reporter. He still had no idea how empty the arena was. Meanwhile, I spotted Alyssa and Kayleigh McEnany, the White House press secretary, huddled together in the back. I went over to them and said, "Alyssa, you should talk to the president."

"Why me?" she asked, giving us a look. I shrugged. I was not sure why I suggested she talk to him, but I thought he would appreciate some news coming from her. He had grown to respect Alyssa and appreciated her insight on touchy subjects. "Okay, fine. I'll do it." Alyssa approached the president with the daunting task of asking him to face reality—then got a last-second reprieve when, just at that moment, he got a call.

I went in the opposite direction and sat in a chair alongside the back wall of the backstage area. I didn't want to be anywhere near the president when he saw all the empty seats. It was not his fault that the arena was not full. He did push for an indoor rally during

COVID, but it was the campaign's job to provide an accurate estimate of crowd size.

The president was fired up, and he spotted me by the back wall and yelled for me to call Mark. I fumbled with my phone. "He wants you," I reported to Mark. He hung up and called the president.

My head volleyed from one cluster of people arguing with each other to the next, everyone shouting opinions, casting blame. I wished Tony were there, to point out the obvious: we never should have scheduled an indoor, mask-optional rally at the height of COVID in the first place.

———

The president's Fourth of July event at Mount Rushmore was far more successful. Mark sat onstage with the president, so Tony and I were free to watch the fireworks from the VIP section. We found Dan and Tara Crenshaw. Dan was wearing his Captain America glass eye. Tony snapped a photo of the three of us and I sent it to our group chat with Kevin.

"Don't burn everything to the ground," he wrote back.

CHAPTER 10

A Seat at the Table

COVID HAD RANSACKED the economy, killing jobs, crippling businesses, and clogging supply chains. The initial CARES Act passed in March had provided temporary relief. But with the pandemic in its fourth month and no end in sight, and unemployment benefits and eviction protections about to expire, we urgently needed a second relief bill.

The White House and congressional Republicans would have their usual fights with the Democrats over the size and scope of what to offer, and which programs were more important than others. Freedom Caucus members distrusted Treasury Secretary Mnuchin, who they believed had given too much in earlier deals with Democrats. Mark's participation in the negotiations was meant to signal that it wouldn't happen this time. But the political reality was an unpopular president running for reelection in a pandemic, which required us to try to find a way to cut a deal with Democratic leaders on a package that extended unemployment benefits and the moratorium on eviction notices, and push it through *before* the election.

We started negotiations with Speaker Pelosi and Chuck Schumer, Senate minority leader, in mid-July 2020, and the talks continued for nearly three weeks. Mark made me the White House point person for the negotiations. Normally, the director of OLA would be at the table in these kinds of meetings, but Mark had completely frozen out OLA.

Amy had shared an email from Senate staffers with me about starting negotiations. I showed the email to Mark, who agreed we would negotiate but instructed that he and I were the sole White House representatives. I felt split in my allegiances. When Amy would ask for updates on the progress, Mark reminded me not to share any details, citing his desire to avoid leaks.

Amy was understandably frustrated, but I was not in a position to prevent that, and sometimes her irritation irritated me. She would eventually convene a call every night with Treasury counselor Dan Kowalski, Larry Kudlow, and Francis Brooke, Kudlow's deputy, to stay up to speed on the negotiations. Francis, whom Ben had introduced me to, told me about the call. I would go to his office and listen in.

I was in a difficult position with my former colleagues in legislative affairs. I was seen as Mark's person, which I was. They felt I overstepped my authority, which I now appreciate in hindsight but resented at the time. If I overstepped, it was because the president's chief of staff explicitly instructed me to. Mark had already fired Chris Cox for sharing information with lobbyists. A few days later, when we were traveling on Air Force One with the president to Florida, Mark showed me a text from the Freedom Caucus staff director, who recommended that he fire three more OLA staffers—three of my closest friends, and more important, three of the most competent staffers we had. "You cannot gut OLA before the election," I protested, trying to buy time in the hope that Mark's attention would shift to more pressing matters. He agreed, and dropped the issue for the time being.

That same Air Force One flight was the last trip we took with the president before Mark and I would be on the Hill every day meeting with the Democratic leadership until Congress recessed in August. At the second stop, for a fundraiser, Mark instructed staff to stay on the plane after learning that some of the attendees had tested positive for COVID. This is when we heard that the president was going to commute Roger Stone's sentence. I didn't know much about Stone or the crime he had been convicted of, but I knew he was trouble. That seemed to be the consensus among most White House staff not named Donald Trump.

Alyssa was upset by the news, as were Kevin and Elise when I called to warn them before it became official. We all, in part, blamed Matt Gaetz.

———

The COVID relief bill negotiations were in full swing. Besides Mark and me, others who gathered in the Speaker's office each day included Secretary Mnuchin and Dan Kowalski. On the Democrats' side of the table were Schumer and Pelosi and their senior advisors.

I always sat close to Mark and the secretary. If Mark was unable to attend a meeting, I went with the secretary in Mark's stead. I grew to admire Secretary Mnuchin—he was quirky, and I appreciated that there was no artifice with him.

At times, I felt like I was in over my head, and thought Mark would be better served in these meetings if he were staffed with OLA staffers with years of expertise in fiscal policy and experience with budget negotiations. My workload had effectively doubled. While it was stressful, paradoxically, I was self-assured and confident in my standing with Mark, so I could serve effectively as a bridge between the West Wing and Congress.

We regularly briefed Leader McConnell on our progress or lack of it. I also took it upon myself to brief other members, like Josh Gottheimer and Tom Reed, the Democratic and Republican chairs of the bipartisan Problem Solvers Caucus, who I knew could be instrumental in passing a deal, should we ever agree on one.

I made sure we kept Kevin in the loop as well. If I had not stopped in his office in the morning before the negotiation meetings began, I made sure to bring him up to speed on the phone. And we talked again most nights. On those evening calls, Kevin gave me advice on how to make myself more valuable to Mark and to the process. He never thought the negotiations had a chance of succeeding. He would laughingly remind me that Mark had never brokered any major deal in Congress, and he "definitely won't with Pelosi and Mnuchin in the room."

Our political goal during the negotiations, we assured skeptical Republicans, was to stand firm as conservatives and battle Pelosi and Schumer's liberal idealism. In reality, all the players at the table were respectful of each other. The meetings could become contentious at times, sometimes out of genuine frustration on someone's part, other times as a performative gesture. Mostly, though, the parties to the talks were courteous and shared the overall objective of bringing relief to Americans in need.

The issue wasn't only how much to spend but how to apportion the spending. The numbers didn't always matter as much as how priorities appeared to be ranked. To me, the negotiations should have been a process of compromises to address the nation's needs in an order that could be defended to voters of both parties.

Every day, I took detailed notes. Every night, I went back to the office and tried to make sense of them. I created a separate binder for every possible program, from paid maternity leave, to extending unemployment benefits, to renovations of ventilation systems in office buildings.

The work continued on weekends. On Saturdays, I updated our

policy papers for each program. On Sundays, we had a staff conference call that included Pelosi's and Schumer's senior aides and Dan Kowalski. The idea was to set priorities for the week ahead. I often leaned on Speaker Pelosi's chief of staff during these negotiations. She knew I was in over my head, but she respected the authority Mark had conferred on me and appreciated my professionalism.

One night, Speaker Pelosi and Secretary Mnuchin had been going back and forth for hours over a single item. It was late. We were all exhausted and hungry. I was sitting in my chair, looking out the window at the blinking red lights on the Washington Monument. I remembered the joy I felt during my first visit to Washington as a child. Everything I had done had brought me to this moment—one I had dreamed of since I was a child: to serve my country.

Nearing the end of the first week of August, it became clear the negotiations were failing. A few deals on smaller items had been notionally agreed to, but none of the major issues had been resolved. Mark and the president knew we were not going to strike a deal, and they were preparing executive orders to extend some relief benefits without Congress's agreement.

One night returning from the Hill, the stress of the negotiations sank in, and I felt responsible for why they were failing. I felt I had not adequately prepared Mark for the meetings that day. I started apologizing to Mark profusely for letting him down.

He shut the main door to our office suite. "I don't know what you're apologizing for," he said. "For not being cut out for the job, for letting you down," I replied. Mark looked at me with genuine sadness and concern and pulled me in for a hug. "Oh, Cassidy, you have nothing to apologize for. I'm so sorry for putting too much pressure on you. You're doing a great job. Really, you are."

I reacted harshly, telling him not to lie to me, that we were both better served when he was a straight shooter and told me where I was failing. He told me to go home and get some sleep. That's all he wanted me to do.

I didn't answer Kevin's call when I got home. I stewed over my conversation with Mark, and my shortcomings that I thought had precipitated it, for the rest of the night and off and on for months after.

When negotiations ultimately ground to a halt, I would not have much time for regrets or second-guessing in the aftermath of our failure. Mark left for a family vacation at Yellowstone National Park, and I took my first days off in many months. When we returned to Washington, we would spend most of our time focused on the president's reelection campaign, and the challenges of holding political rallies, not to mention a national convention, amid a pandemic.

By now I had become a more familiar presence to the president, and he to me. Right before I took a few days off, I popped into the dining room with a few staffers to share some updates about Congress's fall legislative schedule. The president looked at me and then turned to Hope and asked if she would give me her hair stylist's contact information. He turned back to me and said, "Cassidy, you should get some of her highlights. I think they would look really nice on you."

That weekend, Alyssa and I lightened our hair. When we showed up at work on Monday with our new blonde locks, we got a lot of laughs.

"You two took some time to get pampered this weekend," Mark observed. "That's why you weren't at my house. You got a little blonde in there. I like it. I'm glad to see you're taking care of yourself."

When the president saw my hair, he loved it. "Cassidy! You did it! I was so right. Wasn't I right?"

"Yes, sir, you were right," I said. Actually, blonde hair did not suit me. After a couple of months, I returned to the dark side.

CHAPTER 11

On the Trail

"YOU'RE QUITE THE FIGHTER," Mark told me. "You sure are loyal to me." I glanced at him before I resumed typing.

We were at the airport in Mankato, Minnesota, where the president held his first campaign rally after the failed COVID relief negotiations. I had not realized until we landed that OLA neglected to invite all Republican members in the Minnesota delegation to fly with us on Air Force One. I called to berate them for the lack of oversight; my temper was boiling almost as hot as the airport tarmac. I must have been loud, because Mark heard me over the loudspeakers that broadcast the president's speech.

"No," I said, and wiped a bead of sweat off my upper lip. "I'm dedicated. And I'm astounded at the lack of dedication from some of your staff."

Mark returned my stare and said, smiling, "I know, that's why I trust you. You're dedicated and loyal."

I turned toward the stage and pretended to listen to the president's speech. I was past the point of denying my growing dedication to Mark and the president—to them personally and not strictly to their office, as I had initially pledged. I was proud of this at the time, and felt recognized when Mark acknowledged it. But he wasn't supposed to acknowledge it. We both fell silent.

"Would you take a bullet for him?" Mark asked. My head snapped toward him in surprise, but his eyes were fixed on the stage. I tried to make a joke. It was the only thing I could think of on the spot. "Yeah, sure, but could it be to the leg?" He laughed.

As the president began to wrap up, we walked toward the stage. "Would you?" I asked him.

"I would do anything," Mark answered, looking over his shoulder at me, "to get him reelected."

On the flight back to Washington several days later, I joined Doug Mills, a highly respected and legendary *New York Times* photographer, for a glass of bourbon in the press cabin on Air Force One. Minutes later, Mark came back to talk with the reporters. He spent most of the rest of the flight chatting with them off the record.

Doug mentioned several times during that flight how impressed he was with Mark's openness to the press. Some of Mark's predecessors were far less forthcoming, and the friendly demeanor he maintained went a long way with the reporters. I felt proud of Mark as I listened to Doug.

Toward the end of the flight, after a second bourbon, I blurted out, "Mark asked if I would take a bullet for the president." I felt I could trust Doug. He looked at me with utter confusion and asked me to repeat what I had said. So I did. He asked how I had answered the question. "I said I would . . . to the leg." He broke into a smile that quickly faded as he shook his head.

"He shouldn't ask you things like that," he said. I felt defensive and for a moment regretted telling Doug. *He doesn't understand how important loyalty is*, I thought. But I caught myself in midthought before I said anything else I'd regret. I wondered when I had started to think of loyalty in such terms, but I shook the thought away.

———

The coronavirus uprooted plans for the 2020 Republican National Convention (RNC), as it had public gatherings all over the country. Instead of one large hall in a city chosen for political and logistical reasons, the convention that renominated Donald Trump would be scattered in multiple locations. And instead of giving a single acceptance speech on the fourth and final night, as was customary, Trump would appear in person at the convention on three of the four nights, and by video on the other one, which was fitting, given his love of the limelight.

The convention opened August 24, in Charlotte, North Carolina. When we arrived at the convention center, Kevin was waiting for us offstage, and we caught up as we waited for the president and Mark to enter. The president shouted, "Kevin! My Kevin!" when he arrived. Mark and I made eye contact, but he would not come say hello to Kevin himself. He knew it was important that the president understand that Kevin and I were close. He wanted Trump to believe that he was close to Kevin as well, and that I had been instrumental in building that relationship.

Alyssa and I shared a bottle of wine and watched the vice president's speech at Fort McHenry in the comfort of her West Wing office. We chatted with Rep. Lee Zeldin, of New York, and Elise, both of whom Alyssa had helped prepare for their convention speeches that week.

We seemed to be the only people in the press office who were paying attention to what the vice president was saying. Alyssa asked if I thought we would win the election. "Of course," I answered. She didn't say anything in response, which worried me. I asked her what she thought. She hesitated for a moment. "He only has a fair shot because of Mark," she began. "Mark just can't screw this up." For the first time in months, I began to worry that we might not win the election after all.

When Mark and I had pulled onto West Executive Avenue earlier that evening, he'd asked me to turn on my cell phone's voice recorder. Confused, I asked why. I made eye contact in the rearview mirror with a Secret Service agent, whose look seemed to say, *Why are you questioning his authority?* But I did not back down, considering the request bizarre. Mark had never directed me to do anything like that. When I did not immediately do as he asked, he turned on his own phone's recorder before calling Speaker Pelosi to discuss a COVID-related issue.

I felt unsettled. Mark knew I worked hard to build a semi-trusting relationship with the Speaker and her staff. The agents got out of the car, and I tried to follow, but Mark held up a finger, motioning for me to stay. When he finished the call, he told me never to be too trusting of people. "You never know when you'll have to show your own receipts."

Mark wanted to grab a bite to eat at the Trump International Hotel before people began gathering at the White House for the president's RNC acceptance speech on August 27. I sat in the hotel lobby with his security detail, waiting for him to finish. I felt a tap on my shoulder. Matt Gaetz was standing behind me. He asked if he could ride with us back to the White House, a few blocks from the hotel. I looked him up and down and replied, "It looks like your legs are working just fine." He said he was going to tell Mark I had been rude to him.

People were already assembling in the West Wing when we got back from the hotel. Holding an explicitly political event at the White House was controversial. The campaign had intended to stage the president's acceptance speech at the hotel. But DC mayor Muriel Bowser had put in place strict COVID guidelines for indoor gatherings, which had ticked off the president, and he had decided to hold it in the White House, critics be damned.

Tony had played a key role in organizing the event. Before the festivities commenced, I caught up with him in his office, since we hadn't seen each other much that week. I told him what had happened in Mark's limo that day. He laughed, and jokingly said, "Chief knows what he's doing. I wouldn't question his decisions if I were you."

Most guests had gathered in Mark's office suite before heading to the South Lawn. But Kevin arrived late, running down the hallway to our office, after everyone else had left. I stood up from my desk to meet him in the hallway. "No, no," he said breathlessly. "Is everyone outside?" I nodded. He laughed and said, "We'll never have a chance to do this again," and he started posing for photographs in Mark's office. He told me to show them to Mark and say, "The president's fifth chief of staff."

I watched most of the president's speech from the Rose Garden with several Secret Service agents. Everyone was awed by the fireworks after, as was I, until one display spelled out "Trump 2020" above the Washington Monument. I began to fret that the evening's military-parade-like pageantry had been too nakedly political and self-congratulatory for an election event held on the White House grounds.

I tried to reassure myself that Mayor Bowser had given us no choice. This was the president's event, and he could kick off his next four years in office wherever and however he wanted.

We flew the next day to a rally in New Hampshire. It was the first time I could remember that the number of people allowed through the magnetometers became an issue. New Hampshire Republican governor Chris Sununu imposed strict regulations on how many people would be allowed into a security-screened area of the airport tarmac. The president fumed about it on the flight, and his ire spiked when we received word from campaign officials on the ground that the number of people in the overflow section (where there were no mags) was greater than that of the magged crowd. Mark tried desperately to resolve the issue, but New Hampshire officials would not budge.

The president demanded we do something to make the people in the overflow section feel important. Mark decided to join the overflow crowd, which presented a security challenge for his Secret Service detail. Mark never quite grasped that the Secret Service protected his life as well as the president's. An un-magged crowd was just as much a threat to Mark as they were to the president. His detail leader begged me to try to persuade him not to do it. I pleaded with Mark, as did Alyssa. But his mind was made up, and we followed him into the overflow section.

Flanked by security as he entered, Mark was greeted with roars from the crowd. I commented to Alyssa that half the attendees probably had no idea who Mark was, but thought he must be important to the president because Secret Service agents were protecting him. That, she reminded me, was the point he was trying to make.

Mark shook hands, took photos, and signed autographs for everyone behind the bike-rack barricade. We spent more time with the overflow guests than we did watching the president's speech. I kept dousing Mark's hands with sanitizer. He asked me a few times to stop. He didn't want people to think we were afraid of COVID. I reminded him of the serious repercussions if he were to give the president COVID. He had no response to that, and I continued the dousing.

———

Laura, a Category 4 hurricane, made landfall on the Gulf Coast toward the end of the convention and devastated communities in Louisiana and Texas. We flew to the disaster sites on August 29 to witness the damage and meet with local law enforcement. En route to Lake Charles, Mark and I went over the day's plans with the president, letting him know who would greet him on the tarmac. We gave him an idea of what he would see at the disaster sites we were visiting, and we went over his talking points for roundtable discussions with local officials and relief workers.

I could see the president's attention drifting throughout the briefing. He was not particularly fond of travel on Saturdays, especially to disaster sites. He kept interrupting Mark and asking me which elected officials we had invited. I reminded him that we had, at his request, invited Republicans and Democrats to meet with him, to avoid criticism by the media for making a catastrophic event into a partisan spectacle. The president stressed that he wanted the event to be professional and controlled, which meant no glad-handing with unnecessary guests. I nodded in agreement and assured him that it would not be an issue.

In Louisiana, Governor John Bel Edwards, Senator John Kennedy, and Rep. Mike Johnson would be on the tarmac. Governor Greg Abbott would greet the president on his own when we landed in Texas. Steve Scalise or Ted Cruz were included only in the roundtable discussions. Each time I gave the president an answer he liked, he commented to Mark, "See. She's a doer. I like it. I like her."

This was my first presidential trip to the site of a natural disaster. As Air Force One descended I was glued to my seat, staring out the window at the devastation Laura had caused. Once we were on the ground, the damage was even more overwhelming. *All these thousands and thousands of people*, I thought, *their lives turned upside down in an instant.* In a year consumed by the deadliest pandemic in a century, and given the countless family tragedies it caused, it was good for Americans to see that government leaders of both parties could come together in crisis, committed to rebuilding the disaster-hit communities, and function effectively in an emergency.

We helicoptered to Orange, Texas. While we were in the air, an advance staffer texted me news I didn't want. Ted Cruz had pressured OLA to get local law enforcement and the Secret Service to allow him on the tarmac to greet POTUS. I had relayed to Amy very strict instructions from Mark and the president, yet there he now was as we landed, standing next to Governor Abbott, ready to grin and grip with the president, who was expecting him only at the roundtable. I was infuriated. I was not in the same helicopter as Mark and the president, and I felt sick that I would not be able to give them a heads-up in person before they landed.

The helicopter I was on landed first, and when I got off, I spotted Cruz and made a dash for him. The advance staffer who had texted me matched my stride and pleaded with me not to say anything to the senator. He told me that he had already tried to get Cruz to leave, and had made the senator angry. "I don't give a damn about Cruz's feelings," I snapped. "When he wins a presidential election, he can dictate events however he wants."

Marine One hovered above as I caught up with Cruz. I was cordial at first. I thanked him for meeting us there, and promised him I would let the president know that he had joined us for the entire visit. But the president had a vision for the touchdown, having specifically instructed that only Governor Abbott greet him.

Cruz, dumbfounded, looked at me and then stared into the middle distance. I repeated myself a bit more forcefully. He asked me if I liked my job. "Yes, sir, I do," I answered. He nodded and said, "I'll keep that in mind," and turned in the direction of Abbott.

I grabbed his elbow—I was angry now—and warned him that if he ignored my instructions, it would be "the last presidential event you ever receive an invitation to."

"Tell Mark that," he replied with a sneer. "He'll never take your side." And he stormed off.

When we got to the roundtable, I took Mark aside and raged about Cruz's behavior. He told me to calm down, and said that it wasn't a big deal—the president did not seem to notice that Cruz was even there. That was not the point, I reminded him. By disrespecting my authority, Cruz was disrespecting Mark's. That seemed to register with him. After the roundtable ended, I watched Mark take Cruz aside. When they finished talking, Cruz walked over to me and warned me not to be a "tattletale" again. I warned him not to disrespect my authority. That was the last time I spoke to Ted Cruz.

———

The following week we were returning to Washington from a campaign rally in Latrobe, Pennsylvania, when Mark rushed over to my seat on Air Force One, looking upset. I was sitting next to Bobby Engel, and Mark asked me to get in touch with Tony right away. Bobby asked Mark what was wrong and wanted to know if he could help.

Mark told Bobby no and instructed me again to call Tony. The *Atlantic* was about to publish "a hit piece on the boss," he explained, about his trip to France for a World War I centennial celebration two years earlier. The magazine alleged that the president had canceled a trip to an American cemetery because he was worried that the wind would mess up his hair. Worse, the story claimed that Trump had made disparaging remarks about dead American soldiers. Mark needed information from email correspondence in Tony's possession that he could use to push back on the story.

I called Tony, and Bobby started searching his emails for any useful information. A few minutes later, we both went to see the president in his office aboard the plane. He was visibly distraught. I had never seen the president so upset about something that inflicted a wound on his prized tough-guy image. There was usually at least a kernel of truth in even the toughest articles about the president, which we acknowledged by trying to spin it. But in this instance, he insisted this story was completely false, and he appeared more concerned that the article would hurt the military. He was proud of the military, he vowed, and proud to be their commander in chief. He was distressed over the damage the story could do to that relationship.

It was a side of the president most Americans never have an opportunity to see—sympathetic, concerned, and apprehensive. It's a side the media doesn't see or doesn't report. It's a side he keeps well disguised, for fear, I suspect, of appearing weak. But it's a side of him that exists.

We promised him that we would do our best to push back on the story. He nodded in appreciation, but the pained look on his face indicated that he was skeptical we would succeed. For once, he didn't end the discussion of a negative news story by demanding we figure out who the leaker was. He just wanted the record corrected.

———

We were scheduled to fly to Shanksville, Pennsylvania, for the annual September 11 remembrance ceremony. I had been coordinating for several weeks with OLA, September 11 organizations, and local entities to come up with a list of members to include that all parties would approve. This was not a White House–hosted event, and we did not control the invitations. The president was an invited guest. A week before the event, a House member texted Mark to say that he had received an invitation, but that he was also aware that he had not been invited by the organization hosting the ceremony.

Mark called me into his office and diplomatically asked if I was maintaining adequate supervision over OLA. I was embarrassed. I had been working closely with OLA on the event. But I just apologized to Mark, promising him I would correct my mistake.

I suspected Amy had done it to make a point. Earlier that week, she had asked for a one-on-one meeting with the president to brief him on the "fall legislative agenda." It was an election year. There was no fall legislative agenda—not a real one, anyway. I denied the request. She followed up with an email to Mark, copying me, again asking for a meeting with the president, either one-on-one or with the entire OLA team. I responded to her before Mark had a chance to respond himself. I reminded Amy that I had already declined her request, and reiterated that if she had any questions about the protocol in relations between our office and OLA, Mark and I would be happy to sit down with her and discuss the boundaries of her position.

After walking outside, trying to cool down, I reminded myself that Mark had not hired me to cool down. He hired me to organize things and maintain control. I stormed back into the West Wing, past Amy's assistant's desk and straight into her office. I closed her door behind me. I had tried to protect her for months, I insisted. I had tried to make our working relationship manageable. But now I was at the end of my rope. I could not protect her or OLA if she continued to sidestep me.

Amy is not by nature confrontational. I had never heard her raise her voice, so when she rebutted me that day, I was caught off guard. She was the director of OLA, not me, she asserted. I tried to steady myself. Her assertiveness had taken me by surprise. "You're the *acting* director of OLA," I reminded her.

Our relationship never fully recovered after that confrontation. It was clear to her and to me, from that day on, that my loyalty was to Mark and not to my former colleagues in legislative affairs.

I arrived at the White House early on the morning of September 11. The West Wing was nearly empty when I walked in, with all the office doors shut except for the ones in the suite Mark and I occupied. Tony was in Mark's office. They both summoned me in when they saw me. Tony shut Mark's door after me.

The president was going to Las Vegas the next day on a two-night, three-day trip. I was supposed to be accompanying Mark. In a hushed, careful voice, Mark informed me that he was no longer going to Vegas, because he had to stay in Washington "to deal with some things that came up." He declined to specify exactly what things he was referring to. I could feel Tony staring at me, and I did not know how to react. I assumed that this meant I was not going, either. I was about to tell them that I was happy to stay behind when Tony chimed in.

He said that Mark had decided I would go to Vegas in his place. I looked at Tony, taken aback by this sudden responsibility. I had never traveled overnight without Mark or Tony. It felt daunting to represent the chief of staff under these circumstances.

I told Mark that Tony needed to go with me. Mark said he needed Tony to stay back and help with the unnamed "things" that had come up. I looked at Tony, then back at Mark. Caught between the two of them, I felt like I did not have another choice, so I reluctantly agreed to go and asked what they needed from me. Mark answered, "Just do what you always do. We don't need to give you directions."

Tony left a few minutes later, and Mark told me that they were sending me because they trusted me. His words were reassuring, but I wondered what was really going on. I texted Alyssa and she agreed to come with me.

We flew to Pittsburgh and helicoptered from there to the Shanksville memorial site. My and Kayleigh's helicopter landed in a field, and we had to sprint through tall dead summer grass while wind from the propellers blew our dresses up.

It was my first time in Shanksville, the one September 11 memorial site I had not visited. The sky was heavy and dull with gray clouds. *Exactly the opposite of 9/11*, I remember thinking. It was a sobering experience, and I walked a little distance away from other staff to take in the event on my own.

Near the end of the ceremony, I heard Mark's voice behind me. "He trusts you, too, you know." I turned around and Mark nodded toward the president onstage. "I would not send you alone if I did not think you were capable or if he wasn't comfortable with the decision." I nodded. It would be the first time I was Mark's sole surrogate. I was more than just eyes and ears.

Kayleigh, Alyssa, and I decided to share a suite at the Trump Hotel rather than retreat to our separate rooms. We quickly changed clothes and went to the Wynn to meet Secret Service friends for drinks. They drove us back in their armored vehicle, and we ordered wine from room service and stayed up late watching movies. It felt like a slumber party. We were dead tired the next morning for the president's first event of the day.

Mark called every hour, or so it seemed, to check on how

things were going. The president overheard a few of the calls, and scolded me once for taking up Mark's time. "Tell him to stop jerking around," he ordered, "and get done what I asked him to do." I still had no notion what Mark was doing that weekend.

Kevin called frequently, too. He was amused Mark had sent me alone, and he wanted me to share any gossip I'd picked up on the trip. I begged him to come to Vegas, wanting help to manage Trump just in case. It was a short flight from Bakersfield, California. He declined. "I have too much money to raise," he explained. "Tell POTUS. He'll like that."

Trump hated fundraisers—he was expected to flatter people he thought should be flattering him. Mark had scheduled one in Vegas before a rally in a nearby suburb. The president was in a foul mood and kept asking me, "Why would the chief schedule this? Ask Mark why he thought this was a good idea."

———

Trump was onstage September 18 at a Bemidji, Minnesota, rally when we learned the sad news that Supreme Court Justice Ruth Bader Ginsburg had passed away. I admired Justice Ginsburg, a brilliant, trailblazing woman. No matter your political views or judicial philosophy, her character and accomplishments deserved respect.

My first concern upon hearing the news was how could we be respectful of a legendary American's passing while we searched for a conservative replacement. My second concern was how much would my workload increase. I expected Mark would want me involved in Hill outreach as we vetted possible nominees for the Court. With campaign travel now consuming more and more of our time, I didn't know how I would be able to take on additional responsibilities. Thankfully, the White House counsel's office took on the task with great success.

On September 26, the president announced Judge Barrett's nomination from the Rose Garden with about two hundred guests in attendance—many maskless. Judge Barrett became a frequent presence in the West Wing in the days following her Rose Garden nomination. We bumped into each other in the crammed hallways one afternoon. The day had been emotionally draining. I forced a smile, but I was already bleary-eyed. She told me a few stories about her children, a gesture that conveyed a depth of humanity and compassion I was no longer accustomed to.

The president held another crowded indoor White House event the day after Judge Barrett's announcement in the East Room for Gold Star families. Few wore masks. It was September 27, Mom's birthday.

Mom was proud I worked for the president, whom she admired, though I knew the true source of her pride was that I felt fulfilled in my job. She would support whatever career decision I made. But there was one politician Mom truly adored: Kevin McCarthy. I typically kept my professional and personal lives separate, but knowing how much Kevin loved birthdays and making people feel special, I asked him for my first favor.

Within minutes, he sent me a heartfelt video, singing Mom happy birthday. Kevin had made her feel more special than Mark or even the president could have. Amidst the grandeur of power and politics, it was the moments of sincerity and human connection that left a lasting impact on both our personal and professional journeys.

———

The first debate with Joe Biden took place in Cleveland, Ohio, on Tuesday, September 29. The campaigns had agreed that the candidates would be tested for COVID on-site in advance and that audience members would wear masks. Biden was tested, and his family wore masks. President Trump arrived so late that there wasn't time to test him. No one in his family who accompanied him to the debate wore a mask.

The next day, we were returning to Washington from a long

day on the campaign trail in Minnesota that had started with a fundraiser in Minneapolis and ended with a big rally in Duluth. The president had looked and sounded sick at the fundraiser, and appeared worse as the day went on. By the time we landed in Duluth, Hope was very ill. She stayed on Air Force One during the rally and was tested for COVID. The results came back positive. The White House physician separated her from the other passengers. The president did not find out until we were in the air on our way to Joint Base Andrews.

Mark summoned me to the president's office onboard and asked me to brief him on a few upcoming events with House members. That was unusual. Mark typically discussed things with me privately until all the details were finalized.

I noticed right away how exhausted POTUS looked. He hardly made eye contact with either of us. When he talked his voice was very hoarse, his throat tight. He sniffled several times. At one point he cut off Mark and asked if he had sounded sick at the rally. "I think my voice sounded a little bit off," he observed. "Did anyone else hear that? I don't think it was noticeable." He wrote it off to the sudden exposure to cold at the rally. He said he was used to doing rallies in hot weather. "The heat is almost easier sometimes. It was so cold. I wasn't used to it. Did anyone notice?"

Mark said he had not noticed it, and assured him that he had sounded great and there was nothing to worry about. The president was rightfully skeptical, and warned that someone in the "fake news" would notice and "probably accuse me of something ridiculous, like having COVID." Mark laughed and promised him that we would handle it if that happened.

I went back to my seat, worrying about the president's health and the implications if he had COVID. He had been with so many people that day and on the days before. With Hope infected, I knew that there was a very good chance that he was too, which meant that Mark and I might have COVID as well. Or maybe we had given it to him. Or maybe I was wrong, and the president had just been affected by the sudden drop in temperature.

Mark and I got into his limo at Andrews and headed to his condo in Old Town. As we pulled away, I watched Air Force One shrink in the rearview mirror and then disappear. My mind still buzzed with unanswered questions, but I matched Mark's silence. We were about halfway to his home when he asked me what was on my mind. "Nothing, really," I answered. He glanced at me sideways, his face illuminated by his two phone screens.

"Liar," he said with a smirk. "Talk to me." I hesitated a bit and then asked, "You don't think the boss has the coronavirus, do you?"

He considered the question for a moment. "He didn't sound too good on the plane, did he?"

I looked out the window. "No, he didn't. But he doesn't have COVID." I felt pathetic, like I was begging for Mark to reassure me. "He can't, Mark, that's impossible." I turned to him, but he was already scrolling on his phones again.

His silence answered every question I had. The virus had reached the highest echelons of power.

A little more than a year later, Mark would publish a book recounting that the president had tested positive for the virus the day of the Barrett announcement, September 26. He and the president had disregarded the result, blaming it on a faulty test.

Welcoming Uncle Joe home from fighting overseas, age eight.

College internship with House majority whip Rep. Steve Scalise in 2017.

In the Rose Garden with Office of Legislative Affairs colleagues on Ben Howard's last day at the White House.

Escorting Rep. Kevin McCarthy, Chief of Staff Mark Meadows, and Rep. Jim Jordan through to the White House residence to meet with the president.

Dinner with the president during a Camp David retreat with members of Congress.

Flying on Air Force One to Cape Canaveral, Florida, for the SpaceX rocket launch.

With Kevin McCarthy on Air Force One, returning to Washington, DC, from Cape Canaveral, Florida.

Walking with Tony Ornato, a USSS agent, and Mark Meadows to attend a security briefing about the Black Lives Matter protests in Lafayette Square.

Watching the fireworks with Tony Ornato during the president's visit to Mount Rushmore.

On Air Force One, overhearing the president discuss his plan to play a practical joke on me.

In the Capitol, leaving a meeting about coronavirus relief legislation.

Arriving at Speaker Nancy Pelosi's office with Mark Meadows for coronavirus relief discussions.

On Air Force One with President Trump's secret service agent Bobby Engel.

With Mark Meadows at a 2020 campaign stop in Pennsylvania, talking to the USSS special operations division counter assault team.

With the president and Mark Meadows after the president's final 2020 campaign rally in Grand Rapids, Michigan.

With Mark Meadows after a post-election meeting with Senate majority leader Mitch McConnell on November 18, 2020.

In the Rose Garden colonnade in December 2020.

Settling in at the witness table in the Cannon Caucus Room at the January 6th hearing on June 28, 2022.

Being sworn in by Chairman Bennie Thompson for the January 6th testimony.

Looking up at the dais where committee members were seated.

With attorneys Stephen Simrill, Bill Jordan, and Jody Hunt at the Alston & Bird offices following my testimony.

Watching the Atlanta
Braves game in Atlanta
with Jody Hunt and Bill
and Lacey Jordan.

With Rep. Liz Cheney and my
cockapoo puppy, George, after
my final interview with the
January 6th Committee.

Meeting Alex Butterfield in
person for the first time.

CHAPTER 12

Fall Campaign

I SAT ALONE AT MY DESK, practically catatonic as I watched the news on the quad screen, four channels streaming video of the president climbing the stairs of Marine One. Mark, his ever-loyal chief of staff, boarded the helicopter with him. Tony walked into the office just as the helicopter's propellers roared to life. We looked at each other for an unnaturally long moment, only breaking eye contact when we heard the familiar sound of Marine One lifting off from the South Lawn.

We were by Mark's side all day Thursday and into the early morning hours of Friday as we grappled with how to confront our October Surprise. I watched as the president's helicopter became a silhouette against the bleeding fall sunset. "Say a prayer he comes home," Tony said.

The president's condition had rapidly deteriorated after we had returned from Minnesota on Wednesday, but he had been determined to ignore the bleak prognosis and carry on, business as usual. It was wishful thinking, but it was impossible to change his mind. He had insisted on keeping a scheduled fundraiser at his golf club in Bedminster. By the time he had returned to the White House, Mark cleared the West Wing of most staff for the evening. He wanted to keep the diagnosis quiet while we awaited the president's PCR test results to come back from Walter Reed National Military Medical Center.

We waited anxiously in Mark's office, trying to devise a plan for an impossible task—convincing the president that he needed to notify the world that he had contracted the deadly virus, and even more importantly that he needed emergency medical treatment.

The test results confirmed what we had anticipated for several days, but they still sent a wave of terror through us. Tony and I ran handwritten draft tweets from Mark's office to the residence, where the president was receiving early intervention treatments. Dr. Sean Conley, the White House physician, cautioned us to wait to release the news until morning, when the president might be more alert. But Tony knew it was imperative to tweet the president's illness before the news leaked. The president reluctantly agreed. We held our collective breath as we watched the news break in the early hours of Friday morning.

I received scores of text messages from staff, members of Congress, family, friends, and reporters inquiring about the president's condition. While some expressed genuine concern, I felt most people let their notions of the president's attitude toward the virus taint their reaction to his illness. I lost my temper with some of them, arguing that this should be a moment for people to come together, to set aside our differences and pray for the commander in chief. I was distressed that no one seemed to realize how dire his condition was, but I knew that, regrettably, that was intentional.

Mark, Tony, and Dr. Conley spent most of Friday trying to convince the president that he needed medical attention at Walter Reed immediately. He refused their entreaties until his condition became so dire that even he realized his decision could be a matter of life or death. The virus was trying to kill him. We were trying to keep him alive.

From the moment the president was diagnosed, I knew Mark would not leave his side. He told me that he planned to stay at Walter Reed for as long as the president was there. I told him I would see him Saturday morning.

When I arrived at the hospital the next day, Dr. Conley offered me a mask but warned that Mark was not wearing one. I declined Dr. Conley's offer. If Mark was not afraid of catching the virus, neither was I.

Mark remained by the president's side almost around the clock, but we saw each other for a few brief exchanges. I drove to Chick-fil-A before I went home that night and bought him a few sandwiches and Diet Cokes. I left them in his makeshift office at the hospital with a note that I would be back in the morning. He texted me later that he was impressed I knew he had not eaten since he left the White House Friday evening.

The days bled together, with the president's condition beginning to show improvement. As his illness abated, he focused on a familiar purpose: making sure he did not look weak. He wanted to convey the image that his strength alone, and not medical intervention, had defeated the virus. The heart rate monitor continued to beep, and nurses replaced IV bags, as he formulated a scheme.

Bobby Engel told Tony and me that the president wanted to go for a drive to greet his crowd of supporters outside the hospital gates. I urged Mark to dissuade him, but it was too late—the president had made up his mind. He tweeted a video of himself: dressed in a blazer and open-collar shirt, he announced that he was about to pay a surprise visit to some "great patriots that we have out on the street." Moments later, news cameras focused tightly on his SUV, with the president waving to his fans, the face mask he wore the only concession to his illness.

By the next day, October 5, the president had had enough of Walter Reed. His doctors pleaded with him to remain for another day of treatment. He defied their orders and the odds.

I was driving down Constitution Avenue on my way back to the White House from Walter Reed when I heard Marine One overhead and saw it land on the South Lawn. But it wasn't until I was back at my desk that I saw the president's grand return, when he appeared on the Truman Balcony and dramatically stripped off his mask, his labored breathing evident for all to see.

Mark walked into the office as the cable news channels replayed the footage on a loop. "That was pretty good, wasn't it?" he asked.

I thought we were handling the president's condition foolishly. We were showing the world he was fine with putting other lives at risk to project an artificial image of strength and wellness. His strength would make a better impression if he had expressed empathy for his fellow COVID sufferers, if he had listened to his doctors and not put others' health at risk when they had transported him while he was sick. I began to understand just how much appearing strong—or *not* appearing weak—motivated the president, and it worried me. But I kept my opinion to myself and nodded in agreement. It was clear that projecting an image of strength mattered greatly to the president, and we needed to navigate this aspect of his personality carefully.

The next day, the West Wing sprang to life as the president entered the Oval Office for a day of work. It was as if nothing had happened.

———

Business as usual in the Trump White House often involved chaos. And it was even more chaotic the week following the president's return. With only three weeks before the election, there appeared to be little, if any, consensus on the major issues we were facing: the status of his participation in the final debate, whether we would resume negotiations for a COVID relief package, our plan to withdraw troops from Afghanistan, the president's travel schedule, and the campaign's final closing message. The one thing everyone agreed on was that getting Amy Coney Barrett confirmed could be a make-or-break moment for the president's reelection.

It was deemed so important that Mark decided he needed to be seen sitting in the front row on the first day of her Senate confirmation hearing. I was taken aback, not able to find another instance of a White House chief of staff attending a Supreme Court nominee's hearing. I told Mark that it was enough that Pat Cipollone, the White House counsel, was there, but he dismissed my concern, stressing how important it was that he represent the president.

I saw Mark that night, October 12, aboard Air Force One on our way to Sanford, Florida, for the president's first post-COVID rally. He practically glowed as he filled us in on the hearing that morning. I was about to remind him that it had been livestreamed and we had all watched it. But the president interrupted and began questioning Mark on the evergreen concern of how many people were lined up at the rally's magnetometers. Florida's lackadaisical coronavirus policies meant we should have minimal issues at the mags.

After we landed, Mark and I worked our way through the crowd as he thanked hundreds of supporters by taking photos with them, signing autographs, and shaking hands. I reminded him that despite our risk level, we were among the few West Wing staff who had yet to contract COVID, and that he should be really careful so close to the election. Mark asked me to locate a MAGA face mask for him, and to squeeze sanitizer on his hands between greetings.

We slipped somewhat effortlessly back into the rhythm of long workdays ending in nighttime campaign rallies. Mark's mood became more frequently volatile as the president continuously berated him about rally crowd sizes. Surrounded by such instability, I fixated on doing my job better. The course of American history, I told myself, depended on the president's reelection. Without Mark's leadership, the president would not get reelected, I told myself. It was my job to make it easier for him to succeed.

On the morning of the final presidential debate, Tony informed us that the debate commission was requiring the candidates to stand behind Plexiglas shields to prevent the spread of the coronavirus. If there was one PPE item Trump disdained more than face masks, it was Plexiglas. I couldn't do much to help Mark prepare for the president's reaction, which made me anxious. I rode in silence to the debate. Fortunately, Alyssa was on the trip, and I knew we could rely on each other.

When Max Miller, the lead advance staffer on the campaign, and I reached Mark, the president was berating the commissioners over their decision. I could tell Mark was tempted to pull out of the debate. To my surprise, the president shouted at Mark to call Dr. Fauci, who could explain that Plexiglas "is completely worthless," adding, "Maybe you'll listen to your savior, Dr. Fauci." Mark eagerly complied with the president's request, and the commissioners were caught off guard when Dr. Fauci agreed with the president's assessment. Still, they would need to get the Biden campaign's permission to remove the shields, and they weren't sure they could.

Mark advised the president to go to the hotel for a last round of debate prep while we stayed behind to sort out the controversy. He reluctantly agreed, and instructed us that he wanted David Bossie, a Republican activist and the former president of Citizens United, to stay with us.

I was not thrilled by Bossie's presence. I thought that he played into the president's and Mark's worst instincts, and I worried that he would do more harm than good as we tried to negotiate a satisfactory resolution of the dispute. Mark needed to build camaraderie with the commissioners, not alienate them. But the two prevailed: the commissioners returned with the verdict that the Biden campaign had agreed to forgo the shields.

Bossie rode with us to the hotel, telling Mark that he would deliver the good news to the president. I lost my self-control before Mark could respond, my thoughts spilling from my lips. I told Bossie that he would not decide how the chief relayed information to the president. If he wanted that kind of power, he should lobby the president to make him his fifth chief of staff.

Bossie and Mark made eye contact before turning to look at me, each with a slight smirk on his face. "She's pretty good,"

Bossie told Mark. "I know," Mark replied, adding, "Let's tell the president together." He winked at me.

Matt Gaetz was lurking in the hotel lobby when we arrived and spotted us right away. He wanted to come with us so that he could give the president debate tips. I could see that Mark was trying to ignore him. I intervened and suggested that Matt find Kimberly Guilfoyle, Donald Trump Jr.'s then-girlfriend, and take her for a drink in the hotel bar. Mark, David Bossie, and I got on the elevator together, letting the doors close on Matt. As we ascended, Mark thanked me, and whispered that I should keep my distance from Matt. It was a protective order, and I understood.

Mark went to brief the president, and I found Alyssa and snuck away from the stress with her for a few minutes. When we got to the debate that night, we sat in the hold room and hardly uttered a word, knowing how much hinged on the outcome. While we didn't say it out loud, there was a silent consensus between us that the night wasn't likely to help the president's reelection prospects.

The president was never a big fan of retail politics, the baby-kissing, the feigning of interest in subjects—things that most politicians master early in their careers. But he did agree to do a campaign stop in Maine's Second Congressional District, which he had won in 2016, Maine being one of two states that split electoral college votes.

We started the day with a rally in Manchester, New Hampshire, and flew next to Bangor, Maine. From there we traveled by motorcade to an orchard in tiny Levant, Maine, about ten miles from the airport. The visit had been added to our itinerary at the last minute, so Tony had scheduled it as an "off-the-record" (OTR) movement. Since the press and public are not aware of OTR movements until the time of the event, they are pulled together quickly and require fewer security assets, like Secret Service personnel and magnetometers, than a scheduled movement. No one was especially anxious about that, believing that the crowd for the un-publicized event would probably be pretty modest.

We were wrong. As soon as we landed, we received word from staff on the ground that the orchard was packed. On the drive there, the roads were lined with Trump supporters, and the front yards of almost all the homes we passed had Trump signs and flags. We were in Trump country. The president had started the day in a bad mood. By the time we arrived at the orchard, his dis-position had brightened considerably.

It didn't last long. To get from our vehicles to the spot where he would address the assembled crowd, advance staff had routed the president through a large, picturesque barn, decorated with a huge American flag above the entrance. The orchard owners, the Treworgy family, escorted the president. The president does not like animals, and Mark and I exchanged a nervous look, each of us hoping there weren't any in the barn. There were.

Not only was the barn filled with livestock, but orchard founder Gary Treworgy stopped at each pen to tell the president some-thing about the animal in it. I was about twenty feet behind the president and Mark, and I could tell that Mark had no idea what to do. They both looked so disoriented—the president because he was fighting to pretend he was interested in what his host was telling him, and Mark because he could not figure out how to get the boss out of the situation. I was standing with Johnny McEntee and Kayleigh, trying unsuccessfully not to laugh.

When we reached the place where the president would make his remarks, there was not a microphone and speaker set up. In-stead, a staffer handed him a bullhorn. Trump scowled at it. He was extremely particular about microphones, with a certain type he preferred and a specific volume level so his voice did not project gravely through the speakers. He did not like it when people could hear the "rumble" in his voice, which most microphones exacer-bated. Mark shot me a look, and, again, I had to bite back a smile.

I told Johnny that this was the president's chance to have a

George Bush moment. He looked at me, confused, so I clarified. "Like at Ground Zero after 9/11, when President Bush used a bull-horn to address the rescue workers—"

"The boss hates Bush. He wouldn't want to have a George Bush moment."

———

The president was scheduled to do three rallies in Pennsylvania the next day, October 26, during the last week of the campaign. Pennsylvania was maybe the most critical swing state. As we flew to the first rally, in Allentown, Mark pressed me for details about the magnetometers.

I was prepared for his questions. I had been in contact with the lead advance staffer and the Secret Service agent on-site since early that morning. The weather was not ideal, with downpours expected all day. I also wanted terribly to tell Mark that the over-flow crowd was small, and the lines at the mags short. But that would have been a lie. The lines were long—we would likely be able to see them from the air as we landed. Making matters worse, the campaign hadn't rented enough magnetometers for the size of the crowd. The designated rally space, which could only accom-modate a smaller number of attendees than the president wanted because of local COVID protocols, was at capacity. I dreaded Mark's and the president's reactions.

I tried to break the news to Mark diplomatically. He was re-sponding to a text as I started to brief him. He stopped typing when I told him the part about not enough magnetometers. He locked his phone and looked at me over his glasses, which were resting on the end of his nose, and his expression prompted me to stop speaking.

Calmly, he asked why I had not instructed the campaign to rent more magnetometers. I did not know what to say, so I said noth-ing. He asked me again, louder. Max Miller was on the plane and tried to stick up for me. He explained that the other rally sites had enough magnetometers, and that it was the job of the Secret Service and the campaign to determine magnetometer allotments. Max joked that I wasn't experienced enough to know anything about magnetometer capacity and control. Mark did not look at Max once but said, "Thanks, Max, but she knows what she's supposed to be doing." Then he launched into a lecture, telling me that I needed to stay on top of the job better.

I wanted to break the airplane window with my elbow and launch myself into space. I was so embarrassed and battled two impulses. The first, to concede that Mark was right, and that he had every right to chew me out in front of senior staff. I had not done a good enough job. I was tired and distracted by other duties. I had taken my eye off something that mattered to the president, thus I was undeserving of my job.

I also knew that Max was right. The acquisition of magnetometers was not my responsibility. I had no campaign experience, and was doing my best to keep up with unfamiliar tasks that were proliferating in the final days. But that voice in my head was more subdued than the first one.

I apologized, and he erupted. "Don't apologize to me. Just do your dang job!" I went back to my seat and tried not to cry for the rest of the flight.

By the time we landed, I had arranged for the lead advance and Secret Service staff to walk Mark and me through the magnetometers and the overflow crowd. I told Mark this as we got off the plane. Mark gave me a stiff nod. Max and I looked at each other, and Max said, "Damn, Chief, normally you only put one of us in a body bag." I laughed, and Mark looked confused. "Body bag?" he asked. "That's what Max and I say when you yell at us," I said, jumping in.

"Oh, okay," he said. "Body bags. I like that. At least you guys are still a little afraid of me."

We almost had to cancel the third and final rally of the day, in Martinsburg. The weather was awful when we landed Air Force

One at a regional airport, where we were supposed to board heli-copters for the flight to the smaller municipal airport close to the rally. The pilots wanted to cancel the flights. Visibility was too poor to fly safely, they argued. I did not hear Mark when he de-manded, on the president's order, that the pilots figure out how to fly us there. There was not going to be a motorcade. I was told that he was stern, brief, and not interested in debating the issue. The pilots relented.

By the time the rally ended, flying was out of the question. We could see lightning in the direction of where we would fly, and the rain was pouring steadily. Secret Service made the call—we would motorcade back to Air Force One. Mark didn't say anything when I gave him the news. He knew that the decision was out of my control, but I could tell he feared telling the president. It would be an hour-long drive on winding country roads and up and down hills. Mark met the president at the back of the stage and had to physically redirect him to the motorcade. I was probably a hun-dred feet away, but I swear I could see the president's eyes widen, and feel his wrath.

As we drove to the airport, my phone rang with a call from the White House operator. The president was trying to get ahold of Mark, who wasn't picking up. I was not in the same car as Mark. We ended the call and the operator called back several more times, so I called Mark myself. "Tell the boss I'm on the phone with Congress," he instructed, after picking up on the first ring, "trying to get things done for him. I'll talk to him on the plane." I knew he wasn't talking to Congress. He just did not want to be on the receiving end of the president's anger.

When we got back to the plane, David Cho, who was filling in as detail leader for Bobby Engel, looked rattled. "Rough ride?" I chuckled. "You have no idea," he answered.

I chose not to check in with Mark on the flight to Andrews. But when we got off the plane, he murmured to me, "No more motor-cades. Please just help make sure, no more motorcades." I said,

"Yes, sir." He added, "And do better for the rest of the campaign. Don't start letting us down."

We were back in the air the next morning for campaign stops in Michigan, Wisconsin, and Nebraska, and then on to Las Vegas, where we would spend the night. My mind and body were worn down with exhaustion from all the travel. I was grateful Tony had agreed to come with us on this swing. I had prepared the materials Mark would need for the trip before I packed my own belongings. My sole priority was Mark at this point. I could make do with the bare necessities for the next few days.

Mark was preoccupied with something back in Washington during our stop in Michigan. I did not know what it was, but I was relieved he was not paying attention to the magnetometers. It was sleeting, and I had not dressed for the weather. Mark spent most of the rally making calls in the control vehicle while I stayed in the offstage announcer's tent, huddled under a heat lamp with Secret Service agents.

Back on Air Force One after the rally, the president was in a surprisingly good mood. We all expected him to be annoyed because of the miserable weather he had just endured. But his only reference to the weather was a request that his valet blow-dry his leather gloves so they wouldn't "turn frozen solid" at the rally in Wisconsin.

His mood darkened, however, when he saw media reports seeming to discredit the Hunter Biden laptop story. He had Kayleigh print out dozens of copies of a Fox News article that linked to video of a Tucker Carlson report of the controversy. The president asked Johnny McEntee to forge "MUST-SEE TV!" in his handwriting on each copy of the article. Kayleigh and I then placed a copy on every reporter's seat after they had disembarked.

The president was excited about Wisconsin. The rally was to be held at a raceway, and he was going to ride in the presidential limo ("the Beast") for a lap around the track before his remarks. Back on the plane, he claimed that he was disappointed. The ride had been less climactic than he had thought it would be.

Mark started pressing me about the magnetometers on our way to our final rally of the day, in Omaha, Nebraska. When he called me to his office on the plane, I knew what was coming. I asked Tony to come with me, having told him about Mark's earlier outbursts. I think he thought I was exaggerating. The event had been a mess in terms of logistics. The parking areas were three to four miles from the rally, so the campaign had chartered buses to bring people to the site. But there weren't enough buses. Tony let Mark vent at me for a bit before jumping in to redirect Mark's displeasure, and Mark retreated.

I looked at Tony after we left Mark's office on Air Force One. I was stressed but satisfied and smiling. He shook his head and laughed. "You weren't kidding, kid."

Despite the mishap, the president was thrilled with how well the Nebraska rally went. Tony and I spent the rally checking out the view from different vantage points, avoiding Mark.

When I woke up in Las Vegas the next morning, I saw reports from campaign officials about the calamity that had followed the rally. Many attendees had been stranded in near-freezing temperatures because of the scarcity of buses and the bottleneck. Mark was having breakfast in the hotel restaurant, and I was supposed to join him. I contemplated skipping it. He had already done television interviews that morning, so I was sure he knew about the buses. But if for some reason he hadn't heard, it was my responsibility to tell him. I packed my belongings in my travel bag and headed to the restaurant.

Tony was already there, thank God. He glanced at me as I walked in and smiled, a look that said, "I've got your back."

We had two rallies in Arizona that day, the first in Bullhead City and the second in Phoenix. After we landed in Bullhead City, we lost electricity on Air Force One, which I couldn't recall ever happening before. I didn't think much of it, but not long into the president's speech, we received word that there were mechanical errors that might not be fixed in time for our departure. When Mark learned that we would have to motorcade back to Vegas, he erupted.

The Secret Service interrupted his tantrum to tell him that there was an unidentified aircraft flying over the rally. Word had been sent to the unknown pilot to leave the area immediately. If they didn't comply, the military might have to shoot them down. Mark erupted again, and then began scrambling with the agents to find a way to let the president know what was going on. I told him that if they typed a message for the president on his teleprompter, he would likely read it out loud. Suddenly, as we were talking, air force jets fired warning flares at the intruding aircraft, and they left the area. The president explained to the crowd that the great US military was putting on a fireworks show. It wasn't until we were back on Air Force One, which had been repaired in time, that he learned about the incident and that it was an aircraft that accidently flew into our airspace.

Kevin was waiting for us in Phoenix—he would fly with us to Florida for our last rally of the night. We had not seen each other in a while, and I was comforted by his company. Tony was not around when Mark started talking about magnetometers, so I was left to fend for myself. It wasn't that bad at first—we chatted more about travel plans for the next day than we did about the mags. Near the end of the conversation, he brought up a new complaint, why I had not been communicating with the campaign about updated polling results. Until that moment, I had not known I was supposed to be communicating with the campaign about polling. Somebody had given Trump the latest numbers, I surmised, and he must have brought it up with Mark, who was taken unaware. Kevin overheard Mark chastising me and walked away. I did not expect him to interject; I doubted he even knew what we were talking about. But walking away had irked me. When Mark finished, I found a seat that was not near Kevin's.

Kevin texted and asked if I was okay when we arrived at Trump National Doral in Miami after the last rally. He said I seemed stressed. I was ticked off, so I answered curtly that I was fine and said not to worry. He wrote back and assured me I could tell him the truth, and added that despite thinking a few days before that the president was not going to win reelection, he felt the prospects had significantly improved. I did not reply, but his text was reassuring.

I woke up the next morning to several messages from Florida governor Ron DeSantis, urging me to make sure he and "the first lady," his wife, Casey, were mentioned in the president's remarks at a rally in Tampa that day. I had known Ron since I was an intern for Scalise and Ron was in his third and final term in the House. I ignored his texts. Ron texted Mark and me all the time. I had repeatedly asked him to stop, but he disregarded me.

When we landed in Tampa, we had a short motorcade ride to the rally. I put my earbuds in and started blasting gospel music, which I didn't listen to often but felt I needed that day. I was physically and emotionally exhausted, especially from having to anticipate the needs of multiple principals when I did not know what to expect myself. I did not realize how loud my music was playing until White House political director Brian Jack tapped my shoulder and asked if everything was okay. I removed an earbud for a moment to hear him. I smiled and told him everything was fine, and put my earbud back in.

Mark got out of his vehicle before I got out of mine, and it took me a few minutes to catch up to him. When I did, he told me to find Ron DeSantis. Ron had found Mark, but Mark had told him I would handle whatever he needed—that he had other things to do. I found Ron and Casey. He asked if Trump was going to mention him in his remarks, and if so, how many times. I lost my temper. I told him that he had to learn boundaries—that he was acting as if he were still a junior member of Congress. He started to apologize like a child who'd been caught misbehaving, but I walked away.

We postponed a rally in Fayetteville, North Carolina, that night. The weather was awful, high winds and driving rain, and the arena wasn't full. Afraid that canceling would make him look weak, Trump wanted to go ahead with it anyway. But Mark had me call a few members from the North Carolina congressional delegation, who assured the president that calling off the rally was the right decision. He reluctantly agreed and decided to pay an unscheduled visit to Fort Bragg army base instead.

Tony texted me the night of October 30 with good news: the White House Military Office had procured a smaller, private aircraft that would fly ahead of Air Force One. From now on, Tony and several Military Office aides and Secret Service agents would land at the campaign stops in advance of the president to make sure each rally met his expectations. We had to keep the arrangement quiet, Tony explained, to avoid negative press attention because we were chartering additional aircraft at public expense.

If I were to fly with them, he said, I would still be responsible for communicating logistics updates to Mark. But the arrangement would at least remove me from the line of fire of Mark's sporadic outbursts.

———

The pilot announced that we were preparing to land after one of the shortest flights I had ever experienced. I glanced out the window as the plane cut through the thick morning clouds. In the distance, I saw a familiar place from a new vantage point: Pennington, New Jersey.

I had been excited when I'd learned earlier that week that we would be landing at Trenton-Mercer Airport, only a few miles from my mom's house and Jack's college. I had texted my family the news before the trip was publicly announced, and offered them VIP arrangements of their choice—watching Air Force One land from the tarmac; a ride in the motorcade to Upper Makefield Township, Pennsylvania, where the rally was; a private tour of Air Force One. The only stipulation was that they needed to let me know by midnight, October 30, so I had adequate time to notify the appropriate personnel.

I did not hear from Mom until shortly before we left Andrews on the morning of October 31. She asked to meet me on the tarmac. She was parked at a Marriott across the street from the airport exit, where she had spotted Dad, leaning against his white pickup truck. As the plane flew over the Delaware River, I texted Mom back to tell her that it was too late to make the arrangement. Then I slammed shut my window blind and closed my eyes for the final moments of the flight.

Tony and I got off the plane together, but I walked off on my own once we were on the tarmac. Noticing that I was acting strange, Tony motioned me over and introduced me to a Secret Service agent from a local field office, who stared at me and said I looked familiar. I answered, "As an average brunette with brown eyes, I get that a lot." Tony laughed, but the agent kept staring. "Where are you from?" he asked. "New Jersey," I answered. Then: "What part?"

I let the veil drop. "Here. Pennington." I added that I'd graduated from Hopewell Valley Central High School not all that long ago. As the agent congratulated himself for recognizing me from "somewhere," I felt Tony's energy shift and his eyes lock on me. I ended the conversation as soon as I could and boarded my vehicle to wait for the president to land.

Once the president was in the Beast, Tony joined me in the car. "Why didn't you tell me this was your hometown?" he asked, as our SUV rolled off the tarmac. "I didn't think it was a big deal," I said, and rested my forehead against the window. As we passed through the gates, I could see Tony out of the corner of my eye, shaking his head. "Where are your folks? We could've arranged something special for them. I can't believe you didn't tell me," he said, though his voice seemed distant from my thoughts.

Hundreds of Trump supporters gathered outside the airport gates, but my eyes locked on just one. Dad. He was wearing his formal clothes—a purple Ralph Lauren polo, dark wash jeans, and sneakers. His hair was neatly combed and thick with pomade. One of his arms was extended toward the sky, waving dramatically. He held his cell phone in his other hand, video-recording the motorcade. Our SUV rounded the corner, and I was close enough to see the lines on his face, the divot and tan line on his ring finger. I saw pride in his wide smile, too. Pure pride.

I spotted Mom a few feet away, leaning against her car, holding her phone with both hands, also recording. I might have missed her had I not known she was there. My forehead left a mark on the window as I turned to Tony and said, "I'm not here to entertain. This is work."

Once we arrived at the Upper Makefield Township rally, I could block out the earlier scene as a skilled compartmentalizer. But when we drove back to the airport, my mind started buzzing. I was traveling with the president of the United States, driving down roads I knew by heart, about five miles from the town that raised me. I did not feel nostalgia, though, or pride or gratitude. I felt detached, as if I were watching myself from above robotically move through the scene.

As we approached the gates, Tony nudged me. "What," I said dully, my eyes fixed on the road ahead. "Why didn't you want your family to come?" he asked softly. My vision blurred, and I knew my tears would stream down if I looked at him.

I wanted to tell him I had tried. I did invite some of my family, but the dynamics are complicated, the personalities tough to balance. I wanted to tell him everything, but that would have required lifting my façade to bring my past into my present. I glanced at the Marriott parking lot. Most of the cars and supporters had cleared out, including Mom. But not Dad. He was still there, still smiling, still waving frantically at the motorcade. I bit the inside of my cheek so hard that my mouth filled with the metallic taste of blood. I looked at Tony and said, "I told you, this is work." I forced a tight smile I knew looked fake.

Throughout the day, Dad sent me dozens of texts with videos of the motorcade, pictures of homemade signs people had brought, voice notes saying how proud he was of me, and that he wished he had seen me through one of the windows. "My Sissy Hutch, the Apple of My Eye, with the President . . . you work so hard, Sissy . . . ," one message read.

We were flying to our final rally of the day when I received one last video from Dad. It was of the C-17 aircraft that transports the motorcade vehicles, taking off against a stunning sunset. I stopped watching it when I heard Dad sniffle and begin to talk. I didn't want to hear what he had to say. In a way, I preferred his cruelty. I was proud of the life I was building, but I couldn't risk contaminating that life with the confusing, conflicted reality of my past. He had never shown up before, I reminded myself.

But he had that day. For a moment, I acknowledged that the shame I felt was not Dad's fault, nor was it Mom's. I was desperate to fit in the world that I had worked hard to become a cherished member of, but below the surface I felt displaced and undeserving. I did not know how to marry the two worlds I loved dearly: the world I came from, and the world I now lived in.

I unlocked my phone and began catching up on email.

Tony and I climbed the scaffolding of a makeshift lookout tower and tried to balance ourselves on the unsteady platform. Everyone was looking forward to the rally in Rome, Georgia, two nights before Election Day, especially the president. The campaign estimated that thirty thousand people were in attendance, our biggest crowd yet. As we found our balance, our jaws dropped. "The boss is going to die," Tony said. "He's going to say there were more than thirty thousand people here. He'll tell Max to do a recount." We laughed. From atop the tower it certainly appeared that there were more than thirty thousand. A sea of red MAGA hats, illuminated in the floodlights, stretched farther than I could see. The crowd erupted as Air Force One touched down. The moon hung in the sky. Suddenly the platform we stood on felt safe.

When staff began to deplane, we climbed back down and made our way to the offstage announcement area. A senior campaign official jabbed his finger into my shoulder. Alarmed, I spun around. "Chief's still on the plane talking to the boss," he said. "He's going to meet up with Tony Bobulinski. Can you go get him?"

I took a step back and crossed my arms. "What do you mean?" I asked. He said gruffly, "The boss asked him to meet up with Tony Bobulinski. He's here. It has to be low-key, though, so just find somewhere away from any cameras." I looked at Tony Ornato, expecting him to say something. Instead, he pointed at Mark leaving Air Force One. "He's coming," he said. The aide walked away.

I didn't know much about Tony Bobulinski, just that he was a former business associate of Hunter Biden's and had something to do with the laptop controversy. Trump had brought him as a guest to the presidential debate in Nashville on October 22. I wasn't tracking the story closely enough to know more. But as Mark approached, I had a weird feeling that we were in danger. I couldn't explain it, but the feeling was real. "Mark shouldn't do this," I said to Tony. "He's being set up." Tony shrugged. "Don't overthink things. It's not a big deal. Chief knows what he's doing. Bobulinski came with us to Nashville, remember? Don't worry, kid." He patted my shoulder and walked away as Mark approached me.

"You're not meeting Tony Bobulinski here, Mark. We can send someone from the campaign." I heard my voice whine with child-like desperation. "Please, Mark. This isn't a good idea. Just trust me." Mark looked at his Secret Service agent, then back at me.

"Just go find him, and work with Secret Service to find a hidden spot. Come get me once you have him there."

He walked away, and Brian Jack came to my side and started talking, but I couldn't hear him. I felt his fingers wrap around my wrist as he pulled my arm, yanking me back to reality. "I'll go with you," he said. I snatched my wrist away. "No. Get someone from the campaign to do this. Mark is not going to do this, Brian." I tried to storm away, but Brian moved in front of me. "Cassidy, the boss asked Mark to do this. I said I'll go with you." My throat was so tight I couldn't respond, so I nodded and began walking without knowing where to go. Brian followed several paces behind me.

We were walking behind a set of bleachers when a Secret Service agent appeared and asked if we were looking for the guest with bodyguards. Brian nodded. The agent told us we could find him in a small, fenced-in house near the middle of the crowd.

As Brian thanked him, I recognized a few of the men sitting in idling Secret Service vehicles and rushed over to them. I asked if they could park four of the vehicles in the shape of a square, and explained that the chief needed to have a quick meeting with someone out of sight. They were reluctant at first and questioned why Mark couldn't just meet the person where staff were congregated. "The chief of staff needs to have a private meeting," I said, lying with convincing confidence. "If you want me to ask Tony Ornato to explain more, I'm happy to call him over." They began lining up the vehicles, and Brian and I made our way into the crowd, searching for the fenced-in house.

The farther we got from the stage, the more the event felt like a fair rather than a campaign rally. Attendees were eating food they'd brought with them and listening to music. Children were running around playing tag. Some had their faces painted.

"There," Brian said, and pointed to the house. "I don't want to talk to him," I told him, as three men came out of the house. I tried to pick out Tony Bobulinski, but they were all wearing hats and ski masks. Brian introduced himself and explained that we would bring them to the chief. I spun around and started pushing through the crowd to make a path for the group a good distance behind me.

I made it to the security perimeter before the rest of the group, telling the campaign staffer to let Brian Jack and his guests through when they caught up. The staffer said he could lose his job if he let people in without proper credentials. "You will lose your job if you don't let them through. I promise you that." He quickly nodded. I thanked him and kept walking.

I rounded the corner and saw Mark talking to campaign staff. They all looked in my direction at the same time. As Mark broke away, one of the staffers patted his shoulder. Mark smiled and flashed a thumbs-up in their direction.

"This is really stupid of you, Mark. I don't know what's going on, but it's really stupid," I said. He didn't have time to respond as I ushered him into the makeshift area, away from cameras, as requested, but not from watchful Secret Service eyes.

In the shadows of the bleachers, I observed Mark and Tony Bobulinski's interaction through a gap in the vehicles. When they said their goodbyes, I saw Mark hand Tony what appeared to be a folded sheet of paper or a small envelope. Mark walked toward me, staring at the ground. He was silent for several moments as we made our way back to the staff holding area.

"You and I, we have seen a lot together, done a lot together," Mark said, his head still tilted toward the ground. I cleared my throat. "Yes, Mark. We have." He abruptly stopped walking and stuck his arm out to stop me. Our eyes locked.

"Oh, don't look so frightened." He dropped his arm. "I just want to thank you for working so hard. It's quite difficult to find someone as loyal as you." He flashed a smile, the kind of smile that doesn't change the shape of your eyes. He disappeared around the corner, his Secret Service agents trailing him.

I could hear the president's voice blare through the speakers, and the screams of the crowd. It should have been deafening. But in the moonlight, I felt removed from it all, and alone. Even though I don't know what Mark had been meeting with Bobulinski about, I could no longer ignore the suspicious activity that he, Trump, and others in the administration seemed to be engaged in. I had done what they had asked of me, not questioning it, but now I started to put together all the moments like this one that didn't add up. I could not shake the feeling that I had been entangled in something far more complex and secretive than I had initially realized.

———

I managed to clock about two consecutive hours of sleep to prepare for the final day of campaigning. When I opened my eyes, I felt disoriented, and my heart was thudding against my ribs. It took almost a full minute to remember I was at the hotel in Miami. I sat up and was hit with a pounding headache and chills that shook my entire body. My stomach growled, but I felt like I was going to vomit. I stumbled into the bathroom and hunched over the toilet. When this did not bring relief, I lay flat on the cold tile floor.

I knew I needed more sleep, but I was already running behind schedule. I convinced a Secret Service agent to drive me to a nearby convenience store to buy a few energy drinks and a protein bar. Between my purchases and the warmth of the Florida sun, I started to feel better.

I did not see Mark until Air Force One landed in Fayetteville, North Carolina, for the first rally of the day. We met on the tarmac and I handed him a pack of trail mix. We fell into an uncomfortable silence as he slowly ate. I still had a pit in my stomach from the Tony Bobulinski interaction the night before, but I had a feeling Mark had either already forgotten about it or did not want to talk about it. He crushed the trail mix wrapper and I watched it flutter to the ground as he began to walk in the direction of the overflow crowd. I picked up the wrapper and jogged to catch up with him.

The Mark who greeted attendees in the overflow section was loud, jovial. He patted his heart endearingly when people cried about their gratitude for the president. He offered Sharpies as an unexpected gift after giving his autograph; I traveled with a stash of hundreds of the markers. When cell phones came out for a selfie, he leaned in and flashed a thumbs-up and a wide smile.

I laid eyes on one particular family toward the back of the crowd. They kept getting pushed farther from the security barricade as people shoved their way forward to greet Mark. The father lifted his daughter in his arms so she could catch a glimpse of Mark. She waved eagerly at him every time he looked in her direction, but her smile faded when he didn't notice her. Her father rubbed her back and whispered something in her ear. Whatever he said must have been devastating, because she began to wail as Mark started walking toward the stage to listen to the last part of the president's speech.

"Mark," I said, pulling on the fabric of his suit to stop him. "You're going to ruin that little girl's life if you don't go say hi." I pointed in her direction. The father had already turned his attention to the Jumbotron, but the little girl's eyes were locked on us. Mark's expression softened, and he asked me to run back to the staff tent to collect every gift we had on hand. When I returned, the girl was in Mark's arms on the other side of the barricade. As he introduced us, I slipped an American flag pin into his free hand.

He smiled and pointed to the American flag pin on his suit lapel. She shook her head when he asked if she had a special piece of jewelry like his. Mark put her down and knelt to her height, pinning the flag on her sweatshirt. I heard her squeal, but I was only paying attention to her father. I handed him the gift bag and introduced myself. He threw an arm around my shoulders, then pulled back and told me I had no idea how much it meant to him that such powerful people showed his daughter so much kindness. This was a once-in-a-lifetime experience for someone like him, and he apologized for acting as if he were meeting his favorite celebrity, and for not dressing in fancier clothes. He worked a night shift and had wanted to skip the rally, but his daughter had begged him to go. He laughed and showed me the dirt under his fingernails. "You must be so fed up having to put up with folks like us, telling us how grateful you are for our support," he said. "But you'll never understand how you just changed my little girl's life. You'll never understand," he repeated.

I wanted to tell him I did understand—I, too, had grown up in a blue-collar family. I was not the most intelligent or most politically connected person at the White House. Rather, the values imparted to me from my childhood were the reason that I stood in front of him that day. I wanted to tell him that I still had my first American flag pin, that the memory of my uncle giving it to me was deeply ingrained in my memory.

But I did not say any of that. Instead, I gave him a hug and thanked him for supporting the president, just as he had predicted I would. I snapped their photo with Mark, and then we walked away.

———

"Masks are a conspiracy, you know." Debbie was working up to a lecture in the motorcade. I hadn't been aware that she was meeting us in Wisconsin for the final rally before Election Day until I'd crawled into the SUV, exhausted, and found her in my seat. "They spread more illnesses than the coronavirus," she continued. "Talk to Mark about it. Why do you think he keeps getting styes in his left eye?"

I knew better than to press the issue further. "I had no idea, Debbie. Let's talk to Mark about setting up a meeting with you and Dr. Fauci next week."

She rolled her eyes and looked out the window. "Dr. Fauci is the worst of them all. I keep telling Mark he gets paid so much, that's why he's making such a big deal out of this pandemic."

I spent much of the rally alone, wandering through the crowd. I paused to take a long look at many of the attendees. Thick clouds of breath puffed from their agape mouths, and their eyes were glazed over from waiting in sub-zero temperatures all day. They did not notice the deepening rattle in the president's voice, or that his adult children wore outfits worth more than their yearly income. Instead, they were mesmerized and emboldened in the presence of the president. I very much wanted to feel an authentic connection to someone there. But the feeling never came, so I returned to my colleagues and the Trump and Pence families. That was where I belonged now.

"Welcome back, Miss Private Jet," the Air Force One steward greeted me as I dragged my body up the airplane steps. Because Debbie was flying back to Joint Base Andrews with us, Tony manifested me back onto Air Force One. I smiled and found my seat, nauseous with exhaustion.

The plane was filled to capacity with guests from the 2016 and 2020 campaigns, the president's most loyal allies and his family. Everyone was energized and cheerful. People placed wagers on how many electoral college votes the boss would win, and hurled insults at the Biden family. Weeks filled with galas and parties for the second inauguration were discussed. The president's children ordered bottles of champagne for the plane. Glasses clinked and champagne spilled onto the carpet as people chanted "Four More Years!" I shook my head when the steward offered me a glass. Mark looked at me, puzzled, as he held a champagne glass filled with Perrier and told me I was off the clock and could have a drink. I told him I was too tired.

I had never been so physically and mentally exhausted in my life, and I was already worried about driving home. But something had shifted in me the night before when I saw Mark interact with Tony Bobulinski, and my unease deepened throughout the day. The version of me that would exchange champagne toasts to presumptively celebrate a second Trump term was inauthentic, but that was the me I had become.

It was a painful realization, one without rationale. I felt heavy with shame that I had been pulled into the center of the political universe, mostly by my own doing. I did not belong on Air Force One, drinking champagne or musing over ball gowns I could not afford. I was consumed with fear that my past had infiltrated the life I was building. I felt that I had betrayed the world that had made me, and I began to grapple with the question of who I truly was amidst this sea of power and privilege.

As I drove home, I gripped the wheel of my car with both hands and squinted to stay awake. My body had begun to shiver again, ready to collapse, as I wrestled with oppressive self-criticism.

I thought about the little girl and her father in North Carolina. Through her eyes, I saw my own life. I started talking out loud. "She has as much right to a job like mine. She has to work hard. She has to be a fighter. Maybe we did that for her today. Maybe we changed her life."

I continued talking to myself until I reached my apartment around 3:30 a.m. I stumbled in, dropping my travel bags at the front door. Without bothering to take my shoes off or slip under the blankets, I collapsed on my bed and immediately fell asleep.

CHAPTER 13

The Election

AFTER MONTHS OF AVOIDING the coronavirus, Mark and I finally caught it immediately after the campaign ended and we were each placed in a ten-day quarantine. Alone at my apartment with CNN quietly playing on my TV, I found it difficult to distinguish reality from what I heard was happening at the White House. I was discombobulated, disconnected.

Mark beat me to work on our first morning back at the office. When I arrived, he was already in a meeting with Russ Vought, the director of the Office of Management and Budget. I had only been at my desk a few minutes when Russ walked out of Mark's office about an hour earlier than we had expected and closed the door behind him. Eliza and I looked at each other, confused.

A moment later Mark popped his head out and asked, "Could you both come in here for a minute?" And then he closed the door. He was seated with his elbow propped on the arm of his couch, his forehead resting on his hand. He wasn't holding his phones. "Oh my gosh," Eliza whispered. I asked him, "Is everything okay?" Eliza nudged me, and Mark pointed to an open can of White Claw, the hard seltzer, sitting on his coffee table. I gasped and then started laughing as Eliza began apologizing profusely.

As a dedicated and faithful Southern Baptist, Mark had never drunk an alcoholic beverage in his life—until mid-November 2020.

And he consumed his first alcoholic beverage in the presence of Russ Vought, a dedicated and faithful Mormon, in the morning hours during a consequential period of American history.

I hadn't been at the White House on election night, quarantined and accidentally sleeping through most of it, but staff had an election watch party in the West Wing. Eliza had stored some of the alcohol she had purchased for the party in Mark's office refrigerator, forgetting to remove the leftover cans of White Claw while we were out with COVID. She kept apologizing, and I was still laughing until I managed to ask Mark, "How much of that did you drink?"

"Well," he answered, picking up the can on the table and swishing its contents around, "this one's about halfway empty." He went over to his garbage can and held it up so we could inspect its contents. I counted three White Claw cans. "I was sitting here with Russ," Mark explained, "and started to get thirsty. I know you girls keep my fridge stocked with sparkling water, so I went and got one. I sat back down and took a sip and thought, 'Wow, this is real good!' I looked at it and saw it was Blackberry, and thought, 'The girls never got me this one before.'" I'm laughing so hard at this point, there are tears in my eyes.

"I liked it a lot and drank it pretty quick, and went and got another. Grapefruit! Another new flavor! Then I got a third, and I remembered I hadn't offered Russ one, so I did, and he looked at me all weird and said no." Mark started laughing then, and continued, "So Russ is talking, talking, and I'm sitting here sipping my water, and Russ says to me, 'Sir, I know times are hard now, but are they really that bad?' And then . . ." He paused to snap his fingers and widen his eyes. "It hit me. My head started feeling funny, and I look down at the can and saw that it was alcohol. I'm drinking alcohol on a Monday morning, and I've never even had a drink before."

We were all cracking up when suddenly my radio bleeped and we heard, "Mogul, moving elevator, ground-floor residence." Mogul was Trump's Secret Service code name. The president, who rarely left the residence before noon, was on his way to the Oval. That wiped the smile off Mark's face. "Does that mean the president is on his way here?" he asked, looking kind of helpless.

"Yes," I answered, struggling to stop laughing, "yes, it does."

"Can you ask Molly to tell him I have a bunch of election calls and I'll see him later? I need to sober up, I think."

———

The president and his legal advisors—led by Rudy and Sidney Powell, a former federal prosecutor—would file ninety "Stop the Steal" lawsuits. The slogan was in support of the president's claims of a stolen election. The same day the news networks declared Joe Biden the president-elect, this group held a press conference about various legal challenges. They stood in front of a Philadelphia landscaping company building in a strip mall next to an adult entertainment shop and a crematorium.

At a press conference that week at RNC headquarters, Rudy and company made a number of uncorroborated accusations about voter fraud, many of them outlandish. Rudy rambled on about "one of my favorite law movies," *My Cousin Vinny*, while streaks of what looked like motor oil streamed down his face. Sidney Powell raised the dreaded specter of George Soros, and Jenna Ellis, another of Trump's lawyers, likened their legal team to an "elite strike force." Mopping his face with a handkerchief, Rudy exclaimed, "This is real! It's not made up! There's nobody here who engages in fantasies!"

Everyone in the White House, including the president, was both fascinated and appalled by the spectacle. Like most Americans who watched it, I thought the lawyers were humiliating for the president, a sentiment he shared. I heard him shouting from the Oval dining room as Giuliani spoke, "Somebody make this stop! Get him off! Make him stop!"

I didn't think there was anything wrong or unjustified about challenging the results of an election when the counts were within the margin of error. Every person who runs for office has the right to do that. It didn't bother me that the president was exhausting every option before conceding he lost the election. I couldn't imagine him doing otherwise. But the erratic, to say the least, performances of the campaign's lawyers and the rhetoric from some of the president's surrogates were starting to worry me.

I didn't blame the president for any of it yet. I didn't want to blame him. I felt strongly that he should concede the election, and I worried that we were surrounding him with people who fueled his most impulsive behaviors. I knew things could get out of hand, and fast.

As we lost each lawsuit, I thought there was a clear end in sight. But, despite our unbroken string of legal defeats, the battle continued, and the president's core staffers stood by him as he decided to settle in for a long fight.

In mid-November, Mark and I went to the Hill for various end-of-year policy negotiation meetings. We stopped by the office of Leader McConnell, who earnestly pleaded with Mark to tell the president not to meddle in the upcoming Georgia Senate runoff elections. Mark assured the leader he would do his best. I struggled to remain stone-faced—I knew Mark had been discussing the president's involvement for days.

As we walked through the Capitol, Mark asked if I had given any thought to what I was going to do if Biden was inaugurated. I told him I'd heard from a few members and their staffs about openings in their offices and in the offices of incoming freshmen members, but there was also another job opportunity on my mind.

I reminded Mark about a conversation the president had had with me when we were in his office on Air Force One flying to Wisconsin for a campaign rally. He sometimes struggled with phonetic pronunciations, so I had been briefing him about the members in attendance and how to properly enunciate their names. A devious smile crept across the president's face, and he complimented my skill set and mastery of Congress. He joked that if the Democrats stole the election from us, he would probably need me to remain on his staff, since it would be difficult to find someone who knew the members like I did. Mark and I laughed, and I assured the president that while I served at his pleasure, he was not going to lose the election.

But we had lost, and now I was trying to figure out my next move. While I had reservations about remaining in the president's circle after January 20, there was something attractive about helping build his post-presidential operation. On one hand, I worried that moving away from Washington would tarnish the network I had spent the last few years building, and it might then be difficult to land a job on the Hill if I decided to return.

I also felt I could be an asset to him. The president needed strong-willed, sane people surrounding him, and I was confident I could fill that role. Mark listened intently and reminded me that we were not yet at a point to have proactive conversations about anyone's life post-presidency. But, he added, he was sure that the president would welcome me to move with him, if I was willing to pause networking for other job opportunities for now.

I was willing—and I did. I assured Mark I would stay until the very end.

————

On Thanksgiving Eve, Mark was scheduled to fly to Florida. We kept having to push the departure time while we made arrangements for the president to meet with a group of Pennsylvania legislators. Rudy and former New York City police commissioner Bernie Kerik had brought the lawmakers to the White House following an election fraud hearing in Gettysburg, Pennsylvania.

Dan Scavino and I were among the few stragglers in the West Wing that day. "Look around, Cass," Dan said. "No one is here. No one sticks by the boss's side when things get hard. It sucks. I feel bad for the guy." He looked at me closely. "You actually care about the president, don't you?"

"Yeah, I do," I said. "But Dan, this is getting a little out of control. I mean, look at us. We're here on Thanksgiving Eve, and now we're entertaining Rudy's cast of characters for a meeting without purpose."

Dan conceded. "I know, but the president needs loyal people, like you, surrounding him now more than ever. And in Florida, if we end up having to move down there in January. You see who's actually on our team on days like this," Dan said. "But who knows. Maybe we'll actually pull this off."

I had to coordinate the logistics with Trump advisor and Rudy Giuliani protégé Boris Epshteyn for the impromptu meeting. When the guests arrived, I brought them to the White House Medical Unit for routine COVID screenings. Several tested positive for the virus, which complicated matters. The president was impatient, and I worried that Mark's travel window to get out in time for the holiday would close.

I was ready to escort the last group of COVID-negative legislators when my phone buzzed with a call from Molly. When I answered, the president was on the other end, scolding me to hurry the remaining guests to the Oval Office so the meeting could begin. I explained that a few guests had tested positive and that I'd be there with the last of the negatives in about two minutes.

"I said everyone!" he yelled. "Bring them all! Bring them all now!"

Several doctors had overheard him and immediately urged me to push back. While I agreed with their assessment, I was not in the business of defying the president's orders. I suggested that if they felt so strongly, they should call the Oval Office and explain their case. We reached out to Dr. Conley, who reluctantly agreed with me and cautioned that the COVID-positive guests should wear N95 masks. I brought every guest, positive and negative, to the Oval Office to meet with the president and Mark.

When everyone had filed into the Oval Office, the president instructed the masked guests to take off their masks. He assured them it was more important for him to see their beautiful faces, and he was not worried about contracting the virus. He explained that since he had recently had the coronavirus, his antibodies would protect him from contracting it again. The guests stripped off their masks.

I pulled Mark out of the Oval Office and whisked him down the hallway. He needed to make his flight, and I assured him I would have everything under control. He slipped into his limo and thanked me.

When I returned to the Oval Office, the guests were shoving their personal items across the Resolute Desk at the president for his signature. Rudy was thrilled at the president's hospitality. But by the look on the president's face, I knew he felt anything but hospitable.

I felt a pang of regret for assuring Mark I had everything under control.

CHAPTER 14

December

THE QUAD-SCREEN TV in the office showed CNN reporting that Attorney General Barr had acknowledged to the Associated Press that the Justice Department had found insufficient evidence of widespread voter fraud that would have changed the results of the election.

Moments later, the president's valet rushed down the hall to say that the president wanted to see Mark in the dining room. I knew the president would be livid about the attorney general's statement and would blame Mark for not alerting him beforehand or quashing it entirely. Mark went to the dining room and returned soon after, which sparked my curiosity. I decided to walk down there to see what was going on.

The door to the dining room was propped open slightly, and I saw the valet rushing to tidy up the space. I stepped into the room and immediately saw a shattered plate to my right, and Heinz ketchup smeared on the fireplace mantel. I grabbed a tea towel from the pantry drawer and started wiping away the condiment.

"Did you see what Barr said?" the valet asked. I nodded. "I think he's at the White House right now. What the hell is going on?" I began to pick up pieces of the shattered plate.

He grabbed the tea towel from me and suggested I return to my office. "The president is really, really angry at the attorney general," he said.

Speculation about the attorney general's job security quickly spread through the West Wing. Many staffers, including me, hoped Barr would stay until the end of the administration.

About a week later, the president tweeted that he had accepted Attorney General Barr's resignation. He appointed Jeff Rosen as acting attorney general, slated to assume duty on Christmas Eve.

———

On December 8, the president's de facto legal team came up with a Hail Mary lawsuit that had an attorney general—Ken Paxton, of Texas—challenge the election procedures of other states, Pennsylvania, Georgia, Michigan, and Wisconsin. He believed that the Supreme Court would hear the case and side with him.

The next day, Mark and I went to the National Archives for a meeting with the archivist of the United States, David Ferriero, to discuss plans for the Trump presidential library and end-of-administration document-retention protocol. The archivist greeted us at the entrance upon arrival, and I tried to lighten Mark's solemn mood by requesting to see the Declaration of Independence and US Constitution, citing that perhaps the White House needed a friendly reminder about our favored founding documents. The archivist seemed eager to comply, but Mark said it wouldn't be necessary and apologized for my inappropriate behavior. I was only trying to lighten the mood, and Mark's spirits.

When we left the meeting, flurries of snow were falling from the sky. "The first snowfall. That has to be a good sign . . . right, Mark?" I asked as we climbed into his limo. He was in a trance, scrolling through his phone.

I let a few moments pass before I broke our stalemate. "Hey, Mark," I began. "Does the president know about the meeting at the National Archives?"

"No, he doesn't," he said. "I'll probably tell him this afternoon. The president probably won't be that happy with me about meeting with him, though. He doesn't want us to work on a post-election plan yet. There are still some pending lawsuits we're working on.

You know the president, he has very strong feelings about how things should be handled."

I understood, but my curiosity grew. "How do you think things should be handled, Mark?" I asked.

"Well," he started, "I had the meeting, didn't I?"

The limo had bumped over the first security checkpoint at the White House complex, and I could tell Mark wanted to spend the rest of the car ride catching up on his texts and emails. I watched the snowflakes float as we drove past the south grounds of the White House, not entirely sure what to make of our conversation.

———

I had been dreading the White House holiday parties. Many attendees were encouraging the president's election theft claims, and the event would open the floodgates to their direct access on campus.

I remained at my desk for most of the evening and spent the time catching up on work. When John Ratcliffe, the director of National Intelligence, stopped by the office with his daughter toward the end of the ball, I felt a calming sense of normalcy temporarily return. John and I were both close with Kevin and spent much of the past year working to build our working relationship. He had become someone I relied on as a mentor and ally.

We showed his daughter around the West Wing. At the end of the tour, I handed her a White House gift bag and brought her into Mark's personal gift closet so she could stock up on gifts that would soon be out of commission. Meanwhile, John and I stepped outside to Mark's patio and strolled to the White House swimming pool.

Delicately, John asked whether I had heard any of the recent advice Mark had given to the president. "I hear a lot of things. What are you referring to specifically?" I asked.

"Well, you know, I'm a little worried about what's going on around here," he began, and explained he had spoken a few times to the president about the election. "He acknowledges he lost, not that he wants to concede, but he acknowledges he lost the election," John said. He looked at me for a reaction, but I offered no comment. "Then he'll immediately backpedal," he continued, "or call the next day and say he didn't lose the election and I should call Mark. Mark has more information. I'm a little worried Mark's not giving him good advice."

I conceded that Mark might be "in that phase of telling people what they want to hear. But," I added, "I don't know everything that's coming across his desk right now." We went back inside, and he promised to stop by the next day to talk with me about my future.

———

I was at my desk when the news broke that the Supreme Court had declined to hear the Texas case. The press, legal experts, and most Americans had expected the decision, and it was a cause for celebration for many. But in the West Wing, it felt like the final blow. I sympathized with my colleagues who mourned our second term, but privately, I was relieved we had reached what seemed like the last impasse. The legal challenges had been disorganized and unserious and had only succeeded in embarrassing the president. I wanted the chaos to subside so that we could prepare for the next phase of our careers, and encourage the president to leave with his dignity intact.

After a Christmas reception in the residence that night, Mark asked if I had thought any more about going to Florida. I said that I had, and that I was leaning toward going. He asked if I had had any other job conversations. A few people had reached out, but there were no offers I was seriously considering, I told him. He said to let him know either way as soon as I decided. I promised I would, and then he told me that Jared had asked whether I might be interested in moving to Miami with him. I declined without hesitation and told Mark that if I were going to uproot my life in Washington, I wanted to continue serving the president. Mark agreed.

Mark and I were walking through the Rose Garden colonnade later that evening when we crossed paths with the president, who was beside himself about the Supreme Court's decision. While they spoke, I stepped back and stood across from the president's valet.

"They got it wrong, Chief. How did this happen? Why didn't we make more calls? We needed to do more. Okay? We can't let this stand," the president raged. Mark tried to reassure the president, asserting there were still other options on the table, and he was going to figure it all out. The president pushed back. "I don't want people to know we lost, Mark. This is embarrassing," he said. "Figure it out." Mark assured the president that he would work on it.

I was irritated that Mark gave the president false hope. Of course, that's what the president wanted to hear, but he was damaging the country by concocting false rationales for perpetuating a fight that was now certainly a lost cause.

It was also upsetting to witness the president so distraught. He looked run-down, defeated, almost frightened, like a hollowed figure of himself. He tried to cancel his trip the next day to the Army-Navy game at West Point, unwilling to be seen in public after the Supreme Court rejected his token election fraud case. Eventually, we persuaded the president that canceling the trip would make him look weak—his greatest kryptonite.

"I think my life is about to get real tough for the next few weeks," Mark remarked to me.

Mark had no idea how accurate he would be. None of us did.

———

While other staffers slowed down in anticipation of the Christmas break, my responsibilities ramped up in mid-December. Mark practically ordered the majority of the staff to go home to spend the holidays with family. I thought maybe he was trying to protect them.

But I was there, every day. So were Mark and White House lawyers Pat Cipollone, Pat Philbin, and Eric Herschmann.

Mark asked for General Services Administration (GSA) staff to light a fire in his office fireplace first thing every morning. He kept a pile of firewood and throughout the day added logs to keep the fire burning. When I went into his office to deliver lunch or a package to him, I would sometimes find him leaning over the fire, feeding papers into it, watching to make sure they burned, and placing logs on top of the ashes.

I do not know precisely what papers Mark was burning, but his actions raised alarms. The Presidential Records Act requires staff to keep original documents and send them to the National Archives. All copies and personal papers were supposed to go into burn bags to be properly disposed of. Mark knew these procedures. Even if he was burning copies, he was still toeing a fine line of what should be preserved, under the law.

―――――

Matt Gaetz started dropping by more frequently. He had asked me several times if I thought the president would issue him a pardon. I tried to dismiss Matt's antics but began wondering why he was pushing so hard for a pardon. I raised the issue with Mark one day after Matt had left and asked if there was anything I should know about.

"Between you and me," Mark said, "DOJ may be looking into something about Matt. Best to stay away from him. Can you do that for me?" I nodded and promised I would.

On the evening of December 18, Mark returned from a meeting in the Oval Office and abruptly asked if I could tell his detail he wanted to go home, as if there was an emergency there. His detail quickly prepared his limo and he left campus without further explanation.

Shortly after Mark's departure, I walked down to visit with Molly and get a sense of the president's evening plans. Usually, if Mark went home before the president went to the residence, I would stay at my desk in case the president needed anything from Mark or me. But since Mark had left early with such confidence, I thought perhaps the president was wrapping up for the evening and I would get to go home early, too.

When I walked into the Outer Oval, I saw that the president was meeting with General Michael Flynn, the former national security advisor who had pleaded guilty to lying to the FBI about his involvement with Russian officials, cutting a cooperation deal in special counsel Robert Mueller's inquiry into interference in the 2016 election. Three weeks before today's meeting, on November 25, Trump had issued Flynn a presidential pardon.

"Why is Mike Flynn here?" I asked Molly.

"I'm not sure," Molly said, then added, "He's just talking to the president about some things." *Talking to the president about some things. Got it.* I went back to my office and settled in.

Molly came to my office soon after and asked if we had a wine opener. "No," I said. "Mark doesn't drink, so we do not keep alcoholic paraphernalia in his vicinity." I tried to joke, but she did not crack even a slight smile. I sighed. "I know the vice president has one. I'll call his assistant." Once we secured the wine opener, we parted ways, back to our respective desks.

A few minutes later, Pat Cipollone, Pat Philbin, Eric Herschmann, and Derek Lyons barreled down the hallway past my office door and rounded the corner toward the Oval Office.

I was imagining various reasons Flynn could have for being there that had the lawyers in a panic, but then I remembered it was Derek's last day at the White House. I figured I was overthinking—Flynn had probably left, and there was a toast for Derek in the Oval Office to celebrate his tenure at the White House.

Liz Horning, Cipollone's top aide and Derek's fiancée, wandered in and asked if I knew what was happening in the Oval Office. She had dinner plans with Derek and could not get in touch with him. "I'm not sure," I said, "but a bunch of people are in the Oval."

On cue, we both turned toward the sound of raised voices coming from that direction. Although the Oval Office was about a ten-second walk from my desk, it was highly unusual to hear any noise coming from there. We could not make out distinct words that night, just people screaming at each other.

Molly called me to come to the Outer Oval. Dan Scavino was pouring the last of a bottle of wine into a glass. The screaming was much louder than I had anticipated. I looked into the Oval Office and saw a larger group. Along with the White House lawyers were Mike Flynn, Sidney Powell, and Patrick Byrne, the CEO of Overstock.com. *How did all those people get inside the building?*

"Can you call Mark?" Molly asked. "I keep trying to get him, but the call keeps dropping."

I was confused. "That's weird, Molly. Mark is at home. The call shouldn't be dropping. I'll get him on the line and patch him over to you." I tried several times to reach Mark, but had no immediate luck.

I could tell the meeting was growing more contentious, so I decided to text Tony. "Flynn is still here. And Powell. There's a brawl." He responded, "Oh holy hell." He immediately called and asked if I knew what they were brawling over. He had been in the Oval Office earlier that day and heard the president talk about invoking the Insurrection Act or martial law. If that's what they were arguing over, Tony said, I needed to get Mark back to the White House as soon as possible.

Eventually, I got ahold of Mark, who seemed reluctant to get on the line with the president. I urged him that it sounded like it was a matter of national security.

A Secret Service agent who was standing outside the Oval Office came by. "I don't want to hear all of that," he said. "It's really upsetting. I wouldn't recommend going down there."

The West Wing was officially unhinged.

Things seemed to be breaking up as people filed out of the Oval and walked by my desk. Molly told me that the president wanted to have dinner in the residence and was planning to reconvene the meeting in the Yellow Oval after he finished eating. I told her I would stay in case something happened. She wished me luck, and then left for the night.

Dan Scavino stopped by on his way home and said, "This is fucked up."

Eric Herschmann walked into Mark's office in a fury, pounding his fist on the wall. "This can't be fucking happening," he said. "This is fucking insane."

Pat Cipollone, looking traumatized, said to me, "This is nuts. Mark needs to come back."

"Does the chief really need more of a reason to come back?" Derek asked. "Here it is. Martial law. I mean, for God's sake, we called Rudy to come help us do damage control. Rudy Giuliani. You know it's bad when we call Rudy for backup. The chief needs to come back!"

I called Tony and told him what Derek had said, and that I was having trouble getting ahold of Mark. I asked Tony to come back, but he said this needed the chief's intervention. I agreed, and continued to call Mark.

He continued ignoring my calls, so I called one of the agents on his detail. "Go pass your phone to Mark, now," I ordered.

"Seriously?" the agent asked. "What if he's in bed sleeping? What do you expect me to do? Shake him awake?"

"Yes," I responded. "This is a matter of national security. You need to put me on the phone with him."

After a few minutes, I had Mark on the line. "Mark, the president is reconvening the meeting in the Yellow Oval. Rudy is on his way as backup for Pat Cipollone. *Rudy, for Pat Cipollone.* We're talking about the Insurrection Act, seizing voting machines." I felt my voice begin to sound desperate. "Please, Mark. You need to come back here."

He said, "Alright, I'm on the way."

When he got out of his limo, he said to me, "I thought they'd be able to handle it without me there. I'm not going to lose my job because of these guys. We've got to fix this. We've got to fix this."

I walked with Mark to the residence, and he had asked me to come back at midnight to break up the meeting if it had not already ended by then. I heard the president scream, "I don't care how you do it, just get it fucking done." Mark and I exchanged a pained look, and he disappeared into the Yellow Oval.

My hands were sweating as I walked back to my desk. I had never heard the president sound so desperate before. Somebody needed to give the president good advice, and I worried that he was surrounded by too many people who were misleading him. But at the same time, I knew that it was the president—not his advisors—that was not only enabling, but encouraging this to happen. He was in control.

I went to the residence around 11:55 p.m., but the meeting had begun to end. I used my key to the Rose Garden colonnade to unlock the door to let everyone out. Mark escorted Rudy off the premises to make sure America's Mayor didn't wander back to the residence.

One hour after the meeting broke up, my watch buzzed with a Trump tweet alert. "Peter Navarro releases 36-page report alleging election fraud. 'More than sufficient' to swing victory to

Trump. A great report by Peter. Statistically impossible to have lost the 2020 Election. Big protest in D.C. on January 6th. Be there, will be wild!"

Wild.

––––––

Mark and I were back in the West Wing less than twelve hours later. He had scheduled a meeting with Devin Nunes, who at the time was the ranking member of the House Permanent Select Committee on Intelligence (HPSCI), as well as the committee's top Republican aide, George Pappas.

I glanced at Mark's office door when I received a notification from the Secret Service that our guests had arrived. His door had been closed since I had arrived, and I was not sure whether he remembered about the meeting. With my coat folded over my elbow, I peered through the peephole on his door. Mark was nestled in the corner of his couch, scrolling through one of his cell phones. I drew in a deep breath and pushed the door open.

"Morning, Mark," I said. "Devin and George are here for your meeting. I am going outside to get them now. Are you ready for the meeting, or would you like a bit more time to yourself?"

"I started the fire on my own this morning, since you or Eliza didn't have the GSA guys come start it for me," he replied. *I wanted to say, I should have known your first concern the morning after the United States was on the brink of anarchy would be your fireplace.* But I bit my tongue and walked out of the office to retrieve Devin and George.

"Morning," I greeted them on West Executive Avenue. "Sorry to keep you waiting in the cold." As we walked into the West Wing, Devin asked how everything was going. I stifled a laugh and asked, "Do you want my honest answer?" Devin shook his head and said, "I'm sorry. I shouldn't have asked."

Mark was leaning against my desk watching the TV when we walked into the office. Without saying hello, he motioned to bring them into his personal office. "Cassidy, you're coming, too, right?" he asked.

I studied his face, wondering what purpose I would serve in that meeting. Mark knew I preferred to limit my exposure to conversations about classified material. He and the president were constantly hunting for administration staffers who were leaking classified information to the press, and while I would never do that, I never wanted them to speculate that I was a source. I shook my head no and told Mark he knew where to find me if something came up.

About twenty minutes later, Devin popped his head out of the office. "Hey, Cassidy?"

"Yes, sir? Does Mark need something?" I asked.

"No, no. He's handling some things on his phone. We haven't started the meeting yet. But, uh, I was wondering if we could open one of his windows. It's a little smoky . . . ," he said. I followed Devin into Mark's office, where the fireplace was lit. "Mark, what is going on?!" I snapped as I propped open the door to his patio. "You're going to set off a smoke alarm!" Mark was startled. "Sorry, sorry," he responded. "Sorry to keep you guys waiting. Let's get this meeting started."

As I went to leave, Devin whispered, "How often is he burning papers?" I glanced at him pointedly, then rushed out of Mark's office.

I sank into my desk chair and buried my face in my hands. I did not understand what was going on. Assuaging the president's impulses took precedence over order and protocol, and we were the enablers. I needed to correct course with Mark before we let things completely spiral out of control—before it was too late.

In the recesses of my mind, I wondered if we had already reached that point, and I was just too naive to see it.

After a few hours Mark called me into his office, now cleared of smoke but, with the patio door still propped open, nearly as cold as it was outside. He explained that immediately after Christmas, HPSCI would come to the White House with boxes of classified documents to sort through. "We're hoping to declassify some of this material before the end of the administration," Mark said. "I'll help them when I have time in my schedule, but I want them to do it here. I need you to coordinate everything with George."

I looked at each of the three men in front of me, blankly. I was confident Mark knew this request was completely out-of-bounds. HPSCI's protocol for reviewing classified documents was independent of the White House, and if Mark needed national security staffers with the appropriate clearance, we could work with Robert O'Brien and the National Security Council team. But I could tell by the look on Mark's face that his mind was made up, and trying to give him a lesson on protocol would only infuriate him.

I was floored. For the president's sake, I felt burdened with the responsibility to restore order.

I knew it would be an impossible task.

———

Rudy convened a meeting in the Cabinet Room on December 21 with about a dozen members of Congress. The vice president and Marc Short, his chief of staff and former OLA director, also participated in the meeting. The president and Mark made sporadic appearances. I was in and out of the meeting and understood Rudy was primarily discussing the vice president's ceremonial role of certifying the election results on January 6, which I would come to associate with John Eastman, a lawyer advising the president on the 2020 election.

Coincidentally, after this meeting, the White House began filtering several "preemptive pardon" requests from members of Congress. A preemptive pardon, they argued, would prevent a potential Biden administration from prosecuting them in a political witch hunt for their efforts to save democracy.

To me, "saving democracy" should not require a presidential pardon.

Mark left that night for Georgia, where he was spending Christmas with his family. He had asked me to stay at the White House until the president and First Lady left for Mar-a-Lago, on the twenty-third. I didn't watch Marine One take off, but I heard the call signs on my radio, and the rotor wash whipped tree branches against the West Wing windows. I sat alone at my desk. The West Wing was nearly empty. But I didn't feel lonely. I never felt lonely there. The end of our time in the White House was near, and the thought of leaving was weighing on me.

I hoped the president would return from Florida ready to accept his electoral defeat so we could begin preparing him for his post-presidential life. The country was best served if we could all move forward.

It would take a miracle, but it was Christmastime, after all.

CHAPTER 15

New Year

AFTER I SPENT ABOUT forty-eight hours in New Jersey for Christmas, I returned to the office on December 28 with Mark. A week earlier, the Secret Service had informed me that Mark had made an unscheduled visit to a Cobb County, Georgia, vote-counting center, which I wrote off as another attempt of Mark's to placate the boss. He had promised the president that he would visit all the states where the election results were being disputed. I thought that the Georgia stop was unwise; I believed that it would read as an effort to pressure local election officials.

That first week back, at Mark's request, I received regular ballot-count updates from Jordan Fuchs, Georgia deputy secretary of state and chief of staff to Secretary of State Brad Raffensperger. Mark also asked me to put together gift packages for Cobb County election officials and workers, each stuffed full of expensive White House memorabilia that he and the president had selected to send. It might have been a good-faith gesture intended to show our appreciation for their hard work, but both the press and skeptical people could see it as an attempted quid pro quo for a favorable count. It took me a few days, but I managed to talk Mark out of sending them.

To prove he hadn't stopped trying to keep the president in office, Mark stepped up his efforts. "I'll be the best chief of staff if I can keep him in office," he explained to me. "If that's what he wants, that's what I want."

At the end of an administration, if a president has children who are minors, they are given Secret Service protection, which continues until they turn sixteen. Adult children of the president get Secret Service protection for the first six months post-presidency. The issue was raised one day, and Trump said, "If we have to leave here, my children are going to get one year."

I discussed it with Tony. "Adult children getting more than six months is unheard-of," he explained. The demand seemed particularly egregious, since all of Trump's adult children could afford private security.

Mark stuck his head out of his office that same day and said, "The president's real mad at me." By then many of us knew that Trump had accused Mark of "giving up"—failing to continue contesting the election results. "Can you have the staff secretary print the one-year security memorandum for POTUS to sign?" he asked. "I think that'll make him happy."

"I think we need to talk to Tony about it," I cautioned him. "That's never been done before. He's going to get bad press."

Mark shook his head. "He's so angry at me all the time. I can't talk to him about anything post–White House without him getting mad that we didn't win. I'm trying to figure out something to make him happy."

I asked the acting staff secretary to draft two versions of the memo, one that gave Trump's adult children six months of protection and one that gave them a year. The president signed both copies, and told Mark, "You pick which one to deliver."

Mark passed that decision off to me, and I delivered the six-month memo to the staff secretary and put the one-year memo in the archives folder.

Before the new year, I had thought that Mark had just been indulging some of the January 6th plans, but as the days passed, he seemed more prepared to embrace a plan for the vice president to reject states' electoral votes.

On New Year's Eve, he asked me to talk to Tony about a potential motorcade movement to Capitol Hill following the president's rally. Tony and I agreed that the movement would be almost impossible. I hoped Mark would not raise the issue again.

January 1

On New Year's Day, Mark again directed Tony and me to come up with a plan to take the president to the Capitol after the rally on January 6.

I called Kevin. "Hey, I know that you've never personally brought a presidential package up to the Capitol for the State of the Union. But we've used your leadership office as a holding area for the staff. If we were to make a movement from the rally at the Ellipse to the Capitol on January 6th, do you think it would be a viable option to use the same plan? I'm just trying to gauge what your thinking is about this." The Ellipse was the park just south of the White House where Trump planned to hold the rally.

"You guys aren't coming to the Capitol, right?" he replied. "There's no way he wants to do that. Why would he want to come up to the Capitol?"

"I don't know," I said. "Mark just asked me to figure out if there was a plan that we could potentially put in place. Kevin, I assure you this move can't happen as of now. There are going to be way too many people. It's not safe to bring him up."

"So why even ask about it?" he said, losing patience.

"I'm asking you to cover my back so I can tell Mark and the president that I made a call to Capitol Hill about it, and there are people on the Hill who are aware of a potential movement."

"Yeah, okay, no. You guys aren't coming here."

I said, "I know! I just have to ask."

———

I called Mom to wish her a Happy New Year. She made a plea. "Cass, I don't want you to go to work on January 6th. Are you looking at the news? Crazy people are going to that rally. You have to be careful."

"It's okay, Mom," I said, trying to reassure her. "There will be road closures to clear a path for White House staff. And if it gets too crowded, they have a secure car service that will pick me up and bring me in."

I understood why she was worried. The news networks were warning that the crowds on January 6 were expected to be large and militant. She kept texting and begging me not to go to work that day, and I kept brushing off her concerns. But her fear gave me pause. *Why is she so scared? Should I be more scared than I am?*

January 2

Mark spent much of the morning in his office with George Pappas, sorting through the classified documents that had arrived a few days earlier. When I went into his office to remind Mark about an upcoming call he was scheduled to join, there were thousands of papers sprawled across his conference room table. He quickly began to scoop them up in a rush so he could prepare for the call.

"We can get this, Chief," I said. "I'll bring George to the Situation Room to continue reviewing the documents." Mark shot me a sharp glare. "No, no, no. No Situation Room. These documents need to stay up here. Can you unlock Tony's office for him?" *Absolutely not*, I thought, but said, "We'll figure it out."

George and I left Mark's office with arms full of classified documents. I contemplated where he should go before settling him into the Roosevelt Room, a conference room that is not a sensitive compartmented information facility (SCIF), but was close enough to our office that I could keep a watchful eye on him.

As I turned to leave the Roosevelt Room, George invited me to look through the documents with him. "There's a lot of interesting stuff in these. I thought I knew a lot about Crossfire Hurricane, but turns out there is a ton I didn't know. You should read them, too."

"Crossfire Hurricane? What does that mean?" I asked him, genuinely perplexed. He laughed and said I had a good sense of humor. I shook my head and walked out of the room.

I had not wanted to know what was going on before, but I especially did not want to know now.

The call was with Brad Raffensperger, Georgia's secretary of state, and it went on for a long time. I had a backlog of stuff I needed to speak with Mark about and was waiting for the call to end. Mark was listening to the conversation on his desk phone's speaker and had the phone cord stretched to his couch. His door was propped open, and I heard much of the conversation.

When the call ended, Mark asked if I would place the phone back on the receiver for him. He was too wrung out from the call to do it himself.

"Mark, he can't possibly think we're going to pull this off. That call was crazy, right?" I asked, looking for reassurance. The president had pressed Raffensperger to "find" the nearly twelve thousand votes that would have put him ahead of Biden.

Mark shook his head and replied, "Cass, he knows it's over. He knows he lost, but we're going to keep trying. There are some good options out there still. We're going to keep trying."

Pat Cipollone appeared in Mark's doorway and said, "That call was not good." Pat was also dialed in to the call.

Mark gulped. "Maybe I should go up to the residence and talk to the president. I'm worried that call might leak to the press."

The next day, the press reported an audio recording of the call.

That evening, Rudy and associates met with Mark and Senator Lindsey Graham, of South Carolina. I was under the impression they were meeting to discuss allegations of voter fraud, and the plan for Trump allies in the House and Senate to object to certifying the electoral college votes from certain states. As Lindsey left the meeting, Rudy followed him out of Mark's office with a huge binder and asked me to make a copy for the senator. When Rudy went back into Mark's office, Lindsey waved off his request. "Don't waste your time photocopying dead people's names. I'm not even sure these people are really dead."

Lindsey left, and the president convened a call with Freedom Caucus members to discuss the plan for January 6. When the meeting ended, Rudy asked me to walk his group out.

I got my coat and escorted Rudy and his associates out of the West Wing. As we walked, Rudy said, "Are you excited about the sixth? It's going to be a great day. I'm excited. We're going to go to the Capitol, Cass!"

"I'm curious, Rudy," I said. "What are we going to do at the Capitol?"

"It's going to be great. The president is going to be there. He's going to look powerful . . . The chief knows all about it. Talk to the chief about it."

Remarkably, I followed Rudy's advice and went to discuss the topic with Mark. He was still in his office, seated on his couch, scrolling through his phone. I leaned against his doorway and reported that I had just had an interesting conversation with Rudy. "It sounds like we're going to the Capitol."

Mark didn't look up, but he stopped scrolling for a moment. "There's a lot going on, Cass . . . Things might get real, real bad on January 6."

Until then, I'd been apprehensive about the rally—and whatever else people on the Hill were cooking up. But Mark's warning that night made me genuinely frightened that something "real, real bad" was going to happen.

January 3

George brought an entourage of HPSCI staffers to the White House for more document review sessions. Mark met with the group in his office, and after about thirty minutes, he asked me to put them in the Roosevelt Room for several hours. "Just keep an eye on the group and make sure none of those documents leave with them," Mark instructed me.

"What's Mark thinking?" Kevin asked me later that day on the phone. "He's giving the president bad advice."

"What do you mean?" I asked, but I'd had the same conversation with John Ratcliffe.

"When I talk to the president, sometimes he admits he lost the election, and then he immediately says he didn't lose it and there's a way that he's going to stay in office. Where is he getting that? I can only imagine that Mark is lying to him," said Kevin. "Cass, there's no way he actually thinks he won the election, right? Like, he knows it's over."

"I don't know," I said. "I hear a lot of conflicting things, too."

"Well, Mark needs to give him better advice."

"I'll let Mark know that you think he should give the president better advice."

"This is serious, Cass," he said, and hung up.

Tony was back at work. He had information from the Secret Service that worried him. "We have intel about potential violence at the rally," he told Mark. Max Miller had been hanging around our office suite. "It's only going to be dangerous if the Boogaloo Bois come," Max said.

Mark seemed puzzled. "I haven't heard of them. Are they dangerous ones, or is some other group dangerous?"

Max said, "They're all dangerous. Boogaloo Bois, Oath Keepers, Proud Boys."

"Antifa is dangerous too," Mark added.

As HPSCI was ending their review session, Mark notified me there was going to be an impromptu meeting with DOJ officials. The president was considering installing Jeff Clark, assistant attorney general of the Environment and Natural Resources Division (ENRD) and acting assistant attorney general for the Civil Division, as the new attorney general. "Didn't we just hire a new attorney general, like, two weeks ago?" I asked.

"I've got about ten minutes to meet with HPSCI before I have to go to the Oval. Can you please just bring them here so I know where they're at with the documents?" Mark asked. I quickly pulled the group from the Roosevelt Room and ushered them into Mark's office.

When they left, George handed me some of the documents, now bound into a three-inch binder. He let me know Mark wanted me to keep it in my desk drawer, and not to let it leave my sight. I thanked George and immediately locked the binder in our office vault.

It was out of my sight, but not out of my mind.

January 4

We flew to Georgia with the president for a rally to support Republican senators Kelly Loeffler and David Perdue in their runoff elections against Democrats Raphael Warnock and Jon Ossoff. Trump invited Marjorie Taylor Greene, the newly elected congresswoman from Georgia's Fourteenth District, to come onstage with him.

I didn't think having a QAnon supporter onstage with the president was such a great idea, and told Mark as much. "We don't need her," I said. He pushed back. "The boss wants her, so we're inviting her."

Every decision seemed intended to avoid conflict with the president.

Not only was Marjorie invited onstage, but she flew back to Washington with us on Air Force One. She took out her phone and started showing everyone, including the president, photos of her constituents wearing shirts with the letter Q on them. "There are my people," she said. "They're all coming to the rally. It's going to be a great day!"

After a while, Mark went to his office, and I sat on a couch outside it. The president came out and stood in the doorway of Mark's office. I overheard them talking. "Do you think we're going to pull it off?" Trump asked him.

"In case things don't go as we hope, we're going to have a plan in place, sir," Mark said.

"There's always the chance that we didn't win," Trump replied. "But I think the sixth is going to go well. Do you think it's going to go well, Chief?"

Mark said, "Yes, sir, I think it's going to go well."

January 5

I got to work late. We'd gotten back from Georgia in the early hours of the morning, and I had slept in a little. Mark spent much of the day in the Oval Office with the president, talking about plans for January 6.

A few days before, the president had proposed to convene an Oval Office meeting with Rudy and company and several of the most outspoken House members. Mark was tight-lipped about it when I mentioned it to him, dismissing the subject: "I'll talk to the president about that." I don't know if he dissuaded the president from meeting them in the White House or if he tried to. I did learn that they held the meeting somewhere else, probably on the Hill. I did not learn whether the president phoned in to it or not.

The president asked Mark to speak with Roger Stone and Mike Flynn, who would be staying at the Willard InterContinental that night. Also at the request of the president, Mark had already tried to make plans to meet with Rudy and Bernie Kerik at the Willard, where they had set up a "war room" to monitor efforts the next day to delay Congress's certification of the electoral college results.

For days, I had kept Mark apprised of the Secret Service's heightened security protocols around January 4 to 6, and I did not welcome adding that I felt the meeting was a waste of his time. More concerning was the likelihood that reporters would spot him there. "That's not a smart idea, Mark," I argued.

I did not know everything that Rudy and company were discussing at the Willard, but I knew enough to realize that Mark's attendance would be terrible optics. Mark didn't push back very hard. He raised the meeting twice more that afternoon, but didn't insist I facilitate it, and eventually dropped it.

He stayed at the White House late that night, watching the disappointing Georgia runoff returns in the dining room with the president. He dialed in to the Willard meeting from the car on his way home.

Peter Navarro stopped by our office to deliver more materials proving election fraud. Peter was a master at using PowerPoints to describe conspiracy theories. I usually took any items from Peter and, after thanking him, gave them directly to Mark, who ignored them. Peter was more demanding this time. "This stuff is important, Cassidy," he insisted. There was a note of frustration in his voice. "And you should be paying attention. I need to meet with the chief and the president about it."

"Is this from your QAnon friends, Peter?" I asked.

"Have you looked into it yet? I think they point out a lot of good ideas. You really need to read this. Make sure the chief sees it."

"Oh, I will," I told Peter, with no expectation to share the document with Mark.

I struggled to fall asleep that night, unable to turn off my brain. In less than twenty-four hours, the antics of the past several months would finally end—the false hopes, the wild schemes, the futile efforts to keep the president in office after the voters had rendered their verdict. We were finally coming to the end. Until then, we were supposed to act as if the president was going to serve a second term.

Mom and I traded texts. She made a last plea that I call in sick the next morning. She settled for my promise to be careful on my drive to work. I finally drifted off after that. *It will all be over by the afternoon.*

CHAPTER 16

January 6

WHO IS CALLING SO EARLY?
   I snatch my work phone off my bedside table. It's vibrating nonstop. The screen lights up—it's 7:28 on January 6, 2021. I start to wonder when I'd last slept for more than four hours, but stop myself. *I don't need sleep. I need a triple espresso. And a sugar-free Red Bull.*

No missed calls. *Odd.* I have dozens of unread emails from senior staff bickering about the president's "Save America" rally speech.

Damn it, it's the sixth! My heart pounds as I tear out of bed, still reading emails. I cannot be late today. *Did Mark make it to the White House yet?* I flip through my inbox, checking for an email from the Secret Service. He's still at home. *Really odd.*

I jump in the shower, setting my work phone on the bathtub's edge. I can't afford to miss any calls, not in this job, and especially not today. My phone continues to vibrate while I rinse conditioner from my hair. *Soon I'll be in Florida*, I remind myself. *This will all be over soon.*

Around 8:00, I hear from the Secret Service that Mark is on his way to work. *He's running so late.* Any other day, I would call him to make sure everything was okay, but I don't have time to wonder or care. I text Liz Horning that I'm running slightly behind.

I glance at my outfit in the mirror and notice I'm dressed in black from head to toe. *Do I look like I'm going to a funeral?* I laugh to myself. *I guess I am.* I sit on my sofa to pull on my boots, gazing out the window at the world nine stories below. The cold looks harsh, unforgiving. *Is it an omen?* I text Mom that I'll be careful. I find myself wishing that skipping work was an option.

My personal phone vibrates. A message from a Secret Service agent, warning me about the road conditions. I stuff my faux leather blazer, the one that matches the length of my skirt, in my bag, and fold a wool coat over my elbow as I take the elevator to the parking garage.

Liz is waiting outside when I drive up to her building. She struggles to open the passenger door against the force of the wind. I push against the door from inside.

She hands me an espresso vanilla latte. "Drink it slowly, it might be your last," Liz jokes.

I let it warm my hands as she settles in her seat. "Thanks. So sorry I'm late," I say. "Do you have your flip-top?" We were required to show law enforcement our official badges to pass through security checkpoints.

"Yep. You ready for the best day of your life?" We exchange pained smiles. I know how worried she is.

"Have you heard from Pat Cipollone yet?" I ask.

"On his way in. Running late," she quips.

"Mark was late, too." I'm uneasy. Maybe they agonized over their outfits, like I did. But Mark knows I keep extra gloves and hand warmers in my bag for him. I glance at Liz, but she's buried in her work phone, answering emails.

We flash our badges at the first security checkpoint, and the police cars and military vans unblock the entrance, allowing us to pass.

"Life is going to suck once we lose these on the twentieth," Liz says, waving her badge, still typing an email.

"We wouldn't need them today if the boss had any shred of dignity left."

"Fact." Liz rolls her eyes.

We're quiet for a few minutes. I forgot to put on music. Too late now. Trump supporters are everywhere. Thousands, I estimate. They're all walking toward the Washington Monument, like soldiers marching to battle. *Where did they all come from? Where are they all going to go?*

"Cassidy, stop!" Liz slaps my shoulder and braces her right hand on the roof of the car. I slam to a halt, inches away from plowing through a group of around thirty men dressed in military fatigues or wrapped in Trump 2020 flags. They don't appear to notice, or if they did, they are unfazed. But I'm frozen as the group continues to pass. *What the hell is going on?*

"Liz, this is not antifa," I caution, slowly easing my foot back on the gas pedal after they pass. For days, our colleagues were preemptively blaming antifa for violence that could break out today. A few days ago, Mark told me the president agreed.

"Well, no shit, Cassidy. They're *our* people."

We're silent for the rest of the drive. My car is swept three times before we go through our normal security checkpoints. I pull into a parking spot near the West Wing entrance. Liz and I are unloading our belongings when I notice there are SUVs missing on West Executive Avenue. *The president is still in the residence. I guess we're not too late.*

"Do you hear that?" Liz asks, and I listen.

"Is that 'My Heart Will Go On'? Playing at the Ellipse?"

Liz erupts with laughter. "Yes, yes, it is. How fucking appropriate. The ship is sinking. The ship—"

"The ship is the White House."

"And we're in steerage. Nobody cares about us. We're the first to go down."

I know she's right, but acknowledging it makes my stomach twist. "I think Pat would try to save you, Liz."

She gives me a puzzled look, which fades to a sad smile. "I think Pat would try to save all of us." She lightly punches my arm. "Are you going with the boss to the rally?"

"I am." I can't bring myself to make eye contact with her.

"Cassidy," she says sternly. "Do not go to the rally. Bad. Bad idea. No!"

"I have to. Mark is going." I can tell Liz has more to say, but she bites her tongue. Before we split for our offices, we promise to stay in touch.

———

"Morning, T." I flop onto Tony's couch with my second triple espresso vanilla latte. I love spending time with Tony in his office. The built-in bookshelves are stocked with American history books and, in between the books, memorabilia he's collected throughout his career in law enforcement and framed photos of his family. Tucked away from the noise and activity of the West Wing, Tony's office feels safe and comfortable, like home. In a few weeks the new deputy chief of staff, Jen O'Malley Dillon, will decorate the office, and the thought saddens me. I shove it away.

"Hey, kid." Tony places his phones on his desk and sinks into a chair. "Have you seen the chief yet?"

His expression is more stoic than usual. The only time I saw Tony stressed was when the president tested positive for COVID. He has the greatest poker face I've ever seen.

"No, I just got here, and his office door was shut. I was hoping you'd already seen him and could fill me in on how his mood seems." I'm only half kidding.

He smiles and shakes his head. "This day is fucking nuts already. My phones have been blowing up since four o'clock this morning. This rally is going to be crazy."

Crazy? "I've seen the email chain with speech edits. I haven't gone through the rest of my emails yet, though. What's going on?"

Tony reaches behind his shoulder, fumbling for his phones. "Listen to this shit."

He reads correspondence, which I assume is from the Secret Service or local law enforcement agencies, about the crowd. *More* people than expected. *Road closures. Enhanced security measures requested. People climbing trees. Issues at the magnetometers. Weapons.*

"Wait, weapons?" I'm confused.

Tony lists weapons found on rally-goers. *Knives. Bear spray. Military-style body armor. Flagpoles, some sharpened.* At first I'm not sure if he is saying that these were confiscated at the magnetometers or that law enforcement had reported seeing them on people.

"One of these motherfuckers fastened a spear to the end of a flagpole. It's fucking nuts."

I know he's being serious, but I don't know how to react. *Shouldn't we do something?*

"Does the boss know?" I ask. Maybe the president knows. Maybe that's why he's still in the residence. He's giving us time to figure out how to manage the crowd.

"Big guy knows." I assume he means the president. *Okay, good. Progress.* "Want to go see if the chief is free?"

We find Mark's office door propped open, but he doesn't notice when we loiter in the doorway. He's sitting in the far-left corner of the brown leather sofa, his usual spot. The cushion has a permanent imprint of his body, and the leather is showing signs of wear.

"Morning, Mark," I say, putting an empty Perrier bottle in the recycling bin and grabbing a fresh bottle for him from his refrigerator. Tony and I sit in the armchairs across from him. The room is hot. Flames roar from his fireplace. He doesn't respond or look up at us.

"Chief, just a few updates." Tony recites the same information we'd just discussed in his office.

I'm fixated on Mark. I know him so well. Tony speaks, and Mark's bloodshot eyes flick between his personal and work phones as he sends a message on one before turning his attention to the other. His face is splotchy. His suit jacket is covered in white flecks and strands of silver hair. His eyeglasses have slid down to the tip of his nose, the lenses smudged with his fingerprints. *He's stressed—really stressed.*

The room falls silent. Without turning my head, I make eye contact with Tony. My gut twists. *Please say something, Mark. Tell us what to do. Say something.*

"Alright. Anything else?" he says dryly, eyes still locked on his phone screen. *What the hell?*

Tony clears his throat. "No, sir. Unless you have questions, we'll get out of here."

Silence.

I lose my patience. "Mark, Tony was filling you in about what's happening at the Ellipse."

"Yeah." His eyes snap up. *Holy shit, I've never seen his eyes this bloodshot.* "Does the president know?"

"Yes, sir. He's been made aware." Tony's tone is firm. *Good.*

"Alright, good. Thanks, guys." Mark's eyes return to his phones. "Cass, can you shut the door on your way out?" he says.

I ignore him, walk twelve paces to my desk—it's a number I've memorized—and yank open my top-left drawer. Twelve more paces, and I'm back in the doorway.

"Chief." I'm loud, stern. Mark looks up. I toss a tiny bottle of anti-redness eye drops in his direction. He extends his arm, attempting to catch the bottle. It lands on the cushion beside him.

"Put those in your eyes now. Please." I shut the door.

———

"Mogul, Leverage moving from the Oval Office to West Executive Avenue," my Secret Service radio announces. *Finally*—the president and Mark were on their way to the motorcade. The West Wing had erupted in chaos when the president had delayed the rally for an hour. I want to escape it. I'd made a final plea to Tony to come to the Ellipse, which he had refused. I ask for someone from the White House counsel's office to come and am rebuffed again. But one of the lawyers urges me to make certain Mark knows that there will be grave legal consequences if Trump goes to the Capitol: "Just make sure we don't go to the Capitol. Don't let that happen," I'm warned. *I'll do my best. I'll always do my best.*

The West Wing door swings open. The president and Mark emerge in the doorway together. I notice they're wearing matching red ties. "Red power ties," the president and Mark call them. Mark spots me at his vehicle and breaks away from the president. He doesn't say a word to me as he gets in the car.

I make a last-minute decision to ride in the staff van to the rally, hoping to catch bits of information from chatty colleagues who had just been in the Oval Office with the president. I tap my middle finger against my thumb, a nervous habit, as the motorcade slowly makes its way to the Ellipse. Stephen Miller scratches edits to the speech. Eric Herschmann mumbles something about the vice president.

The van bumps onto the lawn. *Oh God, I hope the president's driver went over that bump slowly.* He hates being jostled in the car. *The president is going to lose his mind if he didn't.* My fingers tap quicker.

"Guys, look! This is so amazing!" Kayleigh McEnany gawks at the crowd. "There's no way Joe Biden won. Look at all our people!"

I'm laser-focused on the vehicles in front of me. I see Mark get out of his car and disappear into the tent. *Shit.* I'm out of the van before it's fully stopped, practically running to the tent. *Where did Mark go? I need to find Mark.*

The tent flaps are snapping angrily against the wind, and one of them lashes my cheek when I stumble inside. I press my fingertips against my cheek to calm the sting on my skin. *Where's Mark. Where's Mark. Where's Mark.*

I shove my way to the front of the tent. *Mark isn't with the president. Where's Mark?!*

"Chief!" The president's voice booms through the tent. He looks at me. *Shit.* I turn the other way, searching for Mark, before the president can yell at me. I find an exit near the front of the stage. *Maybe Mark is shaking hands with people in the crowd.*

I don't see him out front. I turn back toward the tent and finally spot him, on the stage, waving to the crowd, as if it's his own rally. *Oh my God.* Moments later, we meet inside the tent.

"Cass, go find Rudy. He's somewhere around here."

"Yes, sir." I duck outside the tent and spot a volunteer working the rally. I wrap my hand around the staffer's elbow so he doesn't slip away. "Hey, do you know where Rudy is? Is he in the VIP section?"

He looks confused. "Rudy?"

The little patience I have left vanishes. "Yes. Rudy Giuliani. President Trump's attorney. The former mayor of New York City. Rudy fucking Giuliani. Do you want me to pull up a photo for you? Would that help you figure it out?" His eyes are as wide as saucepans. I should feel bad, but I don't. "Find him and bring him to the president," I say curtly, before storming back into the tent.

I'm two feet behind Mark, trying to get his attention. I can hear the president roaring, "Take the fucking mags down." He swings his arm toward the TV monitors. "Look at all those people in the trees." He points into the park. "They want to come in. Let them. Let my people in. Take the fucking mags away. They're not here to hurt me."

I've seen him angry before, but this experience is almost surreal. I hear bellowing onstage, music blaring, a cacophony of conversations backstage. I am staring at Mark, trying to get his attention, willing him to look at me.

I hear Mark assure the president offstage, as "God Bless the U.S.A." starts to play, that he's still working on scheduling an off-the-record movement to the Capitol. Dumbfounded, I'm still staring at Mark. *No, you're not.* The president nods and takes the stage.

Mark shuffles over to me.

"Where's Rudy?"

"Mark, we're not going to the Capitol."

No reply. He turns toward the TV and watches the president before turning back to me. "Do you think you and I can go?"

"Mark, no!"

His eyes are on the TV again. "Where's Rudy?"

I turn away without another word. My senses are hyperfocused, but my emotions are in turmoil. I experience anger, bewilderment, and a creeping sense of dread that something really horrible is going to happen. And my patience with Mark is near exhaustion.

I find Rudy in the back of the tent with, among others, John Eastman. The corners of his mouth split into a Cheshire cat smile. Waving a stack of documents, he moves toward me, like a wolf closing in on its prey.

"We have the evidence. It's all here. We're going to pull this off." Rudy wraps one arm around my body, closing the space that was separating us. I feel his stack of documents press into the small of my back. I lower my eyes and watch his free hand reach for the hem of my blazer.

"By the way," he says, fingering the fabric, "I'm loving this leather jacket on you." His hand slips under my blazer, then my skirt. I feel his frozen fingertips trail up my thigh. He tilts his chin up. The whites of his eyes look jaundiced. My eyes dart to John Eastman, who flashes a leering grin.

I fight against the tension in my muscles and recoil from Rudy's grip. "It's faux leather, Rudy. Tell the boss to pay me more and I'll get a real one, just for you." Filled with rage, I storm through the tent, on yet another quest for Mark.

He's at the base of the stage, watching the president, a familiar image. I scan the crowd. They are cheering and screaming for Trump. They sincerely believe that he won the election. This, too, is a familiar scene, with the people at the rally appearing as his rally-goers have always appeared. But this isn't the same. There's something going on, something I'm not clear about but feel a dread of. I look again at Mark. *There's something he's not telling me.* I let him know that Rudy's in the tent, and he leaves to find him.

A half hour later I watch him walk to his vehicle in the motorcade. *Okay, good. He's making some calls.*

I'm back in the tent, trying to refresh my Twitter feed, but the signal is weak. A Secret Service agent rushes toward me, breathless. "Cassidy. Where's the chief?"

"I can get him." I lock my phone and wrap my arms around myself. "What's going on?"

"Mogul just announced he's going to the Capitol. I need the chief to sign off."

No. My heart drums in my chest. *What do I do? Act. I have to act.* I look around the tent. The White House advance staff are gone. *I'll try to handle this myself.*

"We've talked about this. It's not happening. Tell everyone to stand down." The confidence in my voice is gone. I don't feel like I'm speaking with authority.

I text Tony about the off-the-record movement as I walk quickly to Mark's vehicle. Normally I would stand by the door until Mark opened it. But I don't have time now. I try to yank it open, and he pulls it back shut without explanation. A second later, Kevin McCarthy calls me. I run back into the tent and answer. He's yelling at me. He never yells at me.

"Are you guys coming up to the Capitol? You can't come up here." I assure him we're not. He thinks I'm misleading him. "Figure it out," he barks, and hangs up the phone. I don't hear from him for the rest of the day.

From onstage, the president's tone and cadence shift. *His speech is almost over.* I text Mark to let him know, but now I'm already waiting outside his car. He finally gets out, and I brief him on the developments as we walk back into the tent.

"The president said we're going to the Capitol. My phone is blowing up. Secret Service needs you to make a call. I've been trying to get your attention."

He looks at me absently and asks, "How much time does the president have in his speech?"

I glare at him, exasperated. "Mark, we're not going to the Capitol." I feel the beat of "YMCA" vibrating on the ground. *The president has started his exit routine. He'll be back here any minute.*

Staffers and family flood back into the tent to greet Trump when he steps off the stage. He emerges with Bobby Engel trailing close behind. He doesn't look tired. He looks energized. I can tell he wants to keep going, keep playing to his crowd.

Mark walks the president to the motorcade, and Bobby trails close behind. I follow them for as long as I can before I turn toward the staff van. "Talk to Bobby. Bobby has more information," Mark says to Trump. It's the last thing I hear him tell the president.

The motorcade idles for five minutes and then slowly pulls off the Ellipse. We turn toward the White House. *Thank God.*

———

Tony motions me into his office when I get back to the West Wing and shuts the door. Bobby is slumped in the same chair Tony sat in this morning. I decide to stay standing. I glance at Bobby. He won't look up.

Tony, wide-eyed with surprise, asks me, "Have you heard what happened in the fucking Beast?"

"No, I just got back."

He proceeds to describe an "irate" Trump demanding to be taken to the Capitol, and losing all self-control when Bobby repeatedly rebuffs him with "Mr. President, we're returning to the West Wing."

I feel my breath grow shallow as Tony describes Trump grabbing for the steering wheel, and then for Bobby's neck. I don't know what to do.

"Does Mark know?" I ask.

"I don't think so. His door was shut," Tony replies. *Why is Mark letting this happen?*

I sink into my desk chair, transfixed by the television screens. Mitch McConnell is speaking on the Senate floor. In the corner of the screen, Fox News is running a live video of the mob marching to the Capitol.

Mark's office door is closed when I bring him lunch. I open it and find him in his usual pose, on his couch, scrolling through his phones. His television is streaming the C-SPAN feed of the House floor. I abruptly drop his meal on the table without comment. His head doesn't move as he slowly lifts his eyes. His eyes, usually a piercing sapphire, are now the color of ash, blending with his flaking skin and hair. Lifeless.

"Hey, Chief, are you watching the TV?" I make my voice purposefully saccharine to mask my anguish.

"Yeah." He returns his attention to his cell phones.

I open and close my mouth several times. "The rioters are getting close, Mark. Have you talked to the president?"

"No, he wants to be alone right now." His voice is flat, indifferent.

My mind reels. I am trying to figure out a way to get him to pay attention, to care. *Jim. He'll care about Jim Jordan.* "Mark, do you know where Jim is?"

His eyes dart from me to the television and back to his cell phones. "Jim?"

"Yeah, he was speaking on the House floor a little while ago. Did you watch?" I'm desperate to keep his attention.

"Yeah, it was real good. Did you like it?"

"Yeah, it was. Do you know where he's at right now?"

"No," he mutters. "I haven't talked to him."

"You might want to check in with him," I say, extending my arm toward the television. "The rioters are getting close. They might get into the Capitol."

"Alright, I'll give him a call." I'm halfway through the door before he finishes his sentence.

Back at my desk, I hear the news break. The first rioters have breached the Capitol. They're inside. I'm registering the development as Pat Cipollone and Pat Philbin barrel past me and barge into Mark's office.

"The rioters are in the Capitol, Mark. We need to go down and see the president—now," Cipollone insists.

Mark is a statue on his couch. "He doesn't want to do anything, Pat."

Pat calmly gives Mark direction. "Mark, something needs to be done. People are going to die, and the blood is going to be on your hands. This is getting out of hand. I'm going down there."

My eyes are locked on Mark. *Get up. Go with Pat.*

He slowly stands, leaning against the arm of the couch, and walks silently to my desk. He's clutching his eyeglasses in his fist—his knuckles are white. He sets his phones on my desk. "Let me know if Jim calls."

Jim Jordan calls minutes later. I feel a pang of hope. "One sec, I'll go get him." I go to the dining room. "Is Mark in there?" I ask the valet. He nods. I look through the peephole and see the back of his suit. I open the door to get his attention. The group is having a heated conversation about the rioters. Mark sees me, and I point at the phone screen, where Jim's caller ID is visible. He comes over to take the phone, propping the door open with his body as he talks to Jim.

I take a few steps back as Mark takes my place in the doorway and strain to listen to both conversations. The TV in the Oval dining room is blaring, and the president is yelling. *What's he saying? I can't make it out.* I hear him say "hang" repeatedly. *Hang? Hang? What's that about?* Mark hands his phone back to me, the cue for me to return to my desk. *Shit.*

Back in my office, my phone notifies me of a Trump tweet: "Mike Pence didn't have the courage to do what should have been done to protect our Country and our Constitution, giving states a chance to certify a corrected set of facts, not the fraudulent or inaccurate ones which they were asked to previously certify. USA demands the truth!"

I'm struggling to process what's happening as Mark, Pat Cipollone, Pat Philbin, and Eric Herschmann stumble back into the office. I overhear their conversation, and suddenly everything makes sense.

They're calling for the vice president to be hanged.

The president is okay with it.

He doesn't want to do anything.

He doesn't think they're doing anything wrong.

He thinks Mike is a traitor.

This is crazy. We need to be doing something more.

My phone is pinging nonstop with emails, texts, Signal messages, and unanswered calls. Mark's phones are too. I'm devoid of emotion as I consider what I should do, and then, letting what I just heard sink in, I'm gripped with anger and hurt. I snatch my coat and run out of my office to go to the Eisenhower Building. *I need to check in with Mark's Secret Service detail. We need to have a plan in case the worst happens. In case this is the beginning of a coup.*

My hands shake as I punch in the passcode to unlock the door to their break room. Access denied. I concentrate to steady my hands, and the door clicks open. As I enter the room, my cell phone vibrates with a news alert. *Someone has been shot in the US Capitol.*

I feel like the blood is draining from my head. I feel it in my feet, my fingertips. My ears are ringing. *This is it. This is how it starts.* I look at the agents. They're strangely calm.

"Is anybody listening to their radio?" I ask.

They aren't.

I text Tony: "Are we in Condition Yellow?" This is a heightened security protocol for the White House.

"Yes."

Mark needs his security detail at his side right now. "Guys, we're in Condition Yellow. Get to the West Wing." I leave them behind as they scramble to put on their gear. *Who was shot? Do I know them?*

I'm sprinting across West Executive Avenue when a grim memory comes back. It's July 30, 2020. Herman Cain is dead. He had contracted COVID at the Tulsa rally. I had seen him in the risers behind the stage in Tulsa. He grabbed my wrists and pumped my arms above my head, flashing his enigmatic smile as he cried out, "We're going to win! We're going to win! Four more years! Four more years!"

I had slipped into Mark's office when I got the news, my middle finger and thumb tapping together as I gnawed the inside of my cheek, wrestling with my words. "Chief, have you heard about Herman Cain?"

"No, how's he doing? Is he doing alright?"

I lowered my head. "No, Mark, he's dead."

Mark put his phone down as the blood drained from his face.

"He was in Tulsa, wasn't he?"

"Yes, sir. He was in Tulsa."

"That's where he caught COVID, right?"

"Yes, sir. That's where he caught COVID."

Mark had briefly turned his attention to the TV. I had assumed that he was wondering if the news had been made public. He looked back at me and said flatly, "We killed Herman Cain." I could hear him swallow. "Get me his wife's number," he said sadly.

———

Back at my desk, I feel bile burning the back of my throat. Mark emerges from his office with the lawyers.

"Cass," he says, shoving a blank chief of staff note card and one of his pens in my hand, "write this down for me. We're drafting a tweet for the boss."

Hands shaking, I scratch the pen across the note card as Mark begins, "Anyone who entered the Capitol illegally—"

"Add 'and without proper authority,'" Eric Herschmann says.

"—should leave immediately," Mark continues.

Mark plucks the note card from my hands almost before I finish writing, and the group rushes to the Oval dining room. He and the lawyers are still in the dining room when I receive another Twitter notification. The president has tweeted: "No violence! Remember, WE are the party of Law & Order – respect the Law and our great men and women in Blue. Thank you!"

Mark returns, this time on his own, and tosses the note card on my desk. I notice that "illegally" is crossed out.

"No action necessary," he informs me. His tone hints at defeat. He retreats to his office and shuts the door. Every fifteen minutes or so he heads to the Oval dining room and then comes back. People are in and out of his office. I check in with Mark's detail leader, to make sure he's always wherever Mark is.

Mark's phones are on my desk. Members are frantically trying to reach him to get him to put a stop to this madness. Mark returns to his office when the president moves to the Rose Garden to record a video statement, and I beg him to return some of the calls.

The general consensus throughout the West Wing, the White House complex, the entire executive branch, is that the president needs to tell people to stop and go home. The president tweets a two-minute video statement telling the protesters that they are special, and that he loves them, but that it's time to go home.

At her desk behind me, Eliza is watching TV. "There's no way these are our people. This is definitely antifa."

I slowly turn around in my chair. "Are you kidding me?"

"No," she responds flatly. "Our people are peaceful."

Tony enters Mark's office, and they emerge together a few moments later.

"Cass, can you tell the staff to get out of here by five o'clock?" Mark asks, his attention fixed on the TV. I part my lips, ready to snap at him. "We'll also send out an email. We just need you to start spreading the word. There's still protesters out. I don't want any staff trying to get home once it's dark."

Tony casts a "don't you think about it" glare in my direction. I roll my eyes. *You ruined my chance.*

I wander around the West Wing and the Eisenhower Building and alert the scant staff of the chief's order.

————

I lean forward in the driver's seat of my car, pressing my forehead against the steering wheel. Gentle clouds appear and dissolve when I exhale. It's still so cold.

As I pull off campus, military vans pour into the city, unloading hundreds of National Guardsmen. Non-scalable metal fencing is already erected around every street. My soul feels broken. *Washington looks like a war zone. Because of us.*

I'm overwhelmed by the street closings, and end up driving into Virginia. I have no groceries and haven't eaten all day. I find a Harris Teeter and wander the aisles aimlessly. Life feels like a fever dream, completely unreal. I'm detached from myself. I abandon my cart in the middle of an aisle and leave without buying anything.

Mark makes it home, and his detail invites me out for dinner. Wound up from the day, I accept their invitation. *I suppose it's better than being alone in my apartment.*

I meet them at the Guapo's in Arlington. I pick at the chips, licking flakes of sea salt off my fingertips, and lift the margarita glass to my lips. The taste of alcohol makes me nauseous. I pass the drink to the agent next to me.

The agents are talking, attempting to have a normal, light conversation after a long, traumatic day. I can hear them, but I'm not listening. Images of the Capitol flash through my mind. The rioters, like feral animals, ransacking and vandalizing the beautiful halls of our Capitol. Members of Congress, journalists, and career employees sheltering under furniture, in closets, wherever they could find refuge. They're all public servants, afraid for their lives, wondering if they'll see their families again.

I throw a twenty-dollar bill on the table, apologize, plead exhaustion, and leave the restaurant. My lungs fill with frigid air as I walk to my car, tears rolling down my cheeks.

I feel physical pain when I see the Capitol dome as I cross the bridge into Washington. I want to scream, but I feel paralyzed.

I don't turn on any lights when I enter my apartment. My body is on autopilot as I walk from my front door to the living room. I collapse onto my couch, staring at the ceiling. I feel my cell phone vibrate. It's Mom and Paul.

Mom is crying. She's begging me not to move to Florida. Paul interjects, trying to defuse the argument before it begins. He doesn't realize how little I care, how far gone I am.

My tone is flat, uninflected. "I have to go. I've already committed. The boss needs good people around him. The only reason today happened is because we let bad people, crazy people, around him. I need to try to fix—"

"Cassidy. Listen to yourself." My mom's tone shifts to parent mode, and I dissociate even more. "This isn't you. You know better than this. You can't fix him. You know you shouldn't go. Listen to me, Cassidy. Listen to me . . ."

I hang up and put my phone on Do Not Disturb. Heavy, loud sobs escape from my chest. *I have to go, I have to go . . .*

PART IV

ENOUGH

CHAPTER 17

The End

CIGARETTE SMOKE HUNG in the air as Larry Kudlow held me in an embrace on the morning of January 7. He pulled back and gripped my shoulders, and softly asked whether I was considering resigning. I shook my head.

"I can't," I told him. "I committed to moving to Florida with him." Larry took a long drag on his cigarette and stubbed it out. He nodded at the West Wing entrance and turned to walk inside.

"Wait, Larry," I said, reaching for his elbow. "Are you going to resign?" My voice cracked.

"Come on, Cass, let's go in. I want to see if the chief is free." I reluctantly followed, and we rode the elevator together in silence.

Secretary Mnuchin was leaning on my desk, thumbing through a newspaper. Mark's office door was shut.

"Hey, sir, good morning. Are you waiting to see Mark?"

"Yeah," he said curtly. "The Twenty-Fifth." He was referring to calls to use the Twenty-Fifth Amendment against Trump to remove him from power. He didn't look up from the newspaper.

Behind me, I heard Larry whisper that he would return later.

I looked through the peephole in Mark's door and saw him on the couch, clutching both of his cell phones. Without checking his schedule or announcing the secretary's presence, I opened the door for Mnuchin. He folded the newspaper and tucked it under his arm as he entered Mark's office, and the door swung shut.

I settled at my desk and saw Alyssa Farah on TV. I snatched the remote and turned up the volume as she sharply denounced the president's conduct on January 6.

My phone vibrated with a text from Alyssa moments after she was off the air. She apologized for not having given Mark and me a heads-up, and explained that she had felt compelled to say something. My phone clattered as I dropped it on my desk in disgust. *She promised she wouldn't betray us. She promised she would always be loyal.*

Mnuchin emerged from Mark's office, offering a "thanks" over his shoulder as he left without making eye contact.

Eventually I gathered the strength to think about entering Mark's office. Until January 20, I had a job to do. I had made a promise to stay to the end. I pushed his door open with my shoulder and walked in, arms crossed.

"Morning, Chief," I snapped. "Is Mnuchin quitting?"

"Nah, I don't think so." He was still looking at his phones. "What are you hearing?"

"The Twenty-Fifth Amendment. Impeachment. Stuff like that."

"Yeah," he said, turning his attention to Fox News. "I think yesterday was antifa."

I tried to ignore the remark. "I'm hearing from some members. Are you?"

"Yeah, some members." His eyes shifted and met mine. "Do you think yesterday was antifa?"

"No." My eyes narrowed. "I don't think yesterday was antifa." The clock mounted above his door ticked in response.

I turned to walk out. "By the way, Chief," I said, turning back to look at him, "Alyssa just screwed you." He snapped his head in my direction as the door closed behind me.

The lawyers were in and out of Mark's office all day, dropping off amended drafts of the speech the president would record, pressing him to finally concede the election. All they managed to convince him to do was recognize the obvious—that a transition was underway.

Early that afternoon a White House deputy press secretary dropped by the office.

"Hey there. I heard you had a busy day yesterday. What did I miss? Anything big? Catch me up." The staffer grinned. "Did I miss anything big?"

My face flushed. "Are you joking?"

"No," they said, straining to be serious. "What did I miss?" I blinked several times, hoping they would realize the gravity of their mistake. But they continued in the same vein. "Come on, you're acting like there was an insurrection."

My middle fingernail dug against the flesh of my thumb. "Get out," I said, standing. I heard Mark's office door open.

The staffer's smile faded. "Are you serious?"

"Now," I said, pointing at the door. "Or I promise, today will be your final day."

The staffer was out of sight when I dared to look at Mark, and once I did, he retreated to his office. My body shook as I prepared to sit down. Michael Haidet, the president's scheduler, appeared, tapped my shoulder, and suggested we go for a walk.

"Are you still planning to move to Florida?" he asked once we were outside. The cold air was a relief and helped restore my composure.

"Yeah." I sighed reluctantly, wondering if I should reconsider what had come to feel like an obligation. I had committed. If I didn't go, someone else who might not try to hold things in check as much as I would might take my place. I looked up at him and preempted his response. "But you're not?"

He drew a deep breath and stared off at the Eisenhower Building. "I've served the president for almost five years. It's time for a change of scenery." He looked back at me. "Are you sure you want to go?"

It was my turn to admire the Eisenhower Building. "I have to go. I promised I would go. The boss needs good people around him."

We stood outside for a while, communicating in silence our resigned mutual understanding.

Much later, as the final rays of sunlight disappeared, Hope Hicks strolled into our office, carrying several overstuffed bags. My heart sank. *She's leaving, too.* I called Mark to come say goodbye to her.

"Hope, you did a real great job. I enjoyed working with you." He put on his best hail-fellow-well-met routine. "Thank you for everything you did for the president and me."

Hope tapped her fourth chief of staff on the elbow. "Thanks, Chief." Then she was gone.

Thirteen days to go.

———

The next week was a blur of packing, off-boarding routines— everything we should have been preparing for since November 4, 2020.

Debbie, Mark's wife, helped pack his belongings. As she made a final trip to the car, she made one last request. "Cassidy, Eliza, please don't light that fireplace anymore. Mark doesn't need to burn anything else. All of his suits smell like a bonfire, and I can't keep up with the dry cleaning." Mark rolled his eyes when he was informed that his fireplace was no longer to be used.

Less than a week after January 6, the House of Representatives moved swiftly to introduce, without holding a public hearing, a single article of impeachment. Unlike with the first impeachment inquiry, I was resigned to this one. I didn't have the will to fight an action I believed was justified. Kevin called me periodically to relay updates for the president and the chief, neither of whom wanted to speak with him. After the article was passed by the House, Mark asked me to make a chart with headshots of the ten Republican members who had voted in favor of impeachment. Mark gave the hit list to the president, who kept it on the Resolute Desk.

Last-minute requests for favors from members of Congress poured in—everything from departure photos and autographed memorabilia to presidential pardons. Mark spent much of his time fielding pardon requests and deliberating his own. Word came from the White House counsel's office that the blanket pardons those involved in the John Eastman plot had sought were going to be denied. Matt Gaetz made an unannounced visit to our office to lobby Mark for a personal pardon but didn't receive one.

On January 12, my Secret Service radio made an unexpected announcement: "Hoosier, arrived West Wing." I exchanged a nervous glance with my colleagues. Vice President Pence emerged from the stairwell with a coterie of aides and Secret Service agents trailing behind. He looked every inch a president. He stopped at the entrance to our office.

"Is he down with the president?" He nodded toward Mark's office door.

I shook my head. "No, sir. Mark is in his office."

"Alright." He paused for a moment. "And the president is in the dining room?" I nodded. The vice president glanced at Mark's office door one more time, cast a tight smile, and tapped the doorframe as he disappeared down the hallway toward the dining room. I bit my cheeks to hide the surge of pride and admiration I felt for the vice president, and I decided not to notify Mark.

When their meeting wrapped, the vice president ducked back into our office.

"Hey, everyone, take care of yourselves. You all did a spectacular job. The country is grateful." We didn't have a chance to re-spond before he walked away.

My heart ached. I wanted to thank him, too, for the spectacu-lar job he had done, but primarily for the resolve he exemplified on January 6. Because of his courage, our democracy was still in-tact. Bruised, but not broken. That was the last time I saw the vice president.

Eight days to go.

————

John Ratcliffe came to our office two days later. Remembering our conversation a month earlier, I asked John as he was leaving if he had time to go for a walk. "Grab your coat," he said. We picked up coffees at the Navy Mess and walked the White House grounds, talking and taking in the majesty of the place. John recited a quote from the late Tony Snow, press secretary under George W. Bush, describing where we worked: "that grand, glorious, mysterious place where Lincoln walks at night, and our highest hopes and dreams reside."

We sat down on a bench in the East Wing. Silence hung in the air until I mustered the nerve to ask him a question. "Do you think I should go to Florida?"

John thought for a bit before asking, "Do you still want to go?"

"I feel I have to," I answered.

He looked at me sympathetically, told me he understood if I felt God was guiding me there. "But I don't think you'll hurt your-self if you reconsider."

Six days to go.

————

On January 15, Mike Lindell arrived in the West Wing, escorted by Mark, who dropped him off at the Oval. He showed up after his meeting, demanding to see Mark. "We can still win. I have my notes. The president said I need the chief's sign-off." *Oh, for the love of . . . The president doesn't want this nut around anymore.*

When I told Mark that Lindell was in our suite, he rolled his eyes and told me to take him up to White House counsel. I went upstairs, and Pat Philbin told me, "Just try and get him out of here."

I had left Lindell in the West Wing lobby, where I found him waiting, thumbing through his plan to declare martial law and keep Trump in power. "Hey, sir, everyone's tied up right now. Why don't you give us a call later?"

With that, Lindell pushed past me, hustling up the stairs. I was at his heels as he informed me, "No one here cares about the president. No one here is loyal to him. Including you."

He bolted into counsel's office, directing more profanity at me and staff there. Pat Cipollone emerged, and scolded, "Do not talk to my staff like that! It's over. You need to leave."

Later, Liz called me to come upstairs. Everyone in the counsel's office was huddled around her computer, looking at an image posted online of Lindell outside the entrance to the West Wing, holding his notes, which were clearly visible. One line was redacted with black marker. "You know what that said?" Pat asked us. "Fire Pat Cipollone. He wanted me to fire myself."

Five days to go.

"Cassidy, where is that Crossfire Hurricane binder?" Mark hastily demanded. I rolled my eyes. "It's in the safe, Mark. I'll get it for you." I brought the binder into Mark's office, and he looked chastened. "I told you not to let it out of your sight. It should have been in your desk drawer."

"My desk drawer, Mark, is not where classified documents belong. It was in the safe. You have nothing to worry about." I handed him the binder, and I could tell he had something more to say on the subject but let it drop. He fanned through the pages quickly.

"Can you call Sue Bai from the National Security Council?" he asked. "I need her to make a bunch of copies of this. It's ready to be declassified." Rather than call Sue, I walked downstairs to her office and let her know that the chief wanted to meet with her.

I had had enough of the classified documents debacle. When I got to Florida, I reminded myself, I would have a fresh opportunity to restore order so the president would be better served.

———

My transfer paperwork was signed, and Eliza and I had begun looking for apartments in Palm Beach. Even after January 6th, I worried I would look disloyal and become a target if I backed out. I started packing Sunday night. The next morning, Mark called me into his office and informed me that I might not be welcome in Florida.

"The president thinks you're disloyal," he warned. "That you're a leaker." There had been a news article published listing the staffers who were moving to Florida with the president, and he was trying to identify who leaked the story.

I blinked several times, trying to contain my frustration. "I'm not a leaker. I'm not disloyal. You know that."

"Are you sure about that, Cass?"

My frustration turned to rage. "Mark, you can go to hell if you think that." He had crossed a bridge, and I couldn't contain my anger.

"I don't think that, Cass," he relented. "I know you're loyal. You've been very loyal to me."

That afternoon, I had a conversation with Dan Scavino and Tony Ornato. I told Dan, "I feel like there are always knives out for me." He agreed. "Yeah, sometimes it's best to be out of sight, out of mind." That night I went home and unpacked, trying to let the news sink in that I wasn't moving to Florida.

Two days to go.

———

The day before the inauguration, Michael Haidet approached me. "It's a blessing in disguise, Cass," he said sympathetically. "Actually, it's not even disguised. It's just a blessing." I nodded and smiled slightly, but I was torn. I knew if I let myself, I would feel devastated. I had given everything I had to this job and to the president, and it was ending the same way it had for so many others, with an undeserved accusation of disloyalty, and the specter of taking revenge. I knew I would be out of sight, but not out of mind.

The president stayed in the Oval Office all day on the nineteenth, writing a letter he would leave in his desk drawer for incoming president Biden, a practice that had become customary in recent years. The endeavor required the assistance of Pat Cipollone, Eric Herschmann, and Mark.

Staff were off-boarding all day, saying their goodbyes to one another. Mark paced between his office and the Oval. He was quiet and tired. Eliza and Mike were the last staffers to leave that day.

We walked out of the West Wing together and stood under the awning. We could hear the humming of idling Secret Service vehicles, and American flags that lined West Executive Avenue snapped in the wind. Eliza was going to Florida with the president.

"Hey," I said to her, "you're going to do just fine. Just keep your head down, and ignore all the personalities." She cast her gaze between Michael and me. The three of us had been planning to go to Florida together, but now she would have to navigate Trump World alone.

She pulled me in for a hug. "Please come down and visit."

"I will," I said, unsure. "Everything is going to be okay."

To lighten the mood, Michael joked, "And if you hate it, you can move back here with us." I laughed and gave him a hug. They loaded boxes with their office belongings into his jeep and drove away. I stood outside until the car disappeared. *It's just Mark and me now.*

———

Mark was in the Oval with the president, finalizing the letter for Biden. I could hear what sounded like people saying their good- byes to the president, but I couldn't bring myself to join them. I knew the goodbyes being exchanged were tearful, and heavy with grief for the president's loss. I was grieving, too, but for the way the administration had ended, for the wreck we had left be- hind. The president and I never said goodbye. Some goodbyes are better left unspoken.

I heard over my Secret Service radio, "Mogul moving. Rose Garden colonnade." *He left the Oval Office for the last time.*

Mark came back with the lawyers. Pat, who had spent much of the day helping the president with the letter, remarked, "Now I can finally get today's work done." Mark chuckled. It was the first time I'd seen him do that in a while. "Keep up the good work, Pat," he said. "I'm going to head home. Call me if you need anything."

"I'll walk out with you, Mark," I said. We descended the West Wing stairs side by side. "By the way, Cass, I talked to the boss," he said. "He wants to keep you on the transition office payroll until the summer. Is that alright with you?"

"To work out of the Arlington office?" I asked.

"I'm not sure. He said he wants to keep paying you for all your hard work." His eyes narrowed, and he asked again, "Is that al- right with you?"

"Yes, sir," I answered, not entirely sure what I was agreeing to.

I watched him climb into the limo, noticing the original Cross- fire Hurricane binder tucked under his arm. I didn't have time to ask what he planned to do with it as he drove away.

My mind whirred with questions. *Why would he keep me on payroll? Generosity isn't his style. And what the hell is Mark doing with the unredacted Crossfire Hurricane binder?* I started back to my office, but decided to take a circuitous route, through the Rose Garden. I found the blinking red lights atop the Washington Mon- ument, trying to conjure the gravitational pull that place had always had on me. I had burned my candle at both ends, and I had no wick left. My fire was out.

I walked back through the colonnade and into the West Wing, following the steps of American giants but thinking to myself, *I am lucky to be leaving.*

At around 10:30 p.m., I saw Pat Philbin power walking toward my office. *Great,* I thought. *What could possibly be going wrong now?*

"How many copies of that Crossfire Hurricane binder did Mark make? Where are all the copies?" Pat huffed. "How many of them have been distributed?"

"Slow down," I said to Pat, trying to keep up with his questions, many of which I did not have a response to. "How many copies? I have no idea. There are some in our office . . ." I glanced around. There were many binders strewn around with still-classified but supposedly soon-to-be-declassified information, but the Crossfire Hurricane binders were easy to identify because of how thick they were.

"Did Mark already give copies to Mollie Hemingway and John Solomon?" Pat asked, referring to the conservative journalists who the president and Mark were acquainted with. I nodded. "Yeah, he had a few of his Secret Service agents meet Mollie and John in Georgetown earlier tonight while you all were in the Oval Office with the boss." The color drained from Pat's face. "Seriously?" he asked.

I nodded again. "I tried to tell him not to—"

Pat cut me off. "What about the others? What about the binders he said you were giving to Kevin McCarthy and Mitch McConnell?"

I shook my head. "I called Kevin and cryptically described what the binder is. He asked why Mark wanted him to have a copy. I told him I was not sure, but I did not think he needed a copy. Actually, I told him he probably should not take a copy. Kevin agreed," I explained.

"What about Mitch?" Pat asked.

"I did not call him. If Kevin is not getting a copy, Mitch is not, either. What's going on, Pat?" He was scanning the room and asked where Kevin's and Mitch's binders were. I handed them to Pat, and he stormed out toward the staircase.

I followed Pat upstairs into the White House counsel's office. "Pat, come out here," Pat Philbin called to Pat Cipollone. "Explain to Cip what you just told me." I did.

The two Pats exchanged a concerned look. "Why did Mark have HPSCI recommend the redactions? The Crossfire Hurricane binders are a complete disaster. They're still full of classified information," Pat Cipollone said. "Those binders need to come back to the White House. Like, now. Can you call Mark?" *Great*, I thought. *We have about thirteen hours left and of course we sparked a potential national security crisis.*

"Yes, sir. I'll go downstairs and call Mark now," I responded, and started to walk out of his office. "Hey, Cass, while you're on the phone with him," Pat Cipollone added, "can you tell him we cannot pardon Kimberly Guilfoyle's gynecologist? Maybe he'll listen to you."

My jaw was hanging as I turned around to look at Pat. I knew by the look on his face that he was dead serious. "Yeah, sure. I guess I'll tell him that, too."

I stayed in the West Wing until 2:00 in the morning.

Ten hours left.

———

I'm late. I'm running so late. I had overslept, having had only a few hours' sleep. I was about to rush out of my apartment when I heard helicopter rotors whirring. I looked out my window as Marine One passed overhead. I had missed the president's departure to Joint Base Andrews.

Tony had been searching for me. I found him near my desk when I arrived. "You need to be wearing a mask," he said.

"Why?" I asked, confused.

"Take a look around." The desks were all shielded with Plexiglas. "They're going to be here soon," Tony said. "Where's the chief? Klain will be here soon. I'm meeting with Jen in a few minutes." He was referring to Ron Klain, President Biden's incoming chief of staff, and Jen O'Malley Dillon. Klain was not new to the White House—he had been chief of staff to vice presidents Al Gore and Biden.

"Mark's at Andrews," I told him.

We looked down the hallway and watched GSA staffers moving Trump's furniture out and Biden's in. Tony observed, "As hard as the last few weeks have been, usually these walls are the only witness to history like this." He looked at me. "We're pretty damn lucky." I turned my attention back to the Oval. "Yeah, the majesty of the peaceful transfer of power."

I didn't see Mark when he arrived—he went straight to the White House counsel's office. I was looking at my laptop when I heard an unfamiliar voice: "Good morning." *It's Ron Klain. Shit, Ron Klain's here.* "Good morning," I said, summoning my most chipper voice. "Welcome, uh, I mean, welcome back." I expected a conversational response, but he had something else on his mind. "Do you have a mask?"

"Sir, I'll go find one, and I'll find Mark for you." Out of breath, I staggered into the counsel's office. "Mark, Ron Klain's here. Can you come downstairs?"

"Tell him I'm busy. Would you mind showing him around? I'll try to drop by in a few minutes."

I looked at Pat, then back at Mark. "Does anyone up here at least have a mask I can use?"

"A mask?" Pat said.

"Yeah, a mask. But I'll take that as a no," I said, turning on my heel to run back downstairs.

I poked my head back into the office. Klain was leaning against the credenza, flipping through the *New York Times*, a newspaper the president had banned from distribution in the

White House but that was now back in circulation for the incoming administration.

"Sir, I don't have a mask yet. But I do have an update. Mind if I come in? I promise I'll keep a social distance."

He nodded, folding the newspaper.

"So, Mark's upstairs in the White House counsel's office, finishing up a few things. He promised he'll be down in a few minutes. But for now, I'm happy to show you around." I pushed on the door to the chief of staff's office. *Damn it, it's locked.* "Well, I'll find a key for you. How about I walk you down to the Oval?" I suspected he was annoyed, but I couldn't tell for sure on account of his masks. He was wearing two.

"I've been here many times," he reminded me.

"Oh, of course, I understand. Let me go find that key." I found a GSA employee to unlock the chief's door.

I was barreling down the staircase when I bumped into one of the Secret Service agents on Mark's detail. He was clutching a Whole Foods brown grocery bag full of loose documents. "Hey, Cass! Do you know where the chief is? He asked me to go pick this up for him in Georgetown. Sorry it took me so long, there are so many road closures—" I snatched the bag. "Where are the binders?" I asked, glossing over the fact that the agent had agreed to run one of Mark's errands.

"The binders? Oh, yeah, the binders. I don't know. John Solomon said that all the documents are here, though. So there's nothing to worry about," he reassured me. Dismayed, I turned around and sped up the staircase, back into the White House counsel's office.

I dropped the bag on Pat Cipollone's floor. "Here are your classified documents back from the reporters, Mark." I didn't hide my contempt, my words rife with sarcasm. Mark and Pat peered into the bag. I saw Mark swallow hard, and Pat shot me a piercing look. Overwhelmed, Pat agonized, "Seriously? Seriously? We do not have time for this." I was already walking out of his office.

Tony and I were standing on West Executive Avenue with a few of the agents on Mark's detail when he emerged from the West Wing at around 11:45 a.m. There was one large binder tucked under his arm.

Mark turned to the agent who had picked up the disheveled papers from John Solomon that morning. "How fast can you get me to the Department of Justice?" Mark asked. The agent looked at Tony. "They can use lights and sirens, sir. You should make it there before noon, even with the road closures." Mark nodded. "Good, let's do it. I am not going to be the chief of staff who doesn't get this binder declassified." The agent sprinted to Mark's limo to prepare it for departure.

Mark handed me his work phone and said, "Can you off-board me and make sure this is wiped clean?" Tony interjected. "Already taken care of, sir. We have you covered."

Mark nodded, then turned his attention to me. "You and I saw a lot together. You have been very loyal, and I've been very lucky to have you by my side. You take care now." Then he gave me two quick pats on the shoulder and walked straight to his motorcade.

"Thank you, sir," I called after him. "I'm sure we'll talk soon." He turned around and waved before the agent closed his limo door.

Those were the last words Mark and I would ever exchange.

Liz Horning, Pat Philbin, and I were among the last Trump aides to off-board, at around 11:55 a.m. As we walked out of the Eisenhower Building one final time, we passed a color guard already in position, waiting to welcome President Joe Biden and Vice President Kamala Harris to the White House. Pat, Liz, and I hugged goodbye and went our separate ways.

As I pulled onto Fourteenth Street, I pressed my brake and rolled down the driver's-side window. I could hear muffled sounds of the inaugural ceremony at the other end of the Mall, all of the grounds surrounded by non-scalable metal fences. I looked at the clock in my car—12:02 p.m.

My eyes welled with tears as I eased off the brake, passing National Guardsman and military vehicles protecting the peaceful transfer of power.

It's finally over.

CHAPTER 18

Life After the White House

I DON'T REMEMBER MUCH of the first week after Inauguration Day. Mom came to DC that first weekend to help me unpack what I had boxed up to move to Florida. But I don't remember much more.

A Republican member of Congress, Sam, whom I befriended during my tenure at the White House, a member who did not serve on the House January 6th Committee, checked on me the week following President Biden's inauguration. He could tell something wasn't right with me and invited me for a bourbon night. I arrived in sweatpants and sweatshirt. He looked at me curiously but didn't say anything at first.

At one point, Sam started pressing me about January 6. Why didn't POTUS do anything? What was Mark doing? I recited the rationale I had heard Mark and other colleagues make, except for their ludicrous attempts to blame the riot on antifa. In that moment, I detested myself, and I could not bring myself to look Sam in the eye.

Eventually, he looked at me and said, "Please don't take offense, but you look horrible. Like, I've never seen you look like this."

I laughed and said I'd dress nicer next time, trying to shift the conversation away from me. But he was serious. He asked if I wanted to talk about anything that had happened. I shook my head, but the question had released something in me. "It was bad.

Really bad. None of it makes sense to me. I can't make sense of it."
I kept repeating that last line.

Sam asked if I had enough money saved to go on vacation. I
said yes, that I was still on the Mar-a-Lago payroll. "Cass," Sam
said. "No one in the history of the world has ever needed a vacation more than you do right now." He pushed me to go somewhere
warm for a while, for as long as I could.

The next day I made Airbnb reservations on the Gulf Coast of
Florida and started driving south.

———

I spent my first day on Anna Maria Island, where I sat facing the
waves at sunset, a deep stretch of sugar-fine sand behind me, the
beach lined by houses painted in pastel colors. I felt a sense of con-
tentment, and a glimmer of hope that I would recover the balance
I had lost.

The next morning I woke up after the first deep, uninterrupted
sleep I'd had in a very long time and drove to Naples. I began to
come to terms with how lost and directionless I felt, my mind wandering to the final months at the White House. Even if Trump had
won reelection, I knew I would have needed a break. Whether I
would have actually taken one is debatable, but I now recognized
my need to.

I wanted rest and health. Since childhood, I've detested the
necessity of sleep, fearing I would miss out on something. But
a year of nights that ended hours after midnight and too many
predawn wake-up calls had done damage to my mind and body. I
wanted to rediscover what gave me pleasure: long runs, reading,
cooking. I recognized that my terrifying need to be productive,
and the anxiety that plagued me when I wasn't, made relaxation
feel purposeless. I hoped my vacation to Florida would help heal
that.

On warmer days, I sat on the beach for hours, beginning to
understand how precarious my mental health had become, espe-

cially since Election Day. I had been living at warp speed for the last year, and I hadn't had time to process things properly. Now I had nothing but time, and a little distance, to sort things out.

I still had not talked to Alyssa since she'd texted me on January 7, explaining why she had felt compelled to speak out. I really missed her. She continued to appear on several cable networks as a political commentator and was very outspoken about the failings of the Trump White House. It seemed like January 6th helped Alyssa find her voice and calling.

Watching a sunset on Marco Island, I finally responded to her text. I explained that I had been upset that she hadn't shared her intentions with me, and said that my reasons had been selfish. I told her that she meant the world to me. She responded with similar sentiments, and we promised to get together when I returned to Washington.

Some days I missed being at the White House, and fantasized about an alternate reality where Trump had won. Other times, it was painful to remember my time there. I felt a pain I didn't want to numb but didn't want to confront, either. The magnitude of January 6th, the damage of Trump's election denial, and the toll that the stress had taken on me would hit me full force. I'd feel guilt for having played a role in the chain of bad decisions that led to January 6th. I wasn't to blame for it. But I had been there, and hadn't done enough to stop it. I could have resigned, like Alyssa. I could have yelled, like Eric Herschmann. Instead, I was complicit, and called it my patriotic duty. I delicately danced between confronting the truth and seeking refuge in the past.

I left Florida after three weeks. I had a life to rebuild in Washington.

———

One morning in March, Lee Zeldin asked me to meet him at the Capitol Hill Club for breakfast. We had been fairly close when I worked at the White House, and I was looking forward to catching up. We arrived at the same time and walked upstairs to the dining room together.

The first person I saw was national security advisor Robert O'Brien, seated at a table in the middle of the room. His face lit up, and he excused himself from the table to walk over to us. His guest had his back turned to us, but I recognized the figure. When Robert stood up, Mark Meadows turned around. I expected Mark to follow Robert, but the expression on his face conveyed everything he didn't—he was just as shocked to see me as I was to see him. He turned back to his breakfast. The hostess was getting ready to seat Lee and me when Robert reached us. We exchanged a quick hello, and he told me to text him soon, that he and his wife, Lo-Mari, would take me out to dinner. Mark didn't turn around again.

Our table was one of the farthest possible from Robert and Mark's, and Lee asked if something had happened between Mark and me. I wanted to say no, but that wasn't really true. We'd had our moments, especially near the end. But I didn't think the strain of our relations was so bad that he wouldn't even acknowledge me, and I wondered what I had done to make him ignore me so blatantly. I tried to brush off Lee's question. "You know how it is when you spend so much time with someone. You don't always have to acknowledge their presence." Lee quickly changed the subject, moving on to his potential run for governor of New York. Mark and Robert left when we were halfway through breakfast. Mark and I made eye contact for a split second. As if we had never known each other, he walked out without saying hello or goodbye.

———

The country was tearing itself in two as Trump continued pushing the election fraud nonsense. Constant contradictory thoughts pulled me one way and another, anxiety and grief coming in waves. Sometimes I felt the need to unburden myself of what I knew about January 6th—to someone in authority. But who? Even if there was someone I trusted to share the information I knew, I wasn't sure whether I had the strength to share it. I worried that I would be compromising my integrity. If I broke my word now, who would ever trust me again? I thought of Tony Ornato, a man I believed had supreme integrity. He volunteered to put his life on the line for presidents of both parties. We trusted each other.

I had to talk to someone about my feelings, because keeping it inside was toxic. I wasn't open with my parents about my turmoil, and I couldn't confide it to most of my friends. I decided to text Tony. He was the only person who knew how I felt about January 6th who wouldn't chastise or belittle me.

We spoke on the phone while I was driving, and it was great to hear his voice. I started talking to him about January 6th. I asked if he thought we could have done more in the days leading up to the 6th, and on the 6th. He chuckled and asked if I had been overthinking again. I paused to consider his question, but I knew I wasn't.

"Cass, we did everything we could," he assured me. "You have nothing to worry about. You have no reason to bear any of the blame for this. It's mob mentality. This would have happened whether we had the rally, whether we didn't have the rally."

But we helped plan the rally that brought all those people to DC. We organized it. We had to bear some of the blame. "I don't know," I said cautiously.

By the end of the thirty-minute call, I felt a little better. I pulled up at a consignment store and started to wrap up the conversation.

"Alright, kid. Chin up. It could be worse."

I laughed. "How's that?"

"Well, the president could have tried to strangle *you* on January 6th."

I laughed again. "That's true. At least the president didn't try to do that."

He said, "Touch base with me in a few days. We'll chat again."

———

Kevin and I continued to check in with each other frequently. I had been disappointed when, after calling the former president "responsible" for January 6th, Kevin went to Mar-a-Lago in late January to pay his respects. If Republicans won the majority in 2022, Kevin needed Trump on his side to become Speaker of the House. The second impeachment failed to reach a two-thirds majority to convict in the Senate. No one was doing the right thing, including me. No one was being held accountable other than hundreds of protesters who had done what Trump had told them to do.

At times it seemed as if only one person, one Republican, anyway, was determined to hold the parties responsible for January 6th accountable. As the tensions with Liz Cheney grew among House Republicans, Kevin would sometimes ask how I felt about her possible removal from leadership. He complained about how vocal she was, and said that he wished she would just stop talking, because she was putting him in a tough position.

I made it pretty clear that I thought ousting her was a poor political calculation. I said that she was a serious politician, not some fringe character. It would set a dangerous precedent for the party, especially in the first months after the Trump Administration. I didn't argue vociferously or push him when he resisted. Part of me understood his logic—her job as chair of the Republican Conference was to amplify messages that a majority of House Republicans agreed with, not voice her views about Trump, which were, sadly, antithetical to the views of many House Republicans. I was disheartened at how political expediency took precedence over accountability and principles.

On May 12, House Republicans stripped Liz of her chairmanship of the Republican Conference, replacing her with Elise Stefanik two days later. I told Kevin that I was disappointed and felt bad for Liz. I started to sense a significant shift in Kevin, in the kind of politician and leader he was.

Later that week, he told me to reach out to Elise about a job working at Conference. I was still annoyed with him over what had happened with Liz. But I admit that I was intrigued by what a job at Conference would be like, and I liked Elise. In my mind, she wasn't "full-blown MAGA" yet, and I thought she had a bright future in GOP politics. Member services jobs in Conference are highly coveted. It was also Ben Howard's first job on the Hill after he left the White House in 2009, when Mike Pence was Conference chair.

I sent Elise and her chief of staff my résumé. She was enthusiastic and said to follow up the next week. I never did, instead letting the opportunity pass. I don't know if it was because of my feelings about Liz's ouster or my frustration about January 6th, but something about the prospect of it repelled me.

That was the last time I spoke with either Kevin or Elise.

———

Despite the precariousness of my financial position, I hadn't been in a rush to find a job in the summer. I felt guilty about delaying my job search, and the nagging voice in my head berated me for it. But I had stuck with my Florida resolutions and was living a healthier lifestyle. I was running every day, eating properly, sleeping pretty well for me, visiting my parents often. My mental health had improved, too, mostly as a consequence of my healthier physical practices. I also had time to reflect on my life. I knew that in order to grow, I had to put my experiences in perspective so my past wouldn't continue to trouble my future.

I felt the first stirrings of hope at the end of June 2021. Congress approved the formation of the House Select Committee to Investigate the January 6th Attack. I was disappointed when Kevin withdrew his Republican nominees to serve on the committee. But Liz Cheney and Adam Kinzinger stepped up to put country before party.

On August 25, the committee announced that it had sent record requests to eight government agencies seeking documents relevant to their investigation. One of the agencies receiving requests was the National Archives and Records Administration (NARA). The committee requested documents from almost three dozen White House aides, including me.

I suspected the committee would want to talk to me since I had worked so closely with Mark. A few months earlier, in response to a Freedom of Information Act request, the emails I had exchanged with Jordan Fuchs, the Georgia election official I had communicated with after Mark's visit to a Cobb County vote-counting center, had been made public. They didn't draw much attention at the time, but I figured committee investigators were probably aware of those, too.

I immediately reached out to Sam, who advised me to retain a lawyer right away. He sensed my worry, and said there was a slim chance the committee would subpoena me, but that they would definitely subpoena Mark. They would want to talk to me, likely off the record, to confirm or challenge aspects of Mark's testimony. Still, he reiterated that I needed a lawyer in case he was wrong.

I told him I would try. But even if I drained my savings account, which I was currently relying on to live off of, I wouldn't have enough for attorney fees. Dad taught me to decline handouts, especially financial handouts, from everybody. There was no such thing as a handout without strings attached, and I agreed. I knew I didn't want to rely on Trump World for an attorney. I would accrue more than financial debt if I retained one of their attorneys. I didn't owe anyone my freedom and my voice. I risked the fate I was at pains to avoid, and did what a cautious person does: nothing.

———

One Saturday in early October, I woke up to a message from Alyssa. She had been informally advising the committee. Alyssa explained that Liz Cheney was open to meeting with me one-on-one without lawyers, the press, or Democrats. She encouraged me to accept the offer. She didn't want to see me shelling out thousands of dollars for an attorney or, even worse, being dragged into relying on Trump World for protection, as many others were. I knew Alyssa was looking out for me. We had talked about our family histories, and she knew I didn't have people I could rely on financially.

I admired Liz, but I didn't know her as well as I knew other members. I wanted to trust her, but trusting anyone felt impossible. Alyssa vouched for her trustworthiness. I asked for a day to consider.

I immediately called Sam and, as cryptically as I could, described the proposal. He was quick and sure in his response: despite current intraparty politics, he trusted Liz to be true to her word, more than almost any other member. But he was also pragmatic, and in his opinion, I needed to have a verbal or written guarantee that I wouldn't get a subpoena if I agreed to talk to her off the record. It would protect me from unintentionally providing conflicting public and private statements. He cautioned that the stipulation might take the offer off the table, since Liz wasn't the chair of the committee and didn't have the authority to determine who was issued a subpoena. His advice was sound and objective, and he pointed out every angle I should consider to make a decision.

I asked Alyssa to talk to Liz to see if she'd be willing to agree to not subpoenaing me if I agreed to talk with her confidentially. Alyssa said she would.

I did not hear back from Alyssa, nor did I follow up.

I knew then it was just a matter of time before a subpoena made its way to my doorstep.

CHAPTER 19

Served

W ITH MY FINGERS IN my hair and my palms gently squeezing each side of my neck, I paced the length of my apartment. My cell phone had clattered on my kitchen countertop moments ago, and I let myself wait before reading the article linked to the Apple News alert.

I rested my forehead on the window. M Street was congested, and the familiar symphony of impatient drivers honking their horns carried through the glass. I propped my elbows on either side of my cell phone, my palms now massaging each temple. My eyes were frozen on the CNN article illuminated on my phone: "January 6 Committee Issues Ten More Subpoenas . . . ," the headline announced. Except for Kenneth Klukowski, all the names listed as the committee's newest targets were familiar—Stephen Miller, Kayleigh McEnany, Pence national security advisor Keith Kellogg, Trump deputy chief of staff for policy coordination Chris Liddell, Nick Luna, Johnny McEntee, Molly Michael, my friend Ben Williamson, and Cassidy Hutchinson. *Me.*

I read the list over and over, hoping that there was a mistake in the reporting. I had spent the past several weeks, perhaps even months, mentally preparing myself to be subpoenaed by the January 6th Committee. What I had not planned for, however, was what to do when I was subpoenaed. I called Ben Williamson, who invited me to meet at his apartment.

As I entered his building, I thought that if I had one wish, it would be for the ability to fly, so I could soar away from Washington without leaving a trace. "If you had one wish, any wish, what would it be?" I asked Ben as I closed the door to his apartment. He was sitting on the couch, texting someone, his laptop resting on his legs. He was busy, but I didn't care. I grabbed two cans of vodka seltzer from his refrigerator and sat beside him and tossed him one. I opened mine and took several long sips. He was still glued to his cell phone. "Ben!" I said, swatting at the phone. "Did you even notice I'm here?"

"Sorry, yeah, give me a second," he said flatly, sending a text. Then he cracked open his vodka seltzer. "Cheers to our subpoenas. We're officially in the big leagues." I studied Ben's expression and decided he wasn't being ironic. I polished off my seltzer without reciprocating his toast, and grabbed another from the refrigerator.

"Whoa, hard day or something?" Ben said with a laugh.

"I'm nervous, Ben—" I started as Mark's name flashed on his phone.

"Mind if I answer?" Ben was going to answer the call regardless, so I nodded.

"Hey," Mark said. "I just read the January 6th Committee's press release. How do you feel about joining the subpoena club?" I was certain Ben wasn't aware that the volume was loud enough for me to hear their conversation. I felt blood rush to my face as I pretended to be absorbed in my Twitter feed. It was the first time I'd heard Mark's southern drawl in nearly a year.

"Cassidy's actually at my apartment right now," Ben said. There was a prolonged silence. "Oh, was she on the committee's press release too?" Mark asked. Ben was looking at me now. "Yes, sir. She's in the club." I scrolled through Twitter, waiting for Mark's response. "Alright, well, tell her me and Debbie are thinking about her, and we'll say a prayer for her." Mark told Ben to call back soon so they could discuss legal options, and then the call ended.

"Good news. Mark's going to let us know how to get our legal fees covered." I put my phone away and looked at Ben for the first time since he'd answered Mark's call. His expression was unchanged, placid.

I fought the urge to call him out for lying, but then he would know I had been eavesdropping. I forced a smile instead. "That's great, Ben. What else did he have to say?" Ben took a few sips of his seltzer. "Nothing much, really. Stop worrying. Hey, look." He pointed to the TV. CNN was displaying the name and photo of everyone in the committee's latest batch of subpoenas. My thumb crushed a dent in my seltzer can as Ben laughed, saying, "Told you. Big leagues. Shows we were in the know."

My eyes burned, and I knew I couldn't maintain my composure much longer, so I stood up. "I'm going to walk home. I'm getting hungry." Ben handed me his empty can. As I walked to the kitchen, he told me to start reaching out to attorneys. There was a good chance most would be willing to represent me pro bono. "Conservative attorneys will be all over this," he said. "Don't forget, DC runs on transactional relationships. You get legal counsel, they get to make a name for themselves."

"You're right," I lied. "Hey, you never answered my question when I walked in." Ben was back on his phone and didn't respond right away. "Oh yeah. A wish?" I looked down and saw that one of my shoelaces needed to be retied. I started to lean over when Ben said, "I don't know. I guess I've never really thought about that. Have you?"

"No," I said, lying again. I'd retie my shoelace in the hallway. "I don't know what made me think of that. I'll text you later." I left before he had time to respond.

I tried to convince myself that I had misheard Ben's conversation with Mark or that my memory was unreliable—that I was recalling only what I thought Mark would say. But my memory was one of the only things I trusted in this world—it was a steel trap. I could hear Mark's voice in my head as clearly as if he had said it to me. I wanted to believe that Ben hadn't intended to lie to me, but it was implausible that he could forget the important details of the conversation he'd had just seconds earlier. Mark would help *Ben* find a lawyer, not me. He had only offered me thoughts and prayers. He wasn't going to let me know anything.

It was my fault, I reasoned: I must have done something to upset Mark and Ben, which had caused them to reject me. I tried to regain a sense of self-control as the rationalization became more punishing. For a bitter moment, I pictured Mark and Ben anticipating this moment and looking forward to watching me try to retain legal counsel.

I slammed my apartment door shut and stomped into my living room and cursed to stop torturing myself. I laid down on the carpeted floor and tried to clear the fog from my mind. *Mark hired me to be his fixer. If he reached out to help me with this, that would mean we both thought I was too frail to handle it myself. He isn't reaching out to help because he knows I don't need his help. He would be appalled if he had any clue I felt so debilitated and borderline desperate for help.* I winced.

Satisfied, I rolled onto my stomach and began scrolling through my phone contacts to figure out who I could call to connect me to an attorney.

It took me forty-eight hours to come to terms with two things. First, and most important, I could find an attorney without Mark's help. Second, I was probably going to need financial help.

The same night the committee announced my subpoena, I reached out to Liz Horning, Pat Philbin, and Mike Purpura. Like Liz and Pat, Mike had worked in the White House counsel's office. I regretted burdening them with my problem, but they were the only attorneys I knew. I expected to be brushed off, but I was touched when they all took time to explain how the process was likely to play out and gave me contact information for enough lawyers to fill a slim Rolodex.

At the end of each call, I asked for contact information for two or three other attorneys who might be willing to represent me. My network expanded quickly, and my days started to be made up of back-to-back calls. But I kept running into a roadblock—no one would work pro bono or for reduced fees or even accept a long-term payment plan.

I clung to the hope that someone would say yes before I was served the subpoena, but pragmatically I knew I needed a backup plan, so I drove to New Jersey. I turned right off Reed Road toward Dad's workshop.

The sound of gravel clattering against my car prompted a memory of the time I had stopped by his shop after high school track practice to pick up Mom's child support check and he'd heard the gravel spray my car as I rolled to a stop. In front of his employees, he had screamed that if I loved and appreciated him, I wouldn't be so careless as to risk my car being damaged by gravel. He had kicked the wheels of my car and yanked on the door handle to pull me out as I'd pleaded with him to calm down. I don't know if it was the flashback or my nerves in general, but I took care to drive around to the back of his shop as slowly as possible.

I saw a new white pickup truck, which made me happy. He never really bought anything for himself. The last time I had seen him at home or work, years before, he was still driving the same truck he'd had when I was a little girl. The garage door was open, but I didn't see him. I parked my car and grabbed the gift box sitting on my passenger seat.

"Dad?" I called out, walking toward the garage. No response. "Are you here?" This time, I heard a low grunt.

"Hello? Where are you?" Two grunts. I placed the box on the workshop table next to disassembled chain saws and rags coated in oil. "This isn't funny," I said, more sternly this time. "Where are you?" I heard grunts and monkey noises from above and looked up. His head was poking out from the half attic.

"Sissy Hutch! Ooh ooh, ah ah. Come up here!" he called down. I hesitated before walking to a ladder. "What are you now, a wimp?

You don't need a ladder—hop up on the table and pull yourself up here!" I knew better than to think he was joking. I also knew better than to push back.

"You know I'm not as strong as you. I bet you can't even get down without getting hurt," I said, knowing he wouldn't turn down a challenge. He grunted and made more monkey noises as he dangled from the attic before dropping to the floor. "You didn't think Daddy could still do that, did you? Don't lie to me, Sissy. I'm a warrior," he said through more monkey noises. I pulled him into a hug to stop the antics.

"Did you hear I'm a wealthy man now? I finally did it, Sissy. It started when I sold the house down the street. Did you know I sold that property? Did you hear how much?" he asked. I knew the property, but I didn't know he had sold it. I shook my head.

"Aren't you going to ask how much I sold it for?" he pressed.

"Nah, you would tell me if you wanted me to know. Tell me when you're ready. I can't wait to find out," I said, which made him smile. He liked being in control, a now familiar pattern of other outsize figures in my life. "What's in this box?" He picked it up and shook it like it was full of rocks. "Open it up," I said. "It's for you."

He pulled out a silver bowl with an engraved presidential seal on one side and Trump's signature on the other side. When Mark and I had packed up his office in January, he'd given me a few gifts he kept in his closet for guests. Of all the gifts I had, I thought Dad would like the bowl the most. It looked the most expensive. I held my breath as he inspected it, leaving oily fingerprints as he turned it over in his hands. "I saw you made the news this week," he said without looking up.

I pulled out a printed copy of the January 6th Committee's letter issued earlier that week that detailed why I had been subpoenaed. I still hadn't been served, but the letter was public.

"Yeah," I answered, and went to hand the letter to him. He wouldn't take it, so I put it in the bowl, prompting him to pick it up. "I need to retain a lawyer. I've been networking all week to find one, and I have a few decent leads for lawyers who will work at a low cost," I explained. He was staring at the letter, but his eyes weren't moving across the paper. "I still have a lot of conversations scheduled, and I'm hopeful that I'll find one to work pro bono—for free," I added. "But if I can't . . ."

He gave me the side-eye and I tried to stop my voice from breaking, but my eyes welled with tears. "I might need a little help." He looked back down at the letter.

"Is Donald going to run for president again in 2024?" he asked, breaking the silence.

"Um, I don't know. Maybe," I said.

"Why don't you know?" he demanded, shoving the paper back in my hands. "I don't need to read this. You know you don't have to do any of that bullshit, right? Donald told me himself. He'll pay for your lawyer, right? He's a rich man like me. Maybe I'm more rich than he is now, Sissy." He laughed and reached out to tickle me.

"Stop," I said, backing away. "I'm sorry. Please just listen to me. I don't want him to pay for my lawyer. I promise I would pay you back . . ." He grabbed my wrist and pulled me through the garage. "Stop it, Sissy. No stress. Love and peace. I want to show you all my treasures."

His office was just as I remembered it, but more cluttered. A hoarder's paradise. Wire shelves were stacked everywhere, each one lined with cardboard, holding plastic boxes. His desk was piled with paperwork and more boxes. He began to pull boxes off the shelves and told me, in detail, which dumpsters and junkyards he had found each treasure in, and how his research said that each one was worth over fifty thousand dollars. I dug my hands in my pockets and tried to blink back the tears forming in my eyes, but after about fifteen minutes of this, tears dropped to the floor. He dropped the box he was holding.

"Why the hell are you crying? You know my rule. Warriors don't cry. Are you still a warrior?" he asked as he opened the door leading to the front entrance. "The sunlight will dry up those tears."

I stood next to him quietly and kicked some gravel for a few minutes as I collected myself. "I'm really sorry. I'm just stressed about this." He was staring straight ahead, so I looked up. The mid-November chill had stripped the last leaves off the trees separating the properties. Through the bare branches, I saw our old house on Reed Road.

"You were my best little buddy when we lived there," he said. "Do you remember that? Do you remember when you would run outside every day when I got home and we would sing together when I parked the truck?"

We had never talked about my childhood, ever. I found comfort in the fact that he remembered that, too, that he hadn't forgotten. "I do," I said. Instinctively, I closed the space between us, rested my head on his shoulder, and slung my arm around his back. I thought I felt his body stiffen.

I cleared my throat and said, "Do you miss those days? I do." His arms hung at his side and my breath caught in my chest when he twisted away from me. "Hell no, I'm wealthy now. Remember? Will you tell Donald I'm wealthy now? Can you tell him I'll give him a lot of money so he runs for president in 2024?"

I didn't have anything to say, so I walked back to the door to leave. He followed me inside through his office and the garage. "Sissy," he called out once I was close to my car. "Would a lawyer cost a million dollars? More?"

I turned around. "No. Less. I wouldn't ask you for money if I wasn't desperate. I promise I will pay you back. You have my word," I said. "I don't need an answer now. Can you just think about it? Please?" He responded with monkey noises and I got in my car, ready to speed away.

He motioned for me to roll down the window and grabbed the wheel. "Sissy Hutch, you're no fun. I just said 'I'll think about it' in monkey language." I nodded and thanked him, and put my car in drive. "Sissy . . ." I snapped my head toward him. "How much do you think that bowl is worth? Will Donald give you another one?

We'll have to sell those to pay for a lawyer. You're the reason I've always been broke . . ." I drove away knowing I wouldn't survive if I listened to another word out of his mouth.

Somehow I still had a fragment of hope that he would pull through if I needed his help. But I wasn't planning on needing it. I thought my college degree was my ticket to freedom, but I had messed up. I promised myself that if I found a lawyer willing to work pro bono, that would be the final time I let anyone hold my freedom captive. I knew it could be my last chance.

———

I packed my schedule with calls and meetings, virtual and in-person, with attorneys in Washington, DC, Maryland, and Virginia, but I still had not found one who could commit to representing me pro bono. I had never felt like more of an imposter than when I walked into the first few law firms I visited. Alone on my side of the conference table, I tried to imitate the elegant decorum of the lawyers and their associates who stared at me as I tried to make sense of a situation that hardly made sense to me. I didn't know much about proper attorney-client etiquette, but I made sure I was clear about my financial situation and my over-arching goals in response to my subpoena.

I would have retained many attorneys on the spot if money had not been a factor. A former Department of Justice official connected me to an attorney in Baltimore I particularly liked. He made me feel comfortable enough to let my guard down, and I had been more candid than usual about the details of my experience. He spent hours explaining the legal process I would work through in the coming weeks. He invalidated the shame I felt about my financial situation and promised to do his best to work out an extremely low or pro bono rate on a payment plan. His only reservation was that I should wait until I was served my subpoena before he drafted an engagement letter—he explained that there was a chance I would fall off the committee's radar entirely.

I left that meeting cautiously optimistic. Ideally, I didn't want to wait until I was served to retain an attorney; I wanted to be forthcoming with the committee. I knew I would be doing a disservice to myself if I didn't continue expanding my network of lawyers and have a backup plan.

———

Over Thanksgiving, I went to New Jersey to visit Mom and Paul, who constantly asked for updates on my progress. I felt both pressured and encouraged by their faith that I would eventually find a lawyer.

When I pulled into my parking garage upon my return, I sat in my car for a long time, trying to figure out what more I could possibly do. I felt like I was living *Groundhog Day*. Finally I pushed a bin of Christmas decorations and a disassembled tree into my apartment. Mom had sent me back to DC with them.

I was setting up the tree the next night when my cell phone vibrated with a message from John Ratcliffe. "Mark has been making some news. How's everything been going for you?" he texted. Earlier that week, *The Chief's Chief*, Mark's book, had been published. I hadn't had the stomach to read it, but I had read plenty of articles about it. There were reports that Trump was livid, particularly over Mark's description of his appearance when he had COVID. In reaction to Trump's anger, Mark had withdrawn his commitment to cooperate with the January 6th Committee. Ben Williamson had tipped me off before the news was public, but I wasn't surprised.

I was cheered by John's outreach and responded quickly, knowing that the feeling would soon be replaced by shame. I was becoming more aware that my inability to admit I needed help was borderline pathological, and that continuing to belittle myself was self-destructive.

Later that week, I went to Sam's for the first time since the subpoena news. We played card games as we drained a bottle of bourbon, talking about everything except the committee's work. I knew he wanted me to have a normal evening and wouldn't mention the subpoena unless I did. I eventually explained how much I was struggling to find an attorney that I could afford. I became irritable when he followed up with questions—each felt like an accusation. I couldn't comprehend the questions were a proffer to help.

"Do you have any cigarettes?" I asked in response to one question. Sam shook his head, laughing.

"Shut up. You're out of your mind." I repeated my question. He reminded me that I routinely bragged that I had never smoked a cigarette in my life. I pressed him again.

"Yeah, I do." He walked to the kitchen and returned with a pack. "Come on, let's go outside. This is nuts," he said. I followed him out.

The smell of cigarette smoke filled the air, and I savored the childhood nostalgia it summoned. I would sit outside with my grandmother and Mom's siblings while they smoked. Mom would eventually fall into her oldest-sibling-syndrome lecture about the dangers of smoking. I watched Sam's face glow orange from the burning tobacco and longed for one of those summer nights again.

"I don't know what I'm going to do," I said.

"Sure you do. You said you wanted to smoke."

"I wasn't talking about the damn cigarette. I don't know what I'm going to do," I repeated.

He lit another cigarette and offered it to me. "Shut up and smoke it already. You're wasting time. You know what you're going to do."

"Why aren't you listening to me?! You're not listening. You never listen."

I was pissed and snatched the cigarette from him. Out of spite, I drew a sharp, dramatic drag and erupted into a coughing fit. It felt like my lungs were on fire.

"First of all, I'm listening. I always listen. You just don't want to admit that, because you need a punching bag. That's okay, I can be your punching bag," he said. "Second of all, I wasn't talking about the cigarette. You know what you're going to do about an attorney. You're going to keep looking, and you're not going to stop until you have to. Right?"

I couldn't respond. I felt like I was choking up a lung, so I just nodded.

"Third," he said, snatching the cigarette from me and stomping it out. "Don't ever smoke again unless you want to humiliate yourself. You're not a moron, but you're sure as hell acting like one."

————

On December 12, I woke up to a text message with a video my mom had recorded for my twenty-fifth birthday. I had to double-check the date to make sure it was my actual birthday. Time no longer felt real. My days were monotonous and predictable. I spent most of them in total isolation, and my birthday wasn't any different.

I didn't think a quarter-life crisis would be so literal.

————

"A committee staffer texted me today. He said he was reaching out to talk to me or my lawyer about my subpoena," I said. I was on the phone with the attorney I had met with in Baltimore a month prior.

"Don't worry," he assured me. "They're required to do this. There's still a good chance they will never serve you. And if they do, it won't happen this close to the holidays."

I didn't want to question his assessment of the situation, but I had a gut instinct he was wrong. I had had the same gut instinct for months, and it hadn't failed me yet.

"If they follow up after the holidays, are you still willing to represent me? And if you are, I want to let you know now my financial situation hasn't changed. I'm sorry," I said.

He urged me to stop worrying, and said that he would represent me for free if I was ever served. My heartbeat quickened, and I thanked him. I told him I'd pray for a Christmas miracle that I wouldn't get served.

Privately, I acknowledged that my Christmas miracle was having finally secured legal representation if the time ever came that I'd have to use it.

———

A month later, I was on FaceTime with Paul, venting about how worried I was that I would be served the subpoena soon. Ben had been deposed the day before, January 25. In the midst of his deposition, the same committee staffer I'd mentioned to the Baltimore attorney had texted me again, asking where I wanted my subpoena delivered. I hadn't responded.

As Paul was trying to reassure me, I heard four short knocks on my door. My stomach dropped, and Paul and I both fell silent. He had heard the knocks, too. There was another knock, and a voice called out, "U.S. Marshals. Please open the door."

I felt panic rising as Paul urged me to answer the door. "Shh! No!" I whispered. "Maybe they don't know I'm home." More knocking. "Go answer the door, Cassidy. Then call me back," Paul said before hanging up.

Three federal marshals stood in the doorway, one with his arm raised in a fist, presumably to knock yet again. "Sorry," I said. "You're probably here with my subpoena. At least I hope that's why you're here. Well, if I'm being totally honest, I wish you weren't here at all. Sorry."

Two of the three smiled. I thought I saw a hint of sympathy in their smiles. "Yes, ma'am," one of them said, handing me the subpoena. "Do you have any questions?" I thumbed through the pages. "Yeah, a lot, actually. None you can answer, I don't think."

"Understood, ma'am. We'll head out, then." They were walking toward the elevator when one turned around and wished me good luck.

I wanted to thank him—I needed all the luck I could get. But I didn't feel any genuine gratitude, and I couldn't lie to federal officers, especially now. I had a subpoena in my hand.

CHAPTER 20

Pulled Back In

TEARS ROLLED DOWN MY FACE at the Wawa checkout counter, and I didn't bother to wipe them away. I had already cried off my waterproof mascara in the car. I paid, and the clerk shouted, "Next!"

"You too," I mumbled instinctively, thinking she'd told me to have a great day. We looked at each other awkwardly—I was a blubbering, swollen-eyed wreck, and she looked like she had worked a double shift. I snatched my fountain Coke Zero off the countertop and hurried out to avoid further humiliation.

I started the car but stayed in the parking lot for a long time. I was too emotional to drive. I couldn't even pin down how I felt. I just knew that tears were flowing and showed no sign of slowing down.

The night before, I had called the attorney in Baltimore and let him know that the U.S. Marshals Service had delivered the subpoena. He stressed how inappropriate it was for me to have been put in that position. The marshals should have served the subpoena to my attorney, he said. I was confused, since he had advised me that we shouldn't formalize our attorney-client relationship until I had been served, but he sounded genuinely defensive. He told me to come to his office the next morning to sort everything out. I reminded him about my financial situation and assured him I wouldn't be offended if he could no longer represent me pro bono. "Stop worrying," he said. "We'll get you taken care of. Just come see me tomorrow."

When I arrived, a secretary walked me to his office, where he was seated at his desk on the opposite side of the room. Something was off. He greeted me by handing me an engagement letter with a six-figure retainer. My stomach bottomed out.

Since we'd last spoken, a few things had changed, he explained. With Mark no longer cooperating with the committee, the committee would likely want more of my time, thus more of the law firm's resources. We would need to spend days prepping material and doing mock depositions to make sure I was adequately prepared. And, he said, the Department of Justice would probably want to talk with me at some point.

His lecture went on and on. I tried to listen, but I was fixated on the engagement letter. Thoughts spun through my mind so fast that I couldn't process one before another one popped up. I asked him how much time I would have before I needed to pay off the whole retainer. He said that he would need the money as soon as possible. We couldn't start working until the firm received my payment, and we had our work cut out for us.

I was overwhelmed and didn't know what to say. I sensed how slouched I was, but I felt too defeated to sit up straight. He shook his head when I asked about a payment plan, saying apologetically, "If I didn't have lights to keep on and employees to pay, I wouldn't charge you at all. Unfortunately, that's just not how this works." I told him I understood and apologized for being such a burden.

A few days before, Liz Horning had sent me a CNN article about a legal defense fund that Matt Schlapp, the chairman of the American Conservative Union and a Trump World ally, had set up to pay attorney fees for people subpoenaed by the January 6th Committee. Liz had urged me to reach out to Matt, since financial situations like mine were the reason he set up the fund. I told her I didn't want to because I hated asking for help, which was half true. The other half of what I was thinking was that money would come with stipulations. Stipulations were currency in Trump World—but not in the life I was trying to build.

But that morning in Baltimore, a feeling of desperation I had never known washed over me. I was terrified that I would have to represent myself if I didn't retain a lawyer in the next few days, and the man sitting in front of me with his arms crossed felt like the only person in the world who could help. I asked if he would accept payment from a legal defense fund. He sighed and shook his head. "If you were another client, I would probably consider it," he said. "But I want to be candid with you. That money would have strings attached, and I know you wouldn't agree with the strings."

I looked at the engagement letter, unsure how to respond. The attorney said, "Listen, I'm sitting here with you now. In two hours, I'll be at a jail telling a man I can probably get his sentence reduced from life in prison to a couple of decades. I need you to understand this is a business." I nodded in agreement and thanked him for his time, and promised to reach out when I figured out how to get the money.

He followed up with me several times, but I didn't respond. We never spoke again.

I collected myself enough to drive back to my apartment. On my way home, I called Sam to vent about the meeting. He laughed, which set me off.

"I'm not laughing at what happened—that sucks. It really does. I'm laughing because I don't know why you called me. I'm happy to listen to you complain about it," he said. "But you need to do something about it. Pick up the phone and call someone who might be useful. Stop wasting time. The clock is literally ticking. No more bullshit."

I knew Sam was right.

For the rest of the day, I called attorneys I had spoken with in November and December to ask if they had any flexibility with a payment schedule. Nothing had changed, but many were eager to help me expand my network more. Soon enough, I had dozens of new attorneys to call.

Aunt Steph came to my apartment later that night. Even though she had moved back to DC about a year before, I hadn't seen her yet. We had been so close, sometimes it felt like our bond could never be broken. But our relationship had been strained for a few years because we had different political views. While I try never to let politics influence my personal relationships, I couldn't look past hers. I didn't want to damage our relationship beyond repair, so I pulled away. We still spoke, but it was limited to texting, and our conversations were sporadic and surface-level.

She listened as I caught her up on my legal predicament, and when she spoke, she was more encouraging than anyone had been so far. She was proud that I was standing up for what I believed in, and she trusted my judgment. In that moment, I felt more secure than I had in months and regretted the time I had wasted building a wall between us.

We considered what I should do. She offered to talk to my uncle about refinancing their home. If they were approved, she would lend me whatever money they were able to free up. But she wasn't sure if they would be approved, and I could read her expression enough to know it would put them in a bind. I told her about the conversation I'd had with Dad in November, and said that I thought I should talk to him again. She agreed, and reminded me to be firm. It was going to be painful—he would want me to grovel. But she and I both thought that if I remained strong, he would help. So I drove to New Jersey.

———

I didn't tell Dad I was in town until I arrived at Mom's house. If I gave him too much notice, he would find an excuse for why he couldn't see me. He ignored my first text, so I sent another. Then another. And another. After a few hours I began to panic. I told him how intense my anxiety was, and that I needed him more than ever before. I stared at that text for a while before finding the courage to send it. I worried I would regret telling him that, but I was relieved when I sent it. What I said was true. I thought I had made peace with our broken relationship, but I realized there was still a piece of me that clung to the hope that he also thought there was something between us worth fixing.

A bubble appeared, indicating that he was typing. Then it disappeared. And reappeared. This cycle continued until it didn't. I sent a follow-up text. He told me to come to the house. I got into my car without thinking, because if I stopped to consider what I was about to do, I knew I would back down.

From his driveway, I could barely see even the silhouette of the house. That part of town was so dark at night that the only light was from the moon and the stars. For the first time since the conversation with Steph, I worried this may be too much of an emotionally grueling experience for me to handle. I opened the car door, and frigid winter air filled my car, which snapped me back to reality.

I wasn't sure which door to go through, and I didn't have cell phone service to text him, so I took a chance and crept around to the back of the house. The patio light was on. My heart broke at the sight. Nothing had changed, except that even with minimal light, I could see how abandoned the yard looked. The grill was on its side, and the dog statue he had let me buy at the plant nursery before we moved to Indiana was in the same spot, next to the back door. Through the window, I saw him hunched over the kitchen counter on his phone. I walked inside.

"Sissy Hutch, I hope you're here to give me some money. I'm flat broke," was the first thing he said to me. He tried to pass me a stack of envelopes and a pocketknife. "Thank God you came, Sissy. I need you to help me pay all these bills." I didn't take them from him. I felt overpowered in the house and tried to steel myself. I could tell he sensed my emotions—he dropped the envelopes on the countertop and walked toward the basement door.

"Come downstairs," he said. He was halfway down the stairs when I froze at the door. Mom had hung our school artwork on the walls, and every piece was still in its place.

The basement remained unfinished, but Mom had transformed it into a cozy playroom. Now it was dank. He was chucking logs into a woodburning oven when I made it down the stairs. "See, Sissy? See what you did to me? This is how I have to live because of you," he said, handing me a log. "The least you could do is help me stay warm."

I threw the log into the stove and saw his jaw muscles tense. "Now you're going to burn my wood? All you do is take from me. I can barely afford that wood, I'm so broke." I still hadn't said a word to him, but I didn't know what to say, so I apologized. He stormed back up the stairs, and I followed.

I found him in the kitchen pantry. Mom's handwritten labels were still on each shelf, but I didn't recognize any of the food. The shelves were stuffed with mason jars of preserved produce, jams and nuts, countless bags of dehydrated meat, and glass jugs of water. He handed me a jar filled with brown liquid and something I didn't recognize. It looked like meat of some sort, and he told me to try it. I asked what it was. "Chopped-up deer tongue. Good eatin', Sissy." I shoved the jar back in his hands and bolted from the pantry.

"Man, you're such a wimp. You were never a wimp. What happened to you?" he asked. My hands and feet were starting to sweat. I wanted to flee, but that's not why I had come. I pulled my subpoena that I had folded in quarters out of my coat pocket and handed it to him. "Please, I just need you to listen," I said, my voice trembling. He looked at me, expecting me to say more, but I couldn't find my words.

He threw the subpoena in the trash, ranting that I didn't need to do anything it asked me to do. He had read online that it wasn't mandatory to comply with congressional subpoenas. The investigation was a witch hunt to take Donald down, he said. He prayed I wasn't there to ask for money to pay for a corrupt lawyer—any lawyer who didn't work for Donald was corrupt. He had raised me better than for me to turn my back on the people who cared about me, people like himself and Donald. "You didn't raise me at all," was all I thought of to say.

His expression flattened, and for a moment I thought I could leave before he said anything else. I had made a mistake coming here. As I plotted my exit, I saw his jaw clench. Almost whispering, he asked me to repeat what I had said. I asked if he was deaf. "Has anyone told you lately," he said in a low, controlled voice, "that you're an ungrateful, spoiled bitch?"

My fight-or-flight instinct had failed as his words sliced through me and robbed the strength of mind I brought there. I broke down in loud sobs, unable to speak. He stood across from me and stared. My knees felt weak, then my legs gave out and I curled into myself on the tile floor. I felt the floor vibrate as Dad walked around the countertop to stand over me. I covered my face to avoid further humiliation. He stood there for what felt like minutes, watching me. My sobs only grew louder.

He scooped me up, and I thrashed against him before he dropped me onto the couch. I do not know how much time passed before I gathered myself enough to speak, but when I did, my voice kept getting caught in my throat as I made one final plea for Dad's help. I asked if he would cosign a loan if he was not willing to lend me money. I told him that he could charge me an interest rate higher than the bank. I reminded him how he had always told me that I should never accept favors from people—I needed to be self-sufficient. I was trying so hard, I assured him, but I was desperate and needed help. He told me to ask Donald for an attorney. I walked to the kitchen, pulled my subpoena from the garbage can, and hurried out the back door.

"Sissy," he called out, and I turned around. "What if you move back here?"

"If I move back here, will you help me? I could help you with the business—"

"No, Sissy. If you move back here, you won't have to comply with the subpoena. They'll never find you here. Daddy will keep you safe." I started walking to my car.

"Sissy," he called out again.

"Stop," I shouted. "What the hell could you possibly want now? Is it fun for you to see me like this? What the hell do you still have to torture me about? There's literally nothing left. Just let me go."

"You know I love you, right? More than anything in the world?" he asked. I threw my hands in the air and huffed in disbelief.

"Do you love me?" he asked. I looked at him for a long time, then said, "I always have, and I always will. But you don't know how to love without conditions. Please, Dad. Please let me go. You have to let me go."

He walked into the house, and I drove back to Mom's. I couldn't comprehend what had happened, but I knew how severe its effects would be on my future. I felt like a prisoner who had just been handed over to another captor.

———

I continued networking with attorneys once I returned to Washington, but I knew that it was a fruitless effort. I had already resigned myself to reaching out to my contacts in Trump World and filling out applications for legal assistance. There was now a paper trail of my personal financial circumstances and begging for help. I adjusted my language to match theirs; I felt I knew exactly what I had to say to get the help I needed. I held out hope that they would offer me a blank check with a stipulation that they had to approve the attorney I chose.

But when Eric Herschmann said that someone would be in touch with me soon, I knew I had been assigned an attorney—I would not get to choose. A few days later, a man I didn't know named Alex Cannon called, introducing himself as a former Trump Organization and campaign attorney. He was tasked with finalizing details and assured me that I'd hear from someone shortly. I asked for the name of the attorney who would be representing me, and he said that he couldn't tell me yet.

The following Monday, February 7, I received a call from an unknown number. I answered. "Hi, this is Stefan Passantino," the caller said. "I'm your new attorney."

And just like that, I was back in the Family.

CHAPTER 21

Depositions

I SAT IN THE LOBBY of Michael Best & Friedrich's office waiting for Stefan to appear. I brought a laptop and flash drive with screenshotted text messages that I thought might be responsive to my subpoena, but was not sure what to expect out of this meeting. A week ago, I had asked Stefan what he needed ahead of our first meeting, and if I would sign our engagement letter then or if he would email an electronic copy to sign. He said I would not be signing an engagement letter, and to bring whatever I thought might be useful. *An engagement letter would be useful*, I had wanted to say.

"Cassidy? Hey, I'm sorry I kept you waiting," I heard a male voice call out. It was Stefan. I stood up and noticed how weak my legs felt. I reached out and shook his hand, and he led me to a conference room. We sat in leather chairs, and he started to chat about the Potomac River views and how he liked to look out the floor-to-ceiling windows at the planes taking off from Reagan National Airport.

His small talk and easygoing manner made it hard for me to get a read on him professionally. I was expecting a lawyerly seriousness that might have calmed some of my nervousness about the interview, but he came off as very informal, affable. I had expected to see some paperwork on the table, too, but there was nothing other than a black leather padfolio with a notepad inside it, though I do not recall much note-taking during the meeting.

When we finished the introductions and small talk, he asked what I wanted to discuss.

Maybe what the committee is going to talk to me about, I thought to myself. I told him that some of the lawyers I had met with had said that they would help me reconstruct my memories of the period covered by my subpoena, November 1, 2020–January 30, 2021, to prepare me for the questions I might get asked. That appealed to me, because while I have a good memory, my mind operates like an Outlook calendar, where I see things in blocks of time. I like to have an actual calendar in front of me for reference, and for accuracy.

I started to walk Stefan through the relevant dates, beginning with Mark's and my return to the White House after we had recovered from COVID. At one point I asked Stefan if we could print out a calendar.

"What do you need a calendar for?" he asked.

"To make sure I'm getting the dates right with these things," I replied.

"No, no, no," he said. "We want to get you in and get you out."

We were to downplay my role, he explained, as strictly administrative. I was an assistant, nothing more. The committee was dragging me into things I probably knew little about. I should not emphasize my access or volunteer anything I was not directly asked, nor should I try to refresh my memory. "The less you remember, the better," he advised, and added, "Is there anything you're worried they'll ask you?"

"Yes," I answered, "that's why I asked for a calendar." But I relented, and resumed trying to reconstruct events from memory, describing incidents I thought the committee might ask me about, including the president wanting the magnetometers down on January 6, even though people were armed, and Tony telling me about the incident in the Beast.

"No, no, no. We do not want to talk about that," Stefan insisted.

"But what if they ask me about it?" I asked.

"They won't. They'd have no way of knowing that. Have you ever told anyone about that?"

I assured him I had not. He doubted Tony had, either. "That's one of those stories that's just going to give the committee a headline," he explained. "It's not important to anything that actually happened that day." He went on to argue that since I had heard the story secondhand, it was not my responsibility to share it with the committee. I asked where I should draw the line between information I had an obligation to share and information I didn't need to.

"Do I never say anything I overheard?" I asked him. I had overheard a lot of things.

Stefan never told me to lie to the committee. "I don't want you to perjure yourself," he insisted. "But 'I don't recall' isn't perjury."

"The goal is to get you in and out," he repeated. "Keep your answers short, sweet, and simple, seven words or less. The less the committee thinks you know, the quicker it's going to go."

I talked about planning for a possible presidential movement to the Capitol after the rally. He reminded me again that I didn't need to build out timelines. Unless I had clear memories of a specific day and a specific event, "'I don't recall' is your answer." That led to a longer discussion of what was and wasn't appropriate to dismiss with a "don't recall." If I remembered something but not every detail, "Can I still say that?" I asked him.

"Yes."

"Wouldn't I be perjuring myself?"

He assured me that the committee wouldn't know what I could and couldn't recall. If I didn't have a complete memory of something, it wasn't perjury to plead that I had no recollection. If I remembered something very clearly, I should give as short an answer as possible. "You don't want to get ahead of their questioning," he advised. "We'll get into a rhythm, and you'll be fine."

"Okay."

The flash drive I brought had screenshots of texts divided into files. We put it into my laptop, and he started to go through everything. He complimented me on my "great organization." I started reading some of the texts to him. He stopped me after a bit.

"Stuff like that is not responsive, unless it's explicitly talking about planning for January 6th or planning for meetings that were specific to January 6th." He flagged one screenshot I had shown him.

"That didn't need to be turned over?" I asked, slightly confused by his action.

"Was it about January 6th planning?"

"No."

"Only things about January 6th planning."

We continued to go through my files. He said he would make a copy of the flash drive, and that he'd be responsible for sharing the texts with the committee. My thoughts swung back and forth between *this doesn't seem right* and *what do I know, I'm not a lawyer*. I had to take it on faith that I could trust him, and that's hard for me to do. Still, doubts and all, I was relieved and grateful to have a lawyer representing me.

"My job is to be a buffer," he explained. "If they go too far with questions, I'll interject or I'll give you a signal, meaning time for a break or for me to talk." The signal wasn't defined. I guess he thought I would know it when I saw it.

I asked if we could run through a few mock questions about what they might ask me. He told me it would be very straightforward. I was going to get questions about things I knew about and things I didn't know about. Answer the former succinctly, he said, and say "I don't know" to the latter. No need for mock questions. "There must be a trick to it," I said. He repeated his previous advice. "Short and sweet. That's what you do. Short and sweet."

"Would you be comfortable doing your deposition separately?" he asked. "You could Zoom from home, and I'd Zoom from where I am? We could take a break if you had a question, and you could call me."

"Can't we do it together? I want you next to me," I said.

"Alright, sure."

"Can I have notes with me? Printouts of my texts?" I asked.

He said, "Well, you can, but whatever you have in front of you, we have to give to the committee. Better if you don't bring any materials."

It was still light out when I left. *Maybe Stefan was right,* I thought, as I waited for an Uber. *Maybe Trump lunging at Bobby was just a headline, not a crime. Did I need to talk about something I'd only heard about that wasn't even criminal? Maybe I'm over-thinking the whole thing. Maybe they really are looking out for me.*

Before we parted, I'd asked Stefan if there was anything I could do to prepare for my deposition, which was scheduled for the following week. He told me to "get a good night's sleep," and then repeated something he'd said earlier—not to read anything that might jog my memory.

That weekend, I became more and more nervous, still uncertain how to be responsive to the committee without setting off alarms in Trump World. Meanwhile, a quiet voice in my head warned me that I wasn't overthinking. I drove to a Staples in Alexandria and printed more than a dozen transcripts of witness depositions from the Russia investigation. I took them home and read all of them, highlighting passages that could serve as models of diplomatic responses, trying to pick up the rhythm of the exchanges.

Stefan and I met at a café for breakfast the morning of Wednesday, February 23.

"You're nervous," he noted.

"Yeah."

"You have nothing to be nervous about, Cassidy. We're going to have a nice breakfast. We'll Zoom with the committee. We'll break for lunch. We'll Zoom again, and then it'll be over," he said. "Keep your answers short."

"Got it," I said.

"Cassidy, you're a good person," he said. "I don't want you to feel like you have to bear the weight of responsibility for other people. It's not fair to you . . . It's not fair that Mark put you in this position. We just want to protect the president. We all know you're loyal. Let's just get you in and out of this. It's going to be easy, I promise."

I could barely chew the croissant I'd ordered, but I nodded to reassure him that I was okay.

Several months later, I would tell Liz Cheney that I had felt that day as if Donald Trump were looking over my shoulder. Stefan had planted the seeds of old allegiances with his reference to my loyalty: *We know you're loyal. We know you're on Team Trump. We know you're going to do the right thing. We're going to take care of you.* Phrases I heard throughout my tenure in the White House, phrases I had spent a year trying to separate myself from. And now here I was back in their grip, taking care to protect the president, with a lawyer from Trump World.

Was I nervous? Yes, I was nervous. Extremely. And my nervousness wasn't helped by the sense that I was drifting on currents beyond my control back to a port that I could never leave again.

We went back to the law office and settled in a conference room for the meeting with the committee. The members and staff popped up on the screen, and it began. An investigator asked if I had turned over to them all the text messages I had that were responsive to the subpoena, and I told him I had.

I was asked to describe my role at the White House, and to provide context about my background. Then we moved into more substantive questions about events leading up to January 6.

My objective was to be honest and helpful, but I felt like my objective clashed with that of my counsel, which I understood was to say as little as possible. I tried to balance saying "I don't know" responses while giving the committee threads to tug on that might help them in their investigation. I wanted the truth to come out.

Not long into the interview the questions turned to discussions I was privy to about the president's desire to go to the Capitol that day. Members wanted to know who had told the president he couldn't go. After trying to talk around it, I said that it had been Bobby Engel who had told the president no in the presidential limo, as directed by Mark.

Liz Cheney zeroed in on how I knew what had been said in the Beast: "So who relayed to you the conversation that happened in the Beast?" I froze. I thought for certain she had heard that something eventful had happened, and she suspected I knew what it was. I dodged it. I told her I had heard Bobby tell Trump that they would discuss it during the car ride back, which was true, but incomplete. And I had confirmed with Tony later that Bobby and the president had talked, which was sort of true, and really incomplete.

Liz wasn't deterred easily. She rephrased the question several times before turning to my conversation with Mark about whether he and I could go to the Capitol. Then she bore into my knowledge of White House counsel's objections to the president's going to the Hill. I acknowledged that they had concerns, and had raised them with Mark, but when she pressed me to describe those concerns, I responded in the most general terms. They were worried about the "legal implications," I said. Eventually Stefan suggested that it was time for a break.

With the microphone muted and the camera off, I said to Stefan, "I'm fucked."

"Don't freak out, you're fine."

"No, Stefan, I'm fucked. I just lied to them."

"You didn't lie. They don't know what you can and can't recall. You didn't lie."

We went to the office coffee station, and I kept repeating to him, "I lied," and he kept repeating I was fine. "You're doing great, Cass."

There were only three people in the car: Trump, Bobby, and the driver. There was no way Tony or Bobby had talked. The driver, to my knowledge, had not been interviewed, but it was possible he had told someone else about the incident, and that

that person had shared it with the committee. I had never told a soul. But any number of White House staffers could have seen me go into Tony's office right after the rally and come out looking shocked.

My testimony lasted from ten in the morning to nearly six that evening. Many of my answers were longer than seven words, but otherwise, I mostly followed Stefan's instructions. For the record, I said "I don't know" eighty-five times, "I don't recall" seventy times, "I'm not sure" thirty-nine times, "I don't remember" twenty-one times, "I can't recall" twelve times, "not that I can recall" eight times, "I'm trying to recall" twice, and "I don't specifically recall" twice; and I used a dozen other phrases denying knowledge that I possessed. When I genuinely didn't know something, I was practically gleeful in my ignorance, saying, "I have *absolutely* no idea." But I was not, quite obviously, wholly truthful.

I didn't feel good about it. Deep down, I knew my loyalties should have been to the country, to the truth, and not to the former president, who had made himself a threat to both. I tried to repress that realization with rationalizations and with assurances others offered me and I would tell myself, *This isn't my problem. Others will expose it. I'm getting through this the best I can.* But it was always there, not far below the surface of my reasoning: *This is wrong.*

At the end, the committee requested that I testify a second day. My heart dropped. As soon as we logged off Zoom, I said, "I don't want to do this again."

"I'm surprised they asked to talk to you again," he said, frowning.

I was too exhausted to go out to dinner, but Stefan and I had a glass of wine at Michael Best. We went over a few things and talked about scheduling round two. He couldn't decide whether to brief two of his law partners (Alex Cannon and Justin Clark), Mark's lawyers (John Moran and George Terwilliger), and Eric Herschmann. He decided that he would call everyone in a few days and tell them that my interview was scheduled for March 7, believing they would assume it was my only interview. "If they know you went in twice, I don't think it will make Mark happy."

"And let's get started on looking for a job for you," he said. "The committee is dragging this out. It's not fair. We want to make sure that we get you financially set up and taken care of as quickly as possible. Let's chat in a few days."

———

A week later, Stefan called while I was driving to New Jersey. I pulled into a Wawa to take the call. Committee investigator Dan George asked if I was willing to appear in-person for my second interview. "Do you see an upside to this?" Stefan asked, adding, "I don't."

I had a strong preference for an in-person interview, but Stefan urged me to stick with Zoom because it was quicker and we were in control. I could have insisted I do it in person. But I trusted he knew best.

Ben Williamson called on March 6, and I was immediately suspicious of the timing. At first Ben and I just shot the breeze. Soon enough, he got around to the point. "Hey, by the way, Mark told me you have your deposition tomorrow."

"Yeah, it's tomorrow," I answered, intentionally vague about it being my second interview. He reminded me how his deposition had been straightforward and that he could not recall answers to many of the committee's questions.

Ben was my friend, but for months, I had felt like I was under a microscope with him. I worried that if I appeared disloyal, Ben would tell Mark. So when Ben relayed that Mark was sending prayers and was confident in my loyalty to himself and the president—and that we were a family—I worried that my fear of having a target on my back was coming to fruition.

I did not think Ben was sending veiled threats, nor did I believe what he said amounted to witness tampering. I felt like I was being watched—closely.

———

The questions in my second Zoom deposition covered more ground. The committee members asked about the planning for the January 6th rally, and about my communications with Dan Scavino and event organizer Katrina Pierson about fringe elements taking the stage as speakers. Liz Cheney asked about the John Eastman scheme, and which House members were involved in the ploy to use fake electors in states that Trump had lost. They asked about a thirty-plus-page PowerPoint that supposedly revealed how Venezuela and Italy got control of Dominion voting machines. And they wanted to know about Mark's involvement in all of it.

It lasted seven hours, with breaks. This time around, I didn't overuse "I don't know" and "I don't recall." I was still trying to walk the balance beam—protecting myself from Trump World retaliation while dropping bread crumbs the committee could follow up on in depositions with other people. I wasn't being helpful, but I didn't want to mislead, either. I asked the investigators to repeat questions, and I gave more than a few overly parsed answers that were so granular they became meaningless. I was trying to run out the clock, get through it unscathed. Stefan was more active this time, piping up and shifting in his chair if he felt I was getting too specific.

Stefan congratulated me when I finished. "You did what you had to do," Stefan said. "It's done. You're good."

"It's funny. I feel like it's not over," I countered.

"Dan George said they don't need to talk to you again." He repeated, "You did what you had to do."

We said goodbye. "You did great," Stefan added. "I'll be in touch with you if anything comes up."

"Okay," I replied half-heartedly, and walked outside, alone, in the pouring rain.

CHAPTER 22

The Woman in the Mirror

I STRUGGLED FOR SEVERAL WEEKS, but my feelings of guilt over not telling the committee the whole truth eventually began to subside. *Stefan was right. It wasn't my responsibility to volunteer information.* No sooner had I begun to move on than my name was broadcast on the news networks the evening of Friday, April 22. I received a news alert that the committee had filed a motion for summary judgment against Mark Meadows for refusing to comply with a subpoena. The filing included excerpts from my February and March transcripts.

I opened the link to a news article and started reading the filing. When the first page of my transcript appeared, my heart stopped. *I don't want to relive this. What exactly did I say? What exactly was I helping cover up?* I put on a sweatshirt and shoes and went for a walk. I went in circles around the Navy Yard and finally sat on a bench on New Jersey Avenue that had a view of the Capitol.

I know I'm going to have to read this, and once I do, I know I'm going to be disappointed in myself. I did what I had to do, though.

I gazed at the Capitol for a long time, hoping that the view would reassure me. When that didn't work, I retreated to my apartment. *I guess it's time to read it.*

I read through the pages from the beginning, once, twice, and again. I opened my blinds for the first time in months and looked at my partial view of the Capitol, not much more than a bit of the top of the Statue of Freedom on the dome. I felt overcome by the thought that I had become someone I didn't expect or want to be. *There's more to the story than what's contained in these pages. I withheld information from the committee. I protected principals, not my principles. Is it too late to fix it?*

I called Sam, who, as usual, offered sound advice. I asked if he had read my transcript. He hadn't. I told him that I thought I had put myself in a position I didn't want to be in.

"You have a decision to make," he told me. "Go look in the mirror right now. I mean it, I'll hold, go look in the mirror right now. Do you like what you're looking at? And I don't mean your appearance. Do you respect the person you're looking at? Because you're going to have to look at that person for the rest of your life. The only person you have to live with, Cassidy, is yourself. I can't make that decision for you."

I exhaled. "I'm scared."

"You have every right to be scared. I'd be scared too. But are you more scared to live with that person, that person you're looking at, or are you more scared to ask for a second chance?"

The committee's filing was the main news story that weekend. The details reported from my transcripts didn't tell the whole story, and I knew it. But they were covered as if they were breaking news anyway.

I pressed Stefan to acknowledge that my concerns about the depositions were valid, as was my guilt about my testimony. Stefan reassured me by text that no one in Trump World was mad at me, including the president. He'd heard from Mar-a-Lago that if Trump was "ticked off" at anyone, it was former advisor and spokesman Jason Miller, who was also cited in the Meadows brief. "It's a good reminder that the boss *does* read transcripts," warned Stefan. "Whatever he's reading isn't going to put you in a bad situation."

My emotional dam was crumbling, but in my heart, I knew what I had to do.

I almost turned around as I walked up the flagstone sidewalk to Alyssa Farah's Georgetown row house. But she opened the door, holding a glass of wine, and welcomed me inside. It was the first time I'd seen her since December 2020, and the first time in months that I felt I was where I should be. There was a bit of awkward tension at the start. At that point she and I were in two different worlds. She had encouraged me to join her, an invitation I had ignored. Now I was reconsidering, and I needed her help. But was it too late?

After two glasses of wine and an hour spent avoiding the subject, I mustered the courage to address the elephant in the room. "Alyssa, I think I'm on the wrong side of this. I've made mistakes. Probably some bad mistakes. I don't know what to do."

She placed her wineglass on the coffee table and scooted to the cushion next to me. She put her elbow on the back of the couch, and rested her head on the back of her hand.

"Who's paying your legal bills?"

"I don't know," I answered. "I'm not trying to be cagey. I assume someone or something in Trump World, but Stefan won't tell me."

"How much trouble do you think you're in?" she asked, trying to gauge the seriousness of my situation.

"I don't know. Stefan told me I'm not in any trouble, that I did the right thing." Alyssa rolled her eyes and began to respond. I cut her off. "But I don't trust him. And I don't know who to trust. I think I need help."

She asked if I wanted a new lawyer. I told her I needed to do this in a way that wouldn't alert Trump World to what I was up to. I couldn't fire Stefan without tripping alarms at Mar-a-Lago.

"You can make the break, Cassidy," she said, with frustration in her voice.

"I think I'm in too deep, Alyssa. Can we try something else first?"

We talked over my options, and she agreed to contact Liz Cheney on my behalf about scheduling another interview. I cautioned her that there would likely be aggressive resistance from Stefan. I would probably need a subpoena or he would reject the request. I had every intention of complying fully, I told her, but without another subpoena, Stefan may encourage me not to cooperate.

Alyssa nodded and said, "Liz will probably ask for a few things you wanted to talk about before she agrees to do another interview." I knew she was right, but I couldn't proffer information already covered in my earlier depositions. That would tip Stefan off.

"The committee never asked if I went to the Oval dining room on January 6, or whether I heard about Trump's reaction to the rioters chanting 'Hang Mike Pence.' According to Mark, Trump said, 'He deserves it.'"

Alyssa closed her eyes at my revelation about the vice president, her former boss. I wanted to comfort her but hesitated. For too long, and often alone, Alyssa had warned the public about the dangers of Donald Trump, a duty I now recognized as a badge of courage and endurance—of survival. While she refused to surrender, I had been complicit.

"Cassidy, if we do this, you must promise me you'll be forthcoming. If Liz agrees, this will be your only shot at a second chance."

I lifted my glass to my lips and swallowed a mouthful of wine. "You have my word."

I knew what I was about to do would require a level of doubledealing I wasn't sure I was capable of, and I feared getting caught by Trump World—by my own attorney, even. I wasn't sure I had the fortitude to see it through.

———

Filled with anxious energy, I sped to New Jersey to Mom and Paul's house. I needed a guide, a moral compass, to remind me what was at stake. I picked up my phone, ignoring safe driving conventions, and tapped "Watergate" into the Google search bar, looking for someone who'd had a role similar to mine in the Nixon White House.

That's when I discovered Alex Butterfield, deputy assistant to the president and chief of staff H. R. Haldeman. I didn't know it then, but the person whose name I had just seen for the first time would alter the course of my life.

This guy must have written a book. I searched. He hadn't. Nor could I easily find a transcript of his Watergate committee interview, or any interview. I instantly had a good impression of him. I did find a book that had been written about him, by famed *Washington Post* reporter Bob Woodward: *The Last of the President's Men.* It was a look back, fifty years after the fact, at Butterfield's role in the Watergate investigation. I immediately ordered two copies. When the books arrived to New Jersey the next day, I tore open the package as I ran upstairs to my bedroom.

I read the book three times that night—quickly the first time; I devoured it. As I turned each page, I kept thinking, *Oh my God, Alex Butterfield is me.* The position he held essentially as chief of staff to the chief of staff, the way he viewed his role and operated behind the scenes, and how he valued his relationship with the president were all nearly aligned with my experience. In the inner circle, he was close to Nixon, but chose to add a small degree of separation, more than others around the president. He had information that he didn't want to voluntarily disclose because of his loyalty to Nixon, and he valued his anonymity. But his fidelity was to the Constitution, to the country he swore an oath to protect, and to the public who demanded his trust. He felt he owed it to the country and the investigators to reveal the truth or else imperil our democracy.

While I found encouragement throughout the book, the final pages offered a revelation that would change the course of my journey. When asked if he were given the chance to turn back time, Alex declared he would not: "No regrets. If I had to do it over again, I figure I'd do the very same thing."

In that moment, I recognized how fear had restrained me from making the decision I knew in my heart was right. For the first time, I felt empowered to make the difficult choice to correct course and found the strength to see it through. I had rediscovered my moral compass.

I ran down to get a bottle of water and a highlighter; back upstairs, reading the book the second time, I marked passages and created a personal index of sorts. I studied the evolution of Butterfield's thinking about his congressional testimony. He had resolved to give a direct response to a pointed question by committee investigators, which supplied crucial details to the investigation. When I cycled through and started the book the third time, I stuck Post-its on pages I thought were particularly profound.

I was still reading when Paul woke up for work at five thirty. I went downstairs as he was making his breakfast. "Hey, kiddo, you're up early," he observed. "No," I said with a laugh, "I'm actually up late."

The first beams of sunlight came through my windows as I climbed into bed. I knew that what I was going to do was right for my country and right for me. Alex Butterfield would be my guide out of the morass of suspicions and misplaced loyalties that had kept me in a near-permanent state of anxiety. I took one last glance at *The Last of the President's Men* on my bedside table before resting my eyes.

I'm going to pass the mirror test.

———

On my drive back to Washington, on Thursday, April 28, I missed a call from an employee of GETTR, a new social media platform founded by Jason Miller. I was offered a job at GETTR after my second committee interview. When I returned the call, the tone of his voice was different, apologetic. I immediately knew what was coming—GETTR was rescinding the job offer. My heartbeat quickened, and I muted my line while I steadied myself. I had to act natural, disappointed, but supportive of the decision.

It took several minutes for me to calm down after we hung up. Though I was desperate for income, I was relieved that my next paycheck wouldn't come from GETTR. But this call struck me with intense fear that Trump was already onto me. My second chance relied entirely on zero suspicion from the former president and his associates. I had to be more careful.

———

Stefan called the next day to relay the committee's unprecedented request for a third interview, in person.

"What the hell, Stefan! Why?" I moaned, I hoped convincingly. "You said we were done. What could they possibly want to talk to me about?"

He had no idea, he said, after sympathizing with me. He would follow up with Dan to try to get more information out of him. I told him I didn't think I could refuse to cooperate. Stefan's preference was to have me appear extremely resistant to the idea of a third interview. He thought that the committee might back off if we made enough of a fuss. "But," he added, "if we even think about engaging with them, there is no way that we can do this without a second subpoena."

"Trump World will not continue paying your legal bills," Stefan said, "if you don't have a second subpoena."

Any hope I clung to about a proper attorney-client relationship disappeared like vapor. I didn't remark on the disclosure or do or say anything to indicate I was anything other than surprised and frustrated by the committee's decision.

"You're right, Stefan. I think we would need a second subpoena."

I was scared that Stefan would see through me. The news had gotten out that the committee wanted another round with me, and it was making Trump World nervous.

Stefan seemed to become a little distant right about then. He didn't respond to my texts as quickly as he had before—or even at

288 | CASSIDY HUTCHINSON

all, to some messages. He did encourage me to call Alex Cannon and another Trump lawyer, Justin Clark, about a job opportunity, assuring me that everyone was aware that the committee was treating me unfairly, and that everyone was working hard to find a good job for me. I heard from other Trump associates as well, with other job ideas.

Alex set up an interview for me with Red Curve Solutions, a political fundraising and financial services company run by Bradley Crate, the treasurer for Trump's super PACs. "Brad has a really good job for you," Alex promised. "It's going to pay a great salary. We know you're on our team. We know you're going to do the right thing."

Alex added, "Not to get too personal, Cassidy, but do you need anything else? Are you okay financially? I'm so sorry you're in this position. Whatever you need, just tell us. We'll make sure you have it."

I interviewed with Red Curve Solutions on May 10. Their pitch was by now a familiar one: they'd heard great things about me and wanted to hire me, and were working on finding the right position. They'd be back in touch in a few weeks, which I took to mean after my next deposition, if I still had value to them. They wouldn't have long to wait. I received my second subpoena that same day.

———

May 17, the day I hoped to gain a second chance, ideally with my intentions undetected, had arrived. I thought I was ready, but I panicked when I entered the small, claustrophobic room in the Cannon building where Liz Cheney and Dan George, senior investigative counsel for the committee, were waiting for my arrival. Large cameras pointed at where I would sit, on a small sofa with

Stefan seated next to me. Liz and Dan would be on the other side of a coffee table. I dropped my purse and left the room.

I may have left had I not been able to collect myself in the restroom. *Was I making the right decision?* When I returned to the room, I perched uncomfortably on the edge of the sofa cushion. Stefan looked at me with concern. While he had tried to limit the questions in the new subpoena, the committee insisted that the conditions were the same as with the first, which meant that they could ask me anything.

"Okay to get started?" Dan asked. He ran through the preliminaries. Then Liz took over. "The committee has been involved in collecting information in a number of ways," she said. "And additional information has come to light since we talked to you . . . I am going to ask you some questions about both what you may have heard and also what others may have told you that they heard."

I listened intently as I waited for her first question. I expected her to ask a few easy warm-up questions to put me at ease before she dropped any bombshells. Instead she zeroed in, calmly asking: "Did you see or hear President Trump say anything on January 6th after he returned from the Ellipse? . . . Because we have information that the president said, 'Mike Pence deserves to be hung.'"

She sat back and watched, unblinking, as I mustered my response. If she had wanted me to seem shocked for Stefan's benefit, it worked. I was. Stefan knew that story, and he had probably breathed a sigh of relief that it hadn't come up in my first two depositions. But it was plausible that someone else had told the committee that story, and now they needed me to corroborate it.

I replied carefully that I'd heard it "secondhand from Mr. Meadows . . . I don't know if that was the exact quote, but it was something along those lines." Out of the corner of my eye, I saw Stefan looking at me as I talked. *How couldn't he know?* He opened his briefcase and took out a legal pad. He hadn't taken many notes in my previous depositions; now he began to scribble furiously. He wouldn't stop for five hours.

Liz didn't address any of the subjects that I had previously discussed with the committee. But she raised all kinds of new and well-informed inquiries, which I haltingly answered. In response to direct questions, I divulged information about Mark speaking to General Flynn, on January 5, 2021, about his meeting in the Willard Inter-Continental, about burning documents in his office fireplace and taking home red folders with classified documents. I described the meeting in the Cabinet Room, on December 21, where the Oath Keepers and the Proud Boys were discussed, and the "find me the votes" phone call with Georgia election officials, on January 2. I told the committee that Trump had known that rally-goers had brought sharpened flag poles and other weapons with them, and that he had still wanted to get them into the rally on the Ellipse. I confirmed that the Outer Oval had stopped keeping a log of the president's meetings and phone calls. I described the January 4 flight from Georgia with Marjorie Taylor Greene, when she bragged about her QAnon fans. I gave Liz the names of members of Congress and other officials who had wanted blanket or preemptive pardons, including Mark.

We took a few breaks, and Stefan and I walked down the hall to confer privately. Each time, he asked, "How do they know this stuff? Who's talking?"

"I don't know who's talking," I said with faux outrage. "But this is insane."

When the five-hour deposition wrapped up, Dan brought up the possibility of another interview to dig deeper into the classified documents issue. Stefan wasn't happy about that, and neither was I. When they turned off the cameras, I slumped back on the sofa, exhausted. Stefan shook Liz's hand and then talked to Dan about something. Liz came over to me and gave me a hug.

Whispering in my ear, she said, "Thank you."

"I'm really trying to do the right thing," I whispered back.

Dan, Stefan, and I walked out of the Cannon building. I had a split second with Dan to say goodbye. We shook hands, and I said quietly, "I'm about to get nuked."

He nodded slightly. "I'm so sorry." He turned around and went back into the building.

It was 7:30 p.m., still sunny. My ears were ringing from the stress of the day.

When we reached the street, Stefan seemed perplexed. "I don't even know what to do first," he announced to no one in particular. "Let's get something to eat," he suggested. "We should eat." *No. I just want to go home.* I was drained, and every moment I spent with Stefan came with a risk that I would reveal myself. But I didn't think I could refuse his offer without doing just that, so I agreed.

He hailed a taxi and gave the driver the address of Hank's Oyster Bar at the Wharf. As soon as we took off, Stefan's phone started ringing. I assumed it was Eric Herschmann or Alex Cannon, but was surprised when I learned it was a reporter calling.

"Stefan, did you tell the reporter that we were meeting with the committee today?" I asked.

"No, no, but I should probably answer to see if they know, right? I should answer," he responded.

"Stefan, no. I don't think you should answer that call. They probably want to know if we met with the committee today."

"Cass, I'm just going to answer. It will be just two seconds." He answered the call.

I could not hear what the reporter was saying, but I did hear Stefan say, "Yeah, yeah, we did just leave her third interview. You can put it out, but don't make it too big of a deal. I don't think she'll want it to be too big of a deal. All right, thanks." And then he hung up.

"Stefan, were they asking about my third interview?" I asked, though I already knew the answer.

He was distracted, typing on his cell phone. "Yeah, but don't worry," Stefan started. "They won't make it a big deal."

"Stefan, I don't want this out there."

"Don't worry, the reporter is friendly to us. We'll be fine," he said, but that did not really matter to me. What *did* matter to me was maintaining my composure—and cover—which would become more difficult when the public, and Trump World, learned that I sat for a third interview.

The taxi pulled up outside Hank's. We went in and sat down at a table. I ordered an old-fashioned and downed half of it as soon as it arrived.

Stefan didn't order anything. "I really need to call John Moran and George Terwilliger about this," he said, referring to Mark's legal team.

"Stefan, I respectfully disagree. I do not think we need to call Terwilliger or Moran to tell them about this. I think that is actually the opposite of what we should do." I hoped the liquor would bolster my confidence, but it had not. "I do not think that they should know anything of what we just discussed with the committee, and I don't think they have the right to know what we just discussed with the committee."

Stefan argued the contrary. If we don't tell them and the story leaks, "it's going to look like you're working against Mark," he contended, "and then there's a target on your back." *There will be a target on my back either way,* I thought. *I'd rather it not be me or my lawyer who puts it there.*

Stefan's phone lit up: John Moran.

"Stefan—" I started to plead.

"Just trust me," Stefan interjected. "I'm going to take this." I sat at our table, alone, as Stefan walked out of Hank's to speak with Mark's legal team.

I finished my old-fashioned and ordered another. "All good," he announced when he returned a while later. "All good. Don't worry. They know everything. They're not mad at you. They know it's the committee's fault you were asked those questions." Stefan appeared relieved. I was not.

We ordered dinner, and Stefan continued to apologize for the position the committee put me in. *If only he knew,* I thought, *that it was not the committee that put me in this position. It was me. And I am not sorry about it.*

When we finished dinner, I readily called an Uber. I was ready to put this day behind me.

"I should probably tell my law partners, Alex Cannon and Justin Clark, about today. And Eric Herschmann should know about what happened, too," Stefan said. "Eric technically is not my law partner, but I think Eric deserves to know some of this, too."

"Whatever you think is best," was the response I could muster. I was not going to waste more energy trying to convince him to do something otherwise. If past was precedent, my efforts would be moot.

———

Liz and Dan had made clear that they would likely request a fourth interview with me in a sensitive compartmented information facility (SCIF) because of classified documents that we would discuss. Stefan wasn't in a hurry to give the committee another crack at me. "I made you out to be unwilling," he said, of his conversations with the committee.

One week after my third deposition, I received an email from Red Curve, notifying me that they did not have a job for me. With Stefan out of town, Alex Cannon took me out to dinner. He was genial, and mentioned a potential job with the Harriet Hageman campaign. Hageman was running in a Republican primary in Wyoming for the House seat then occupied by Liz Cheney. I had to put on my best poker face for this one.

Stefan continued to be elusive about a fourth interview and

the possibility that the committee would want me to testify in a live hearing. I continued to press him for insights into his conversations with the committee. Despite multiple news reports that my name was on the committee's short list of live-hearing witnesses, he denied having any conversation on that subject. Stefan told me that in his last conversation with Dan, he had emphasized that I would be an unhelpful live witness and would make it clear that I was testifying against my will. While I did not want to testify live, I was not planning to be unhelpful, nor would I accuse the committee of forcing me to testify against my will.

I was determined to uphold the oath I swore to tell the truth about what happened on January 6 and fulfill my civic obligation if I were called upon to do so. But with each passing minute, it was becoming increasingly difficult to dance around the Trump World land mines. I prayed the committee would entrust that duty to someone else.

———

On Monday, June 6, I woke up to a text message that I had prepared myself for but dreaded receiving. Over the weekend, the Department of Justice had declined to indict Mark and Dan Scavino for being held in contempt of Congress. In light of this decision, Stefan suggested that it was in my best interest to stop cooperating with the committee. "There is a small element of risk to refusing to cooperate, but I think it's the best move for you. Do you agree?" Stefan texted.

I did not agree. I tried to set aside what I thought was my lawyer suggesting that a federal offense—which carried the possibility of serving time in prison—was a "small element of risk." But beyond that, my reputation and livelihood would suffer severe damage if I was criminally referred for contempt of Congress. That might be the best move for someone else, but it was difficult to see how that was the best move for me.

I read his text repeatedly, as if the words before me would

change under my gaze. Eventually my phone screen turned black, and I knew that it was time to respond. Rather than address his proposition directly, I asked Stefan, again, whether the committee had reached out about a live hearing. I thought that if he gave me a truthful answer in response, I might be able to salvage what remained of our attorney-client relationship and come up with a plan that worked for both of us.

An hour passed and he still had not responded to my text. I wrote another. "I don't want to gamble with being held in contempt, Stefan. I'm sorry, but I just don't think I can do it." I tapped the words onto my screen and I sent the text without a second thought. Minutes later, my phone vibrated. "They have not," he replied. I kept staring at the screen, waiting for him to acknowledge what I had said about risking contempt. He never did.

I flung my phone onto the couch and began to pace the length of my apartment. For weeks, I had thought about how I would react if this exact predicament were to arise. Practically speaking, I had several choices. I could accept Stefan's counsel and run the "small risk" of a contempt charge, or continue trying to convince him I could comply with the committee's requests and still balance Trump World's interests, or admit to him that a crisis of conscience had compelled me to back-channel the committee to arrange my third interview. With each came risk.

But I knew in my heart that choice was a luxury I did not have. There was only one option—to fulfill my moral and civic obligations. To honor the oath I swore to defend, I had to free myself from Trump World. All I had to do was figure out a way to free myself without doing anything that would draw their attention and arouse suspicion.

Time, too, was a luxury I did not have. I estimated I had twenty-four hours—forty-eight, if I was lucky—before the pressure campaign intensified for me to agree with risking contempt. I found my phone on the couch and scrolled through my contacts to the only person I had not yet turned to for guidance.

I sent a text asking if we could find time to talk on the phone and sent it before I had a chance to proofread it. I immediately began to panic and put my phone on Do Not Disturb before abandoning it on the couch. When I returned to it an hour later, I saw that I had a missed call. I texted again, and we agreed on a new time to talk. I inhaled deeply when Liz Cheney called, right on schedule.

"Hey, Liz. I really appreciate you taking the time to talk to me, and I'm so sorry to bother you."

"Hi, Cassidy. Of course, and you're not bothering me," she replied. I offered a brief synopsis of the predicament I found myself in with my current counsel. I told her that I was not asking her to confirm or deny the committee's correspondence with Stefan. Nor was I asking for a live hearing or additional interviews. But if the committee was interested in continuing discussions, I was not comfortable moving forward with Stefan and would likely represent myself. Her voice grew more serious, which I didn't think was possible, and she suggested that I explore other options before serving as my own counsel.

I briefly explained how *very* unsuccessful my attorney search had been from November to January, and told her that I had only turned to Trump World for an attorney because of personal financial constraints. Since then, my finances had continued to suffer, and I had nothing to offer a new attorney. I asked if she or any of the members or committee staff might know an attorney who would be willing to put me on a payment plan. Liz said that she would follow up after she spoke with colleagues.

The next day, she called and provided me with contact information for multiple attorneys at various firms. I thanked her and promised that I would figure out a way to do the right thing, regardless of the outcome of the search for new counsel. I could not find the words to tell her that the committee was giving me one of the greatest gifts I could have received: hope.

I reached out to the attorneys to schedule calls, then packed a small overnight bag and began driving to New Jersey.

Afternoon traffic delayed my arrival at the rest stop I'd earmarked as the place to take my first call. Panicked I would miss the call, I swerved off the highway and into a Wendy's parking lot just as my phone began to ring.

"Hi, Cassidy. This is Bill Jordan, of Alston & Bird. Hang on one moment, I'm going to patch my colleague Jody Hunt into the call." I waited quietly until Jody joined. Though I strongly preferred in-person meetings over phone calls or videoconferences, I was immediately impressed with how natural the conversation seemed.

Bill and Jody listened intently as I gave them an in-depth recounting of my initial search for a non–Trump World attorney, and how Stefan had come to represent me. I provided an overview of my committee interviews so far, explained my current predicament with Stefan, and said that I was under the impression that the committee was possibly interested in a SCIF interview and live testimony.

There was a beat of silence, then Bill cleared his throat. "Well, Cassidy, it sounds like you've had quite the adventure the last few years." He added that Alston & Bird was not representing any clients involved with January 6th matters, including to the committee. I felt my expression flatten. Back in November, a number of attorneys had said something similar before declining to represent me pro bono or at an affordable rate, and although I had just begun speaking to Bill and Jody, I thought that our conversation was going well.

"So, I'm actually a little tied up for the next two weeks," Bill explained. "By that I mean completely off-grid. I'll be in the desert on a Boy Scout backpacking trip with my youngest son." I was about to thank them for taking the time to speak with me when Jody interjected. "But I'll be around and will make myself available to work with you in Bill's absence, then we'll catch him up when he returns.

"Just so you're prepared, Cassidy," Jody continued, "whether you move forward with us or a different attorney, it sounds like there will be a lot of catch-up for your new team to do. The sooner you can retain a lawyer, the better served you will be." I was encouraged, but we hadn't yet addressed my least favorite discussion topic.

"I need to be up front with you two. I really don't have any money to give you right now, and I do not have any resources to take out a loan. If it's possible and you're willing, I thought we could discuss a payment plan . . ." I began to ramble, but Bill cut me off. "I'm sorry. We should have led with this. There is no universe where you, a former government employee in your midtwenties, should be expected to shell out hundreds of thousands of dollars in legal fees. If you choose to work with us, your legal services will be one hundred percent pro bono."

My mind whirred. I don't remember the sequence of my responses, only that I checked and double-checked that they knew I had been expecting to pay them. When they reiterated the pro bono arrangement, I fought back tears while thanking them. Bill and Jody told me to take some time to think over my decision, and we ended the call.

I rested my head against the back of my seat and watched cars pull into the Wendy's drive-through. Our call had exceeded my expectations. Bill and Jody had met when they worked together at the Justice Department under President George W. Bush. When Bill's tenure at Justice had ended, he had returned to private practice at Alston & Bird, in Atlanta, Georgia. He remained active in Republican politics and had served as general counsel for the Republican Party and head of the state ethics watchdog in Georgia.

Jody had served in senior career positions at Justice for more than twenty years before he was asked to be chief of staff for Attorney General Jeff Sessions. He'd been selected for the job because of his outstanding credentials as a nonpartisan attorney who knew the intricacies of the department. As in my role with Mark, Jody had been privy to a lot of information in his role as chief of staff. He became a key witness during the Mueller investigation. After serving as the attorney general's chief of staff, Jody was confirmed by the US Senate to serve as assistant attorney general for DOJ's Civil Division. He had then moved to private practice at Alston & Bird.

While Alston & Bird had declined to take on clients who were involved with the January 6th matter, there was a rumor going around Washington that one of the firm's attorneys, Bjay Pak, was slated to testify before the committee in the coming weeks. Pak had resigned his post as US Attorney for the Northern District of Georgia when Trump's pressure campaign to get Georgia officials to overturn the election results intensified just days before the riot.

Both Bill and Jody were lifelong Republicans and unaffiliated with Trump World, and in my mind they checked every box—meeting every requirement and wish I'd come up with since I was first subpoenaed in November 2021. I was so optimistic about working with them that I was tempted to cancel the rest of the calls I had scheduled. But I had made a promise to Liz and the January 6th Committee and would follow through, and I fielded attorney calls for the remainder of my drive to New Jersey.

The next day, I called Bill and Jody during their first free moment and told them it would be a privilege to move forward with their counsel. We scheduled to meet in person at Alston & Bird's Washington office the next day. Jody promised to have an engagement letter ready for me to sign when I arrived, and he asked me to bring a copy of the engagement letter I had signed with Stefan, as well as any other material Stefan and I had produced together. "Well, funny story," I said. "I never signed an engagement letter with Stefan. I asked for one, but he said we weren't doing engagement letters, that they weren't necessary." The line was quiet, and I felt an urge to fill the silence. "I'm sorry . . ." I started.

"Don't apologize. But there's really no engagement letter?" Jody asked.

"No, there's not," I replied. "Well, then, just bring yourself! I'll write a draft email for you to send Stefan, if you'd like." I accepted his offer.

I was soaking up the last few minutes of the day's sun in my parents' backyard before I drove back to Washington when my phone vibrated with a call from Stefan. He had been trying to reach me all day. I was trying to put him off until I switched legal counsel the following day. I answered the call and apologized for not having answered. Stefan was unfazed and picked up where we had left off about the contempt charge. I lay in the grass and stared into the cloudless sky, half listening as he droned on about how not cooperating with the committee was best for everyone.

"Everyone" did not include the tens of millions of Americans who had been lied to about the results of a free, fair, and democratic election; it did not include the families of law enforcement officers who had lost their lives defending the Capitol from the mob Trump had called to Washington. "Everyone" did not include the lawmakers, staff, and journalists who feared for their lives as rioters bludgeoned their way into the building. It did not include the investigators who were being stonewalled by former colleagues of mine who dismissed the investigation as a politically motivated witch hunt.

"Everyone" who would benefit from my ceasing to cooperate with the January 6th Committee was limited to people in Trump World whose personal interests could be affected by my testimony. In less than twenty-four hours, they would all find out that I was no longer protecting "everyone." I had found my way out.

I asked Stefan if I could have a little more time to think my decision over. He agreed but repeated, "This needs to end at some point, and I think it just needs to end now."

Those were Stefan's parting words. We would never speak again.

I laid my phone in the grass and shielded my eyes from the sun.

This is going to end soon.

CHAPTER 23

Second Chance

"DON'T WORRY, HONEY, I won't give you a ticket," the parking enforcement officer kindly called out as I sprinted up Tenth Street, my car parked a little too near a fire hydrant. "Thank you," I gasped. I barely made it on time for my first meeting at Alston & Bird, and struggled to catch my breath as I was ushered into the conference room. The receptionist informed me that Jody was running a little behind.

The conference room at Alston & Bird was warm and inviting, unlike the fishbowl austerity of the rooms at Michael Best where I had conferred with Stefan. The table held food and drinks, and notebooks and pens. I sat my bag on a leather armchair and walked to the windows overlooking F Street. I idly gazed at the activity below, consumed with thoughts of how the next few months of my life could play out.

I had learned over the last several years that I thrived when I had someone or something bigger than myself to fight for. I had always wanted to be a bulldog for the truth, or what I believed to be the truth. I realized now that what I wanted most was to hold accountable people who had selfishly risked the country's welfare. They needed to answer for what they had done and what they had failed to do. But to fight for that truth meant I would be up against the president and chief of staff I had dutifully served, the friends and colleagues I had once fought alongside, and my own fears and uncertainties.

I was so deep in my thoughts that I jumped when I heard "Hey there!" I spun around and saw my new attorney, Jody, walk into the conference room. I pushed my shoulders back and stepped forward to shake his hand.

"So, first thing first," Jody said, handing me a printed-out email that I would send to Stefan, thanking him and terminating our attorney-client relationship, as discussed. I was to include Jody's name and contact number. Jody looked over my shoulder as I typed the email word for word on my laptop. My finger hovered above the cursor. I turned to Jody. "Are you sure this is the right decision?" I asked him. "I am," he said. I clicked Send and closed my laptop.

"Well, the hard part is done. Now let's see if Stefan reaches out." Jody slid a file across the table. "Why don't you read through our engagement letter while we wait?"

I felt like I had forgotten how to read, and found myself just staring at the document. A wave of peace and gratitude washed over me. *A real engagement letter.* Jody's phone vibrated, and we exchanged a look. "It's Stefan," Jody said. "I'll be back in a few minutes." He walked out to take the call in another room.

Smoothing my black blazer dress, I noticed that I had scuffed my black heels while running to the office. I took a deep breath and started reading the engagement letter. I searched for the two words in particular that mattered to me: pro bono.

I wondered what Jody and Stefan were talking about. I hoped Stefan wasn't upset and wouldn't take my decision personally. I wrestled with feelings of mercy and compassion for him. I truly believed that he wished he could have done more for me. Stefan was in a hole that he had dug for himself. But Trump had handed him the shovel. They owned Stefan—he had no way out. *That could have been me.*

It almost was. I did not find the path to my newfound freedom—I bushwhacked my way, and was now free to empower my patriotism again and, as Alex Butterfield had, to reveal the truth rather than be a bystander.

When Jody returned, he flashed a thumbs-up. "All good."

"Is Stefan upset with me?" I asked.

"No, he's not upset with you. He understands these things happen, and he honestly sounded a little relieved."

I checked my phone as I listened to his assurances, and noticed a missed call, a text, and an email from Stefan, all sent before Jody had talked to him. I turned my phone toward Jody and smirked. "This is the fastest response I've gotten from him in months."

Jody laughed, and asked if I had any questions about the engagement letter. I flipped to the last page and signed my name. "Nope."

"Alright, then. I guess we should start at the beginning."

"Okay," I said hesitatingly. "But first, would you mind if I go find a better parking spot?"

The rest of that day was spent telling Jody and Stephen Simrill, an Alston & Bird associate, the story of the past twenty months. I was nervous about doing so, but knew I needed to trust them, though they were still strangers to me. I was guarded in the beginning and at times hesitant to reveal all that I had seen and witnessed. It would be the only completely forthcoming account I'd offered anyone outside the Trump administration, and breaking the code of silence felt like deviant behavior.

When I returned to my apartment, I went to a common space to watch the January 6th Committee's first live hearing in prime time. I listened to the testimony of Capitol Police officer Caroline Edwards and Nick Quested, a British documentary filmmaker. Quested had been at the Capitol on the sixth with a crew, cameras rolling. I admired their willingness to testify and their grace under pressure. I was not confident I could ever do it myself.

I cherished my anonymity. I didn't have active social media accounts. There were few pictures of me on the internet. You never saw me quoted on the record in news stories. I guarded my privacy zealously. It was my protection. If my face were plastered all over TV and the internet, I'd lose control of what I laughingly called the mystique of operating quietly behind the scenes. My depositions had been recorded, and I hoped that the committee would be content with using clips from them.

Jody called after the hearing to let me know that by morning the committee would have given us online access to my February, March, and May transcripts for review. He was flying home to Alabama for the weekend, but we needed to spend those days raking through each transcript so that we were prepared to officially begin our work on Monday. All I could think about was the possibility of testifying at a live hearing. "I really don't think I would be able to testify live. Could we please do everything we can to make sure I don't have to?"

He took a moment before responding. "Get a good night's sleep. You had a long day, and we have a lot of long days ahead of us."

As promised, the committee shared my transcripts with us the next morning, and I immediately began my independent review. I was not yet halfway through my first transcript when Jody called and began peppering me with questions about my testimony. I immediately heard his tone shift to apprehension and concern.

I reminded Jody that Stefan and I had not prepared for my prior interviews, and that without notes, a calendar, or anything to reference, I had found it difficult to answer the committee's questions. I had also taken pains, in those depositions, to heed the counsel I had received and the expectations I felt beholden to—while also attempting to honor the truth. Jody understood but acknowledged the reality of what was in front of us.

At that juncture, the committee still thought that they might have to bring me into a SCIF. They were figuring out whether I should testify live. Based on our conversations and his experience dealing with classified matters at the Department of Justice, Jody recognized that there was no need for an interview with the committee in a SCIF. That meant that my testimony to the committee was complete, other than with regard to the possibility of a live hearing. From Jody's perspective, this was a serious issue. I remembered far more than I had testified to in my three interviews before the committee, and I could indeed recall the details I had previously denied knowledge of. Jody explained that my record was incomplete and in some instances inaccurate.

His sole focus was protecting me. For him to protect me, I had to clarify, and in some cases correct, my previous testimony. Without that opportunity, I was at risk for perjury for any future testimony I would give to the January 6th Committee, the Department of Justice, or other investigative bodies. "You have a subpoena. You are under oath," Jody admonished me. "You have no claim of privilege to assert. And so you have one job, and one job only—to tell the truth and nothing but the truth, no matter who the truth may help or hurt."

He was right, and he had to figure out how to convince the committee to allow me to return for a fourth interview.

I spent the weekend combing through every word of each transcript to identify places we needed to expand upon my previous testimony. I put together Excel spreadsheets with dates and key events, reconstructed my calendar, chronologized any correspondence I had to fit the timelines, and wrote detailed synopses of each day.

I arrived at Alston & Bird an hour early on Monday morning. We had blocked out the whole day to go through my transcripts. Jody arrived looking cheerful and carrying a bag of pastries from Tatte Bakery. My eyes lit up.

"Happy Monday! I picked us up some pastries. Have you ever been to Tatte?"

"Yeah, actually, it's my favorite bakery in the city. I haven't gone there since the end of the administration."

"Then it's time to dig in. I have a goal to try every one of their pastries before the end of the summer. Let's do it together." Jody handed me the bag, and I savored my first bite of a morning bun.

Having gone through the prior transcripts, we dug in to cross-compare what we were working with and were meticulous with every single detail. There was too much at stake for our work to be less than perfect.

Once we began to grasp the degree of information in our possession, Jody reached out to the January 6th Committee and suggested that we schedule a proffer session. Our hope was to convince the committee that a fourth interview, in which I could "correct, clarify, and elaborate on" my previous responses, was in everyone's best interests. The committee agreed to entertain a proffer.

Later that week, Jody and Stephen trekked to Capitol Hill for the proffer session with Liz Cheney and senior committee investigators, while I impatiently paced my apartment. Jody called after a few hours to brief me on the meeting. First, after he and Stephen had explained the situation to the committee and had gone over some additions to the record that I was prepared to describe, the members had quickly agreed that a fourth interview was necessary. Before Jody and Stephen left, the committee also broached the subject of calling me as a witness in a hearing. They suggested that I might be able to testify with a group. Or they might ask me to testify on my own. Jody asked for my comfort level with each of the two possible scenarios.

Zero. My comfort level was zero. I suggested that we get through the fourth interview—maybe they would not ask me to testify live after all. Jody was unconvinced of this, but I had made the impossible happen before. Jody just had to learn that for himself.

―――――

I had my well-organized binder in hand when we arrived at the Capitol on the afternoon of June 20, filled with calendars, chronologies, and transcript notes. As we walked across the East Plaza, I stared up at the Capitol dome, and for the first time since January 6, I felt its magnetism and power. And next to my new counsel, I felt empowered. Together we would honor the place that symbolizes, more than any other monument, a free people's faith in self-government.

Dan George escorted us to Liz's hideaway office in the basement of the Capitol. As I entered, Liz embraced me. Her gesture and warmth conveyed a sense of understanding and purpose.

We fell into a quick rhythm as Liz and Dan began to question me, and over the next seven hours, I shared everything I had observed in the post-election period. There was no obfuscating this time. Liz and Dan came with prepared questions, largely based on Jody's proffer. I was able to provide greater context than before, and, often, excruciating detail. We methodically combed through each of my transcripts, and I expanded upon my previous interviews line by line.

While I had hesitated in previous interviews to share details about the president's unhinged behavior, I now understood the gravity of those moments. Trump's temperament wasn't rational, but neither was it unfamiliar to me. His outbursts shed light on how his volcanic temper and egotism had lit the match that set his followers' torches ablaze.

When we left the Capitol that night, I felt that I had finally fulfilled the obligations of my subpoena and the oath I had sworn to the country. The only cloud on the horizon that evening was my lingering worry that the committee would call me as a witness in a future hearing.

Jody and I crossed Constitution Avenue and hailed a cab. We were quiet for most of the ride to Alston & Bird. I finally broke the silence when I asked, "Jody, be honest, how likely is it that they'll call me to testify at a hearing?"

He looked at me over his glasses and said with a slight smirk, "Oh, there's a very good chance."

CHAPTER 24

The Whole Truth

I HAD ADORED THE PRESIDENT. I'd been very close to Mark Meadows. I had loved working in the White House. I deeply cared for the people there. I believed sincerely that we were serving the interests of the American people. I regretted the belligerence and crudity of some of the president's messaging, the inappropriate, unpresidential tweets. But you can become inured to it, and I did. I often laughed with colleagues at his communications, when I should have seen them for what they were—mean-spirited. Politics is a team sport, and I was a willing teammate.

Even Trump's tantrums hadn't made me angry. Whenever I witnessed or heard about him losing his temper, it hurt me to see him upset. My first thought was why had people let it go so far. Couldn't we have done more—couldn't I have done more—to serve him better, to avoid upsetting him.

My views of Trump would change as I witnessed his selfish recklessness threatening the country's constitutional order. My resolve only strengthened when my loyalties to him and my former colleagues were put in direct conflict with my obligations to the country.

———

After my fourth deposition, Jody goes to New York for a few days. Left to myself, I do my best to keep my mind off my situation. I'm frantically cleaning my apartment when my phone rings and

Jody's number appears. I know beyond the shadow of a doubt that he's calling with news about a hearing.

"They want to do a live hearing," he tells me, "and it's going to be next week."

I don't want Jody to think I'm weak. I'm not weak. I know I'm strong. But I need more time. *I just need more time.*

"Jody, I'm worried I'm not going to be a good live witness. I don't want to let anybody down." By anybody I mean almost everyone: the committee, Jody and Bill, the American people. I'm not worrying in that exact moment about the Trump wing of the GOP. I'm worrying about the people I'm going to care about when I am free from that world.

The fourth and fifth committee hearings had been held by then. They had gotten huge ratings—averaging ten million viewers—and momentum and anticipation for more had grown steadily since the first one.

"Cassidy, you're going to do just fine. I'll make sure you're prepared. The committee knows you recognize the importance of your testimony, and that's what matters. You need to have faith." I appreciate his confidence. He continues, "The hearing is scheduled for next Tuesday, and it sounds like you're going to be the only witness."

I think he's kidding. Since changing lawyers, I had stressed to Jody that if I had to testify live, I did not want to be the only witness. I know my life will change drastically after the hearing, and I will, for a while at least, be the subject of intense public scrutiny.

On Thursday night, I pull up to my parents' house for what I know will be my last visit for a long while. I have one weekend left to enjoy my anonymity, but I don't want to be alone. I haven't told Mom about the hearing or what I'd been asked in my fourth interview with the committee. All she knows is that I switched lawyers. I know she's stressing out about it. For one more night, I want to pretend that everything is alright.

On Friday morning, I go to my favorite local bagel shop and get an Asiago bagel with olive cream cheese, my regular order since I was a child. I bring it home and wash it down with a Nestlé Nesquik chocolate milk, another childhood favorite. I spend the rest of the morning and most of the afternoon lying in the sun in my parents' backyard, the same place I'd had my final phone call with Stefan. I coat myself in baby oil to get a deep tan. I'm a Jersey girl. I don't normally burn, but I do that day, and now I have another worry, that I'm going to look like a lobster at the hearing.

My mom gets home from work, and that evening we go to Target where we pick through a pile of T-shirts. Unprompted, I say, "Oh, by the way, I'm testifying next week."

"Another deposition?"

"No," I say. "Live. On TV."

"What? Cass, are you okay? Do you have something to wear?"

I laugh. "Nope. But I'll figure it out. It's not going to be a big deal. Can we please not talk about it?"

"Oh my God," she says, winding herself up. "What are you going to say? What don't I know?"

Everything, I think, *literally everything*. "Drop it, please. I don't have any more information right now."

The committee hasn't announced my hearing yet because of security concerns, which I do not tell Mom. If she knows that, she won't ever let the subject drop.

"I wish you could stay longer," Paul says as he wraps me in a bear hug Saturday morning. "I'll try to come home soon," I tell him. But I know that's not true. I know that won't be an option for a while. I merge onto the interstate. *When will I see my parents again?*

I stop at Zara in the Cherry Hill Mall in New Jersey. I'm worried about my clothes for the hearing. I want to look professional and demure. I don't want to wear anything distracting or anything that would attract commentary, positive or negative. I have only a few hundred dollars in my checking account, so whatever I purchase will have to be at a discount. I see a white blazer on sale. It feels bold and I'm not confident I will wear it, but I buy it in the event I can't find anything in my wardrobe more suitable.

I meet Bill for the first time when I arrive at Alston & Bird's office on Sunday morning, June 26. Until then I had only spoken with him on the phone. He had just returned to Atlanta from the backpacking trip with the Boy Scout troop he led when Jody called him and broke the news about my hearing. Bill booked a flight to Washington that night and hurriedly packed before rushing out the door. It wasn't until he had arrived at the airport that he realized he was wearing a mismatched pair of shoes. It's the first thing he tells me when we meet. He's funny, and I know I will like him, but I'm so spun up with nerves, I have to fake a laugh.

A member of Liz Cheney's security detail meets us when we arrive outside the Cannon building Sunday afternoon and walks us straight to the Caucus Room, where Liz and Dan George are waiting for us. We enter the back of the chamber through the holding room. This is where I will wait out the last minutes before my testimony on Tuesday. Liz and Dan are standing next to the dais. We have to walk the length of the room to reach them. It's been a long time since I was last in the Caucus Room, and I've forgotten how big it is. With every step I take, Liz and Dan seem farther away. I feel as if I'm moving on autopilot, slowly. Suddenly everything feels real—the seriousness of what I'm about to do. I'm nervous, but I know what I'm doing, and I know it's right.

Liz and Dan are matter-of-fact. They show me the space, go over where everyone will sit, where the press will be, who's going to fill the chairs in the gallery behind me, the button system on the microphone, how long the hearing will take. I don't ask many questions. I feel unmoored from my normal sense of self. Everyone makes small talk to ease the tension. I go through several bottles of water. Liz assures me that they will have plenty of bottles stockpiled at the witness table for me on Tuesday. We make plans to meet again on Monday.

Liz and I walk out of the building together. As we talk, I overhear Dan in conversation with Jody and Bill about security arrangements. The committee intends to keep my identity secret for as long as possible, but Dan advises that we should prepare for the news leak. He suggests that they book me into a hotel Monday night rather than risk reporters or worse showing up at my apartment building. Jody raises the idea with me in the car after leaving the Hill, and I welcome it.

I'm at Alston & Bird Monday afternoon when the news breaks that there will be a surprise hearing the next day with an unnamed witness. Reporters start calling, trying to discover the identity of the mystery witness. I get a text from Liz Horning: "Please tell me you're not testifying tomorrow." I don't respond. It's the last time I'll ever hear from her. I toss my phone into a corner of the room. My friends are falling out of my life. I had hoped I could keep them, but I hadn't really expected to. I know I might lose every Republican friend I have, including Tony, a thought that makes me heartsick.

Jody comes to check on me and lets me know that Liz and Dan have decided to come to Alston & Bird for a final walkthrough rather than risk my exposure on the Hill.

I occupy the time by working with Stephen on a statement I will release after the hearing. Stephen tries to take my mind off the proceedings by describing Atlanta and telling me what a great city it is. Jody tries to distract me by asking me to recount stories of working in the White House. After I describe a few favorite memories, Stephen says that what I'm going to do the next day will be more important to the country than anything I had done in the White House. I thank him, but the assurance doesn't do much to reduce my anxiety.

I can't shake the feeling that I'm violating a code. I pride myself on my discretion and trustworthiness as much as my work ethic. I'm troubled by the feeling that I'm about to betray friends and former colleagues, because a higher loyalty to the country demands it.

"Tell me again why I have to testify live," I say to Bill and Jody later. "Why can't the committee use clips of my deposition?" I know the answer, but I want them to remind me. I need the reassurance.

Jody looks at me sympathetically. "There's a power that live testimony has that recordings don't," he says. "The country needs to see you, needs to see your courage. The country needs to hear the truth."

I know he is right. I know the impact I could have, a White House staffer with extensive access testifying in an open hearing to what amounted to, at a minimum, President Trump's shocking dereliction of duty. I know it will expose how much he was prepared to hurt the country to assuage his own wounded pride. I know it will reveal him as a reckless, dangerous man. I see that plainly now. January 6 was a dark day—traumatizing—a genuine threat to the health of the world's greatest democracy.

I'm alone in the conference room watching two Capitol Police officers on the other side of the glass sweep Alston & Bird's office, wondering what they went through on January 6. Minutes later, Bill, Jody, Liz, and Dan join me. There's a quality in Liz's demeanor, her seriousness and purposefulness, her self-possession, that has a bolstering effect on me. We run through the format of the hearing, a list of questions, identifying the video clips from my interviews and from others' testimony that the committee will use. They ask me which questions I'd prefer to answer at the hearing and which I'd rather use the clips for. "When the clips are concise," I tell them, "use those."

"Just so you know," Dan says, "Eric Herschmann claimed he

was the one who wrote the tweet draft on the chief of staff note card."

"If you guys don't want to talk to me about the note card, that's fine. I don't care," I say with a shrug. "But I know for certain that's my handwriting."

And so, the note card discussion stayed in.

Liz plays a clip from my most recent interview describing the president's explosive tantrum in the Beast. I know there will be denials and recrimination from Trump World. Anyone who resents me for disclosing it won't be assuaged by the fact that I had done it behind closed doors and sat there timidly watching the committee publicize it. I had urged the committee to find someone in the Secret Service to corroborate my account. That had yet to happen.

Liz asks if I prefer to use the clip rather than testify to it live. I draw a slow breath, closing my eyes while I consider. I imagine myself alone at the witness table, listening to the recording of my account of the president's rage, while I sit there silently—doing what? *Nodding affirmatively? Staring into space? Looking like a coward?* I summon a little of Liz's steel.

"Don't use the clip. I'm doing this live."

She smiles slightly and nods.

As Liz and Dan finish and we're getting up to leave, I say to Liz, "I have a question my attorneys are going to kill me for asking." She laughs as Jody and Bill roll their eyes.

"I'd really like to know why you have faith in me, when I'm trying to find faith in myself," I say.

"Cassidy, you're doing right by the country," she replies. "You're upholding your oath. The country needs this. You can explain things like no one else can, and that makes you an extremely special person to this committee. You're bringing people into the White House. It makes your testimony powerful. I'm very proud of you, and you need to be proud of yourself."

I don't want her to think I'm afraid of Trump World retaliation, not after the personal cost she has paid to do the right thing. That's not to say I'm safe from retaliation. I'm not. "I just don't want to put myself in the spotlight," I explain. "That's not me."

"You're not *putting* yourself in the spotlight," she pushes back. "You're being called by Congress to do it. It's important that the country sees that. It's important that the country sees *you*, that women and little girls see *you* doing the right thing."

Once she says the last part, I understand. The country needs to see someone from the Trump administration put the country's interests before politics and self.

I say goodbye, declining to go through the questions again with Jody and Bill. I go to my apartment to pack a few things for tomorrow. We plan to reconvene later at the Riggs, close to Alston & Bird. It is where Bill and Jody stay when they're in town.

At my apartment, I throw some clothes and makeup in a little bag. I text Mom that I'm going to spend the night in a hotel. I stay in the apartment about ten extra minutes before calling an Uber to take me to the hotel. With my bag over my shoulder and my hand on the doorknob, I force myself to take a look around. I know it might be the last time I'm there.

I had moved into that apartment when I started working for Mark, and I had loved it. But the last six months had been a time of turmoil and struggle. I hadn't been able to pay my rent in months, and my Wi-Fi had been cut off. My blinds were drawn and had been since the marshals had delivered my subpoena in January. It didn't feel like home anymore. It felt like a prison, and I wanted to get out. Weeks later, Mom and Paul would collect my possessions and move me out. I never set foot in that apartment again.

That night, when I return to the hotel, the news breaks that I am tomorrow's witness.

I turn off the TV so I won't have to listen to speculation about me, and I text Liz Cheney. "Can you call me?" She does, right away. We talk on the phone for a few minutes. Toward the end of the call, I say, "I really hope I don't let you down tomorrow."

"Cassidy, you could never let me down. I'm really proud of you."

Her pride is enough encouragement for me to see this through.

I start considering how I should comport myself at the hearing. I remind myself to listen to the questions carefully before answering and to enunciate, to speak slowly and clearly. I watch an old video on YouTube demonstrating the proper seated posture for women.

I pass the time rereading passages I had marked in *The Last of the President's Men*. The book had practically become my bible, and its subject my unmet friend. I drift off around three in the morning, the book resting on the pillow next to me.

———

I order room service the next morning, but I am too on edge to eat. I nibble on a piece of turkey bacon and drink some juice but leave the rest untouched. I have the news turned on, and most of the chatter is about the hearing and me. A lady who's come to do my hair and makeup works as I think, *I can't do this.* She senses me fretting and suggests we pick out my outfit. I tell her I think I should wear the black blazer, black pants, white camisole, and heels I've brought. They had been in my closet for quite some time. I had also brought along the white blazer from Zara but was convinced it would be too bold. She insists I wear it. "Stop worrying about what people are going to say about what you're wearing." I skeptically acquiesce.

The diamond necklace I wore was a thirteenth-birthday gift from a dear friend of Mom's. It's the only piece of real jewelry I own. When I put it on, I make a mental note to check that it's straight before entering the hearing room. My earrings are rhine-stones I bought at Kohl's.

I'm carrying my blazer when I meet Bill and Jody in the lobby. We walk to Alston & Bird together. Stephen had brought in a supply of pastries from Tatte, including my favorite, a pistachio croissant. I'm still too nervous to eat anything. So I help my lawyers pick out their ties. Later, I won't remember discussing anything with them in great detail. Around eleven thirty, we load into a black Suburban and leave for the Hill. The hearing is scheduled for one o'clock, and I want to get there early to settle in before it begins. In the car, I try to make a joke by imitating Trump.

"I'm the fucking witness, take me back to Alston & Bird now!"

We are laughing when the car pulls through the security checkpoint outside the Cannon building. No turning back now.

Capitol Police officers and Hannah Muldavin, the committee's deputy communications director, meet us in the garage. We take an elevator to a holding room on the second floor. It overlooks the Capitol. Unlike the gray overcast of January 6, the sky on June 28 is a deep blue. Beams of sunlight are reflecting off the Capitol dome. *It's glowing*, I think to myself.

"Cassidy, what do you want to go over?" Bill asks. I clutch the binder that holds my notes and glance around. We're not alone. Police officers are inside and outside the room. Hannah and another committee staffer are there. I start fixating on the fact that I'm going to have to tell the Beast story, and that I had insisted on doing it live. I'm fighting to stave off a panic attack, and I'm losing. I start acting like a brat, and ask that the room be cleared. No one reacts. Dan George stops in to see if I have any last-minute questions. "Do I have to do this?" I ask.

At twelve thirty, it's time to move to the holding room on the third floor that adjoins the Caucus Room. I feel disoriented. I was familiar with the Cannon building. I had been there hundreds of times. But it feels different today. It smells different, it looks different— brighter, strange, foreign. I know where I'm going, not because I'm following an escort but as if I am being guided by a sense of déjà vu, a forgotten glimpse of a previous life.

"Hannah, please make sure we don't come into contact with reporters," I plead.

"The only people you'll see are Capitol Police," she assures me.

We take a circuitous route, and as Hannah had promised, we encounter no one other than the officers. I exchange looks with each of them. They are nodding at me as we pass them.

I pace in the holding room until one o'clock. Bill puts a hand on my shoulder. "It's time to go."

I spin toward Bill. "Do I have to do this?" I break eye contact with him as I hear the door open.

"Yes," Bill says over my shoulder, and he gently nudges me forward.

We walk into the hearing from the back and make our way to the witness table as committee members file onto the dais in the front of the room. The room appears huge, and is silent but for the furious clicking of cameras and the ringing in my ears. I avoid making eye contact with anyone else in the room other than the members. It's harder than I thought it would be.

I take my seat at the table. Jody, Bill, Stephen, and Hannah sit right behind me. I repeat my self-assigned directions: *Sit forward in the chair. Keep my back straight. Place the binder with my notes and a writing pad and pen on the table to my right. Put my hands in my lap.* The cameras click, the flashes overwhelming.

Chairman Bennie Thompson, of Mississippi, calls the hearing to order. I'm trying to listen, but my own thoughts are crowding my mind. I look at each member, take a sip of water, glance at my notes, and adjust my necklace to make sure it's straight.

I steal a quick glance at the photographers wrestling with their gear mere inches in front of me. I make eye contact with Doug

Mills and think of our glasses of bourbon together on Air Force One after long days of travel. We hadn't talked much after I had left the White House. Doug shoots me a quick thumbs-up, pulls down his mask, and mouths, "You're doing the right thing."

I'm still deep in my own thoughts, but I tune in as Liz vouches for my access and influence in the White House, and my network of relationships with members of Congress. "Ms. Hutchinson was in a position to know a great deal about happenings in the Trump White House," she asserts.

Representative Thompson stresses my role in the White House and my work on the Hill, and flashes pictures on the video screen of me smiling with senior members of Congress. They know how Trump World is going to attack my credibility. So do I. I've participated in attacks like it, especially during the first impeachment. They will dismiss me as a nobody, a junior staffer no one took seriously or would ever confide in. I'm grateful the committee establishes I was more than that. I had been in effect "chief of staff to the president's chief of staff." Mark used to call me his "chief of stuff." His "principal aide," Liz describes me.

The chairman instructs me to stand and take the oath, to tell "the whole truth." My sleeve bunches as I raise my right arm, and I question my choice of blazers. *Trump will hate this*, I think. *He hates when women wear ill-fitting clothes.*

The chairman first asks me to explain my role in the legislative affairs office, and I respond by describing my responsibilities in the chief of staff's office. I realize my mistake mid-answer. *Oh well, too late to start over.* He follows up with the question I had just mistakenly answered. It's not that big a stumble, and I'm not too rattled, but it wasn't the most auspicious start. He concludes by showing a photograph of the offices in the West Wing from the vantage point of my office. "It's smaller than it looks," I crack. He notes that it takes only a few seconds to walk from my desk to the Oval Office.

Liz takes over, and she'll guide me through each moment of

the hearing. It's just Liz and me having a conversation. We aren't posturing or hiding or dreading anything. Her straightforward-ness and steady cadence are comforting.

I trust her implicitly. She has asked me to do a difficult thing, and I will do it to the best of my ability. Liz is on the right side of history, and she welcomes me to join her.

She asks about my conversation with Rudy Giuliani on January 2, when I first learned from him that the president might go to the Capitol on January 6, and Mark's warning that things might get bad that day. I acknowledge that the prospect of such a reckless move had made me "scared and nervous." She turns to clips from the video recordings of my depositions before we get to the issue of the president's furor over the use of security magnetometers limiting the size of the crowd at the January 6th rally. She lists the variety of weaponry confiscated from those who went through the mags, and plays clips of police radio reports of weapons possessed by the crowd on the Mall. They would march to the Capitol with everything they had brought with them.

I know the subjects that the clips will address, but I'm listening to most recordings for the first time during the hearing, like the rest of the country. I hear police officers identifying people carrying AR15s, handguns, and other weapons, their alarm unmistakable in the urgency of the reports. It brings me back to the trauma of that day, the dread and terror I felt as I learned of the multiple warnings of violence. I had felt the catastrophe coming, and witnessed the president of the United States not just failing to stop it but inflaming it.

Liz peers at me for a second, asks me to repeat a part of my testimony for emphasis, so that nobody watching will fail to understand the gravity of what is being said.

"Just to be clear, Ms. Hutchinson, is it your understanding that the president wanted to take the mags away and said that the armed individuals were not there to hurt him?"

"That's a fair assessment," I answer.

I know we've reached the headline moments of my testimony, the president's knowledge that his supporters are armed as they marched to the Capitol and that violence was likely. He didn't care. "They aren't here to hurt me," he had said, pushing back.

"I would characterize it as a lack of reaction," I answer, when Liz asks me how Mark had responded to the news that the president had just announced at his rally that he would join the protesters on their march to the Capitol. I remember White House lawyers pleading with me that morning to get Mark to stop the president from going to the Hill. Not only had I failed to get him to intervene, I could barely get him to engage in a discussion of it. "Mark needs to snap out of this," I testify to thinking. "He needs to care."

I know that my association with Mark is finished, if it wasn't already. I'm unlikely to hear from him ever again. But I had been his person, his eyes and ears, his advocate and protector. I was good at it, and I was proud that I was. There isn't much I can do for him now, but I'm not his antagonist. I have an obligation to the truth—though I do not want to be instrumental in his disgrace.

The portrait my answers paint of the president is damning: an unhinged chief executive, willing to overturn the will of the people and plunge the country into chaos and violence on the advice of crazy people. *For what? To avoid the embarrassment of conceding an election he knew he had lost?* That is who he is, and that is how he appears as Liz's questions draw the evidence of his culpability from my testimony.

"Take the effing mags away," I testify hearing him order. And: "Let my people in"—knowing they were armed. "They can march to the Capitol from here."

Using a mix of deposition clips and live testimony, Liz sets the stage for shocking disclosures. By the time the president had left the rally stage, he knew that the protesters were armed, that the police protecting the Capitol were outnumbered, and that those at the vanguard of the marching mob had already threatened to breach the security perimeter. In her level, matter-of-fact tone, absent theatrics, letting the facts indict her targets, she directs me to the scene in the Beast. "Let's turn now to what happened in the president's vehicle when the Secret Service told him he would not be going to the Capitol after his speech."

I've prepared for the question. I understand the effect my answer will have. I'm ready, even though I had been in a panic in the holding room about this moment, fearing I would screw it up, and dreading, too, the thought of hurting people I care about. I remember that when Tony was describing what had happened, that old rationalization excusing Trump's bad behavior was playing in the back of my mind: *Why had people let it go so far?* Until I shared this information with the committee, I hadn't told anyone else about it except for giving Mark and, later, Stefan an abbreviated version. It had taken me three or four attempts to tell Jody about it.

My mouth is dry, and I take a quick sip of water. I gather myself and begin recounting what Tony Ornato told me had happened, as Bobby Engel listened, "looking discombobulated and a little lost." Bobby had done what Mark hadn't the nerve to do: refuse the president's command to take him to the Capitol. An "irate" Trump had fumed in response, "I'm the effing president, take me up to the Capitol now." When Bobby refused again, Trump grabbed at the steering wheel. Bobby grabbed Trump's arm. "Sir, you need to take your hand off the steering wheel. We're going back to the West Wing." And Trump "used his free hand to lunge at Bobby."

"Toward his clavicles," I add, placing a hand on my own neck to imitate Tony's pantomime of the act.

When I finish recounting it, the room feels cold and quiet. I want to rub my hands together, but I know it will make me look nervous. I take a deep breath and feel relief wash over me. I think of the Capitol Police officers sitting in the back row. I had done right by them, the first victims of the catastrophe Trump had caused. Maybe I haven't always done the right thing, but I'm doing it now.

Drawing an even more vivid picture of Trump's volatility, Liz asks me to describe his reaction on December 1 to Bill Barr's statement to the Associated Press that the Department of Justice had found no evidence of widespread election fraud. I describe the loud noise coming from the Oval dining room, the ketchup dripping down the wall, helping his valet clean up the mess.

"Was this the only incident you're aware of where the president threw dishes?" Liz asks.

"It's not," I acknowledge, adding that there had been several occasions when I was aware that the president was "throwing dishes or flipping the tablecloth."

Letting the image linger in listeners' imaginations, Chairman Thompson declares a ten-minute recess. I stand up. I'm dizzy. I fumble with the buttons on my blazer, give up, and leave it unbuttoned. Jody places his hand on my shoulder and whispers, "Just walk." I try to avoid eye contact with everyone. If I could melt into the floor, I would. It's eerily quiet, as if everyone in the room had been stunned into paralysis and silence, except for the photographers taking my picture, and even that sounds muted. I'm used to wearing heels on marble floors, and the thick carpet in the Caucus Room makes me feel like I'm walking on a cushion, in slow motion. It seems to take an eternity to exit the room. We're ten feet from the holding room when the quiet is suddenly interrupted by applause from the police officers, who are then joined by others. I snap back to reality as I cross into the holding room.

"Am I getting nuked?" I press Hannah.

"No, everyone loves you," she assures me, and she reads a few nice tweets calling me brave and courageous.

"I don't feel brave and courageous," I reply. "Is Trump watching?"

"Yes, Cassidy, Trump is watching."

"What's he saying?"

Hannah just waves me off, so I turn to Bill and Jody.

"Tell me what I'm doing wrong. How can I be better?" Smiling, they assure me that there is nothing to criticize. "You're doing so well. We're so proud of you."

I dash to the public restroom near the holding room. When I come out of the stall, there are several staffers at the sinks who can't help but stare at me for a moment before catching themselves. *Are they watching the hearing?* I wonder.

I'm more at ease when I sit back down at the witness table. The second part of the hearing goes by more quickly than the first. I testify to the difficulty Pat Cipollone, Eric Herschmann, and others had getting an adamant Trump to call off his supporters ransacking the Capitol and threatening the lives of members of Congress and the vice president. I acknowledge again how reluctant Mark was to confront the boss's anger and get him to see reason. I recount overhearing him tell Pat that Trump "thinks Mike deserves it. He doesn't think they're doing anything wrong." Liz briefly interjects to make sure everyone realizes what I had just attested to: the president of the United States had told his chief of staff and legal counsel that he was fine with an armed mob trying to kill the vice president of the United States.

She brings up the shameful tweet Trump had sent while would-be assailants hunted Mike Pence: "Mike Pence didn't have the courage to do what should have been done."

"Ms. Hutchinson," Liz asks, "what was your reaction when you saw that tweet?"

I had not expected Liz to ask for my reaction. I had asked her not to ask for my opinions about anything or anyone. I preferred just to testify to what I saw and heard, and allow the damning facts to speak for themselves.

"As a staffer that worked to always represent the administration to the best of my ability and to showcase the good things that he had done for the country," I begin, "I remember feeling frustrated and disappointed, and really it felt personal. I was really sad. As an American, I was disgusted. It was unpatriotic. It was un-American. We were watching the Capitol building get defaced over a lie, and it was something that was really hard in that moment to digest, knowing what I've been hearing down the hall and the conversations that were happening. Seeing that tweet come up and knowing what was happening on the Hill, and it's something that I—it's still—I still struggle to work through the emotions of that."

I confirm how hard it had been to get the president to make a statement telling the rioters to go home, and how even when he relented, he still refused to state the obvious, that the election was over.

Emotionally, the lowest point of the hearing is the clip the committee plays of Rep. Mike Gallagher, a House Republican from Wisconsin and an exemplary public servant, imploring Trump to call off the mob. He pleads to the camera, targeting an audience of one, the president of the United States. "This is bigger than you . . . It's about the United States of America, which is more important than any politician."

It brings me back to how useless I felt that day as members and others frantically texted, begging for Trump to call off the riot. I think of Trump, sitting down the hall from me, unmoved. He thought that the people begging him to intervene were pathetic and weak, and that they should have been fighting for him. He wanted this.

Chairman Thompson and Liz wrap up the hearing with praise for my courage and patriotism. I didn't think then, nor do I think now, that I had done anything that day that deserved praise or merited excess pride. I had done a duty I owed the country, a duty I chose.

———

I've been an idealist since childhood, a romantic about America since I carried the flag onstage at my preschool graduation and sensed a calling to serve my country. I'm gratified that there are people for whom my testimony meant something; listeners whose eyes were opened to the fragility of our democracy. And I'm proud of bringing parts of my story from my New Jersey childhood to that hearing room. I did what was expected of me, what should be expected of an American. I did my civic duty, no more than that. I felt like an American, and I didn't require or deserve anything more than a "thank you for your testimony."

As I leave the hearing, I stop at the dais to thank each member. Liz is last, and we exchange a quick hug and a few grateful words. Whatever I accomplished in that hearing is as much a testament to her patriotism as it is to mine.

On the drive back to Alston & Bird, I scroll through dozens of supportive texts I receive. "Cassidy, go on Twitter," Bill and Jody insist. "Everyone's calling you a hero." I close my eyes and rest my head against the window. I'm so tired I think I'm going to fall asleep in the car.

When we arrive at Alston & Bird, I find bottles of wine and glasses set on the conference room table. I pour a glass. Jody and Bill know I want to be alone for a while, so to give me some space, they leave to handle press inquiries. I pour a second glass of wine and enjoy my brief solitude.

About an hour later, Eric Herschmann texts me. I'm afraid to open the message. During the hearing, Liz had asked me about the note I had written on one of Mark's chief of staff note cards, the one I had been forewarned Eric Herschmann claimed he had written. "Jody needs to call my lawyer right now," he instructs me. I pass my phone to Jody, and he says, "I had a few calls from an unknown number. I didn't know who it was. I guess it's Eric's lawyer. I'll call him now."

Jody went up to his office to return the call and it is indeed Eric's lawyer, and Eric. They're going wild about the disputed note card. In an animated tone, Eric says to Jody, "That's my fucking handwriting. Law enforcement is going to back me up. I've talked to Bill Barr about it. My family knows that's my handwriting. She needs to put out a statement right now that says that's my handwriting. She knows that's my handwriting." He repeats himself several times and then adds, "I'm sixty-one, and I'm a lawyer. Cassidy was a young staffer. If she doesn't put out a statement, I'll be forced to put one out myself."

When Eric pauses to draw a breath, Jody interjects, "Eric, with all due respect, I will talk to my client about this. But my client feels as strongly as you do that it's her handwriting. If we don't put out a statement, and you feel the need to put out a story saying that it's your handwriting, I can't stop you from doing that."

The joke of it all is that when Dan George showed me that card in my very first deposition, back in February, I had felt embarrassed about my atrocious handwriting. I've never liked it. I've tried to make it neat and pretty, but it didn't take. Because of how much I've hated my handwriting for my whole life, I knew it was mine.

Nevertheless, Eric's demand produces the first stressful moment I experience after the hearing. I don't want the controversy to undermine the committee's work.

Jody mentions the call to Dan George, who acknowledges that Eric called the committee about it, too. "Did he say something about law enforcement backing him up?" Dan asks.

Jody answers, "Yeah, he did."

Dan laughs. "What's that mean?"

Jody, his son Gannon, Stephen, and I decide to get dinner at the hotel. Bill had to fly to Nashville that night. As I wait for the elevator to take me to my room to change into something comfortable, several families approach me to thank me for my testimony. I'm grateful but overwhelmed. *I'm so, so exhausted.*

We move dinner to a private room. I sip another glass of wine and revive a little. I ask my lawyers again what Trump is saying. "Don't bother with what Trump is saying," they advise. But we decide to scroll through Truth Social for entertainment. I see his statements, and they are all predictable Trump attacks.

"We should've made up a bingo card," Jody jokes. *I barely knew her, phony, liar, wanted a job I didn't give her, blah, blah, blah.* Bingo.

We're about an hour into dinner when Peter Alexander of NBC News reports that sources in the Secret Service are prepared to dispute my account of the Beast incident. I had expected it, and it doesn't upset me very much. On the contrary, I feel a surge of confidence. I've told the truth not about something I saw firsthand but about something that was told to me in confidence, with an eyewitness to the incident in the room. I had received texts from several friends in the Secret Service that day thanking me for my testimony. I suspect that contributed to my confidence.

I start doomscrolling Twitter after that report, and my fatigue quickly deepens. I can barely talk anymore. I take my salad to my room at around seven o'clock and pass out for a few hours. I wake up feeling disoriented. *Where am I? What happened?* Then it hits me. I check my phone and watch CNN commentators discuss the hearing. I exchange texts with Liz, who encourages me to get some rest. I go back to bed, and wake up the next day at noon.

———

As I had expected, I woke up to a changed life. I was the subject of a major national news story. Millions of people I've never met now knew me by name and had an opinion about me, good or bad. I would be—for the time being, anyway—recognized by strangers, applauded and disliked. I'd be analyzed, disputed, praised, and wondered about. I could look to my family, to Bill and Jody, and to Liz for support.

Which, in turn, also meant I was now an exile.

CHAPTER 25

Adrift

IT'S A STRANGE FOUR DAYS, alternately boring, fretful, and unreal. Quarantined in my hotel room, I feel disoriented, like I have just gotten off a boat after weeks at sea. My world is still rocking as I try to find my footing.

We haven't planned how long I'll stay in the Riggs or where I will go next. Bill, Jody, and I are of the same mind—that it isn't safe for me, physically, emotionally, or politically, to be seen or heard in public or to risk going to my apartment. There have been security threats, they warn, although I don't know the specifics. I don't want to know. Reporters show up at Alston & Bird's office. A few make it past security, hoping for a comment from Bill and Jody.

The scene is worse at my parents' house. News vans are parked in front of their home, cameras positioned to catch a glimpse of someone inside. Mom and Paul are staying home from work. They feel safer that way. Mom opens the door out of habit when she hears a knock.

"Ms. Hutchinson, I'm with the *New York Post*—"

She slams the door shut. Paul draws the curtains closed and insists that Mom stay upstairs with the dogs. He stays downstairs. Someone parks a car in their driveway and knocks on the door. They ignore it. He knocks again. And again. And again. "For twenty minutes," Mom says. She calls to Paul, "Just answer it." He does, and a man in scruffy clothes introduces himself as an FBI agent who's there to sweep the house. Paul asks to see identification. The man declines and tries to push his way in. Paul manages to shove him back and shut the door.

I hate that I put them in that position. I wish I could go home.

Some of the time, I feel I've lost control of my life, and I have a hard time imagining when and how I'll be in control of it again. The pushback from Trump defenders is picking up speed, the attacks led by Trump himself, whose insults are getting cruder. I tried to mentally prepare for breaking with Trump World. I know how they curate vile attacks on their detractors. I was once part of that process.

We released a statement after the hearing: "Ms. Hutchinson believes that January 6 was a horrific day for the country, and it is vital to the future of our democracy that it not be repeated."

Peter Alexander's report about the Secret Service and Eric Herschmann's insistence about his handwriting start gaining traction. Jody and Bill think it's wise for them to release another statement the next day, and I agree. "Ms. Hutchinson stands by all of the testimony she provided yesterday, under oath, to the Select Committee to Investigate the January 6th Attack on the United States Capitol."

I don't need to say anything more. I stand by everything.

Trump continues to hurl insults in my direction. I learn how it feels to be on the other side. But I know enough not to react. That's what he wants me to do. He wants me to be defensive. He wants to know when he's hurt someone or gotten a rise out of them; he wants to project his hurt onto the source of it. Trump doesn't care if you dispute him or call him a liar. Only silence bothers him. Being ignored drives him mad.

I recognize the handiwork of some friends and colleagues who are amplifying Trump's attacks anonymously. They try to impeach my testimony by impugning my character. I'd had my share of detractors among my White House colleagues who resented the authority Mark gave me. They derisively referred to me as "Chief Cassidy," which finds its way into a *Washing-*

ton Post story. But it isn't only my detractors who are busy. I know that people who had been my friends are trashing my reputation, too. I shouldn't let it bother me, but I do. They were my friends. But their abuse is a reflection of their character, not mine, celebrated in the world they are a part of, the world where I had felt I belonged but now know I do not. *I escaped before it was too late.*

———

I feel embraced by the outpouring of support I get from different corners. I receive hundreds of encouraging calls and messages from members of Congress. Some are friends; others I hadn't known well at all. I hear from high school and college friends, former teachers, reporters I'd become friendly with, Secret Service agents, and strangers from across the world, who reach out in any way possible. Alston & Bird's phone lines ring nonstop, hundreds of letters are delivered every day, my lawyers' email inboxes are full. Callers say that they're grateful for my courage. I'm grateful that they listened, that they care about the preservation of our government.

It's strange, though—I still feel that the only people I can talk to about what happened are people who experienced January 6 in the White House with me. And most of them are not calling.

I do hear from several colleagues who left the administration before, or as a result of, January 6. Sarah Matthews and Olivia Troye send encouraging messages and write tweets blasting my critics. Alyssa Farah calls constantly. She is leading my media defense, going head-to-head with Trump and his cronies. Alyssa is as courageous as she is patriotic, and her friendship grounds me. Mick Mulvaney, Mark's predecessor, checks in and defends my testimony in the press.

The person who means the most—who had recognized my passion and potential, and took a chance on me when I made my Washington debut—calls. When I pick up my cell phone to answer, my hands are trembling.

"Ben? Ben Howard?" My voice cracks.

"Cass," Ben says. "I wasn't sure if you would answer. Hi."

"Ben." I sigh. "I never thought I would hear from you again."

He laughs hard. "You're stupid. I'm so proud of you, Cassidy."

We talk for a long time, a pure, genuine conversation between friends. Ben sees me not as Mark's henchman but as the hard-working idealist he met four years ago. He knows me, and I trust him. But when he asks where I am, if I'm safe, I snap.

"Why are you asking me that? What does it matter to you?" I'm so defensive. *Why am I so defensive? Stop being defensive!*

I hate that I'm skeptical of his intentions. He understands, but I'm angry with myself. *I don't want to hurt the people who care about me. I don't want to push them away.*

Sequestered in my hotel room, I'm lonely. But I'm safe here. I pace the room, order room service, watch the news, alternating between CNN and MSNBC. I don't dare risk looking at Fox. I scroll through Twitter, compulsively reloading my feed, and then I don't look at it again for the rest of the day. In the White House, I'd been an obsessive reader of morning newsletters, but I don't read them now.

I have conference calls with Bill and Jody, and they visit my room. When I ask to walk to a nearby CVS to pick up a few things, they offer to send an associate to purchase what I need. *Forget it.*

I talk with Mom and Paul. They send pictures of newspapers that have positive stories about the hearing. Mom warns that Dad has been texting her, demanding a federal government contact. He wants security. *He's insane.* We laugh. While Mom and I are still talking, Jody calls. I put Mom on hold.

Jody explains that he has just gotten off the phone with the

New Jersey State Police, who had been contacted by . . . Richard Hutchinson. He starts to summarize the call, but I cut him off and apologize. I go back to Mom's call.

"Mom, you're never going to guess what just happened . . ."

Liz checks on me every day. She sends encouraging articles, shares stories about the public support we've received since the hearing, and relays messages from prominent figures in the Republican Party, our Republican Party. We talk and laugh, I cry, we laugh some more. Liz is becoming my rock.

A friend alerted me to the speech Liz is giving at the Reagan Presidential Library the day after my testimony. The speech is a summons to defend our constitutional order and a paean to the values that defined the Republican Party under Ronald Reagan's leadership. They are the values that had attracted me to the party— universal freedom, equal justice, private initiative, limited government, a strong defense, and internationalism. I watch her speak from my hotel room and start to cry when she praises my patriotism and the audience applauds.

On Thursday, I wake up with a pit in my stomach. Jody is flying home to Alabama today. I'm afraid to be alone. We meet in the hotel lobby before he leaves for the airport. I'm not surprised when I find him with two big bags from Tatte and Rasika, my favorite Indian restaurant.

"I thought you might be getting tired of room service!" he says with a laugh.

"I don't want you to leave. Where am I going to go?" I'm embarrassed; I feel weak.

Before he responds, he places a hand on my shoulder and guides me to the nearest elevator. *What the hell . . .*

"People are recognizing you. Go back upstairs and relax. We'll call you a little later." The elevator door shuts before I say goodbye.

Bill and Jody call late that afternoon. I know they're calling about my security arrangements, but I don't know what to expect.

"We think it's best to get you out of Washington," Bill begins. "How do you feel about coming to Atlanta for a while?"

Jody chimes in. "I can work out of the Atlanta office, so Bill and I will both be close to you."

Atlanta is far, unfamiliar. But so is Washington now. I can't go to New Jersey and put my parents' security more at risk. I have nowhere else to go.

"I just want to feel safe," I say. It is the only response I can come up with. I worry I will be a burden to them. They've already done so much for me. But I can't protect myself. I feel suffocated.

"We'll talk about details, but you'll be completely safe in Atlanta. I promise," Bill says. He is confident, firm. I trust him.

"So when is my flight?"

"Saturday. We'll talk through all the details tomorrow. Get some rest," Jody advises. He means *this* Saturday, July 2.

The next morning, Friday, Jody offers to send an Alston & Bird associate to my apartment to pack some clothes for me. All I have at the hotel are the few articles of clothing I packed the night before my hearing. I'm grateful for the offer, but I don't want a stranger going through my stuff. And I want to see Mom.

Before I can finish asking her to come, Mom is in her car driving to Washington. When she arrives, the hotel manager escorts her upstairs. *I can't even meet her in the lobby.*

She's eager to go to my apartment to pack. I give her a handwritten list of everything I want to bring. She returns an hour later with everything I had asked for.

After ordering room service for dinner, Mom asks the question I knew was coming. "How are you getting to the airport tomorrow?"

"I don't know. I thought you could drive me. Maybe an Uber." I didn't want to admit it, but I was a nervous wreck over the airport. I can't let her know that, though.

She erupts. "You're crazy. Cassidy! You can't walk through the airport alone. You'll get mobbed. Are you listening to me? You have no idea—"

"Shut up! Just shut up!" I am still scolding her when my phone rings. It's Bill and Jody. I step into the bedroom, away from Mom's nagging.

I'll be escorted from the hotel to Atlanta by Capitol Police, they explain. They'll switch shifts with Georgia State Police once I land in Atlanta. My head is spinning. They preempt my next question— yes, this is necessary. I hang up and return to the living room and sink into the couch next to Mom.

"This pains me to say, but you were right." Mom is relieved. I don't know how to feel.

————

We wake up early Saturday, determined to have a normal morning. We order room service for breakfast, and Mom paints my nails and repacks my bag several times. We lie in bed, chatting and laughing. I feel her anxiety, and I know she feels mine. *But I need to be strong. She needs to know I'm going to be okay.*

We're on the phone with my grandmother when Stephen calls to let me know that the police are ready to take me. Mom looks devastated. I force a smile.

"Come on, walk me downstairs. I want you to meet Stephen. I also need you to carry my bag—my nails are still wet." She laughs at that, and I feel better.

When we get off the elevator, I spot Stephen standing with several uniformed Capitol Police officers. Two black SUVs are idling outside. I introduce Mom to Stephen. Then I snatch my bag, give her a quick hug, and kiss her cheek.

"I love you. See you soon!" I walk outside, flanked by the officers. If I linger, I won't have the courage to leave. Later, Mom tells me how shattered she felt as she watched me drive away.

Motorcades are unremarkable to me. I've been in hundreds before. But this one is strange. Because this time it's me who needs protection. My life is in danger.

I learn that one of the officers in my car is assigned to Senate majority leader Chuck Schumer and another is from Liz Cheney's detail. I learn, too, that I'm the first nonelected official under Capitol Police protection.

"I'm honored," I stammer.

"The honor is ours," one of the officers responds. We make eye contact through the rearview mirror. I know he's referring to my testimony, but I can't find the words I want to use. *You're the ones who suffered, because of us. Because of the president I worked for. You're the heroes.*

As we walk to my gate, I notice how crowded the airport is. I fight the urge to turn around, to run.

"Don't look up," I hear one officer instruct. "People are being shameless right now about taking your picture." *It won't always be this way*, I tell myself. A few people shout my name, expressing their gratitude.

When we arrive at the gate, the Capitol Police officers inform me that there are plainclothes agents who will accompany me on the flight. They have arranged for me to board early. I only have a moment to thank them and say goodbye before I am whisked onto the airplane.

When I reach the end of the Jetway, I find the crew, including the pilots, lining the interior of the plane, each holding a small American flag or wearing a flag pin. For the first time this week, I am truly speechless.

I am seated in the last row, and switch to the aisle seat so the little girl in my row can look out the window. I fall asleep quickly.

A flight attendant wakes me right before we land in Atlanta.

I fight to stay awake as she explains the plan to be carried out when we land. *You're the first to deplane. Your bag is in the front. Move quickly.*

I follow her instructions, and spot the City of Atlanta police escorts as soon as I step onto the Jetway. Without saying a word, they open a door. I struggle to match their gait as they lead me down a set of stairs, onto the tarmac. I am in a vehicle before I even see it, and we start driving.

As the motorcade moves across the tarmac to my next location, I am hit with a realization: The last time I was in Atlanta, I flew in on Air Force One, *with* the former president.

Now I am in Atlanta *because* of him.

———

Bob Woodward describes Alex Butterfield gazing out the window of the plane he was flying in a few days after he had testified to the Watergate committee: "Butterfield dwelled for a moment on the man on the street, the average American. What would he or she think?"

It's my fourth evening alone at the Riggs after my testimony. I'm starved for human connection when I remember this passage. I sink into the sofa, flip to the chapter, and read Woodward's words. Over and over and over. I close the book and walk to the window of my eighth-floor corner suite, staring down at the street scene below, a busy city intersection. People and cars hustle along, engrossed in their business. I stand at the window for a long time, observing the world below.

I spot a mother and her elementary-school-age daughter walk out of the Shake Shack across the street from the hotel. The mother is carrying to-go bags, and the girl is holding an oversized purse. As if she senses me gazing at her, the little girl looks up and spots me. For a moment, I freeze and almost walk away. I feel like I'm intruding. But then, with her free arm, the girl waves. A wave so big it looks like she's painting a rainbow in the air. I wave back. They cross the street, disappearing as quickly as they had appeared. In that moment, I briefly feel normal again.

She has no idea who I am or what I did. She probably won't ever know. But I did it for her. For the country that's her home.

CHAPTER 26

Home

" CASEY! CASEY!" I heard a male voice shout. The atmosphere in Truist Park was electrifying, and I wanted to be back in my seat behind home plate, out of sight of the hundreds of prying eyes on us. Jody, Bill, Lacey—Bill's wife—and I made our way to our row. "Casey!" The voice was louder this time. *Don't look up, don't look up . . .*

I was stopped in my tracks by two hands holding my shoulders in a vice grip. "Casey!" the man shouted again. His seat was elevated—it was several feet higher than our walkway. He leaned over the metal rail to inch his face close to mine. I shouted for Bill, who quickly ran to my side. The man let go of one of my shoulders to point at his son.

"Casey, this is my little boy! You're damn brave, Casey. You gave me a little bit of hope that my son will grow up in the version of America we should be proud of. Thank you, thank you . . ." He clasped his hands together in prayer. I thanked him meekly and dashed back to my seat. Bill joined us a few moments later.

"Well, that was interesting. After you walked away, he asked if I'm your dad." Bill laughed. "One day, you're going to see how many lives you changed. It's truly incredible, *Casey*." He winked.

I was already shaking my head when Jody asked if I was alright. At that time, there was not much in my life I felt certain of, except that I would never adjust to being in the public eye.

Jody patted my shoulder. "Sorry about that, Bill. He probably asked if you are her dad since I look like I could be her brother."

———

"So, fun fact, my congressional district had the highest voter turn-out for Trump in 2016 and 2020!" Jody said, pulling back onto the interstate from our pit stop at Chick-fil-A. At the end of my first week in Atlanta, he had invited me to spend the weekend with his family at their lake house in northern Alabama.

"Great, that's comforting. At least I'll get a warm welcome," I said, rolling my eyes.

"Only one of my neighbors flies a QAnon flag on their front lawn!"

I shrieked his name, and we both laughed.

"Seriously, there's nothing to worry about. We're making sure you're safe," he said. I knew I could trust him. He had promised.

We drove around Boaz, Alabama, the town where he was raised after moving back to America from Taiwan. Jody was the son of missionaries. We dropped by his parents' and his sister's homes. Their love and thoughtful prayers made me feel connected to a world I sometimes no longer felt part of.

As promised, we drove past a QAnon flag rippling in the eve-ning breeze before we pulled into Jody's driveway. I was imme-diately embraced by his wife, Lori, and two of their children, Aidan and McKenna. I was embarrassed to ask if I could do a load of laundry, but my clothes had not been washed for nearly two weeks. Lori brought me to the laundry room, and she in-vited me to tag along with her when she did errands the next day. I thanked her several times, but she was unfazed, as if she regularly cared for political refugees. She left me alone to wash my clothes, and I savored the rich scents of laundry detergent, fresh air, and a home-cooked meal. Their house felt alive; it was a home.

That weekend, I began to heal. When Lori and I were getting manicures and clips of my testimony splashed across every TV in the nail salon, we quietly joked and bit back smiles. Jody swiftly ushered us in and out of restaurants as patrons did a double take when we walked by. We chose seats in the very back of a movie theater so we could see *Top Gun: Maverick*. For old times' sake, we livestreamed a Trump rally, but switched on *My Cousin Vinny* and *Legally Blonde* once he began to berate me.

On our last night in Alabama, we took Jody and Lori's boat out for a sunset cruise on Lake Guntersville. I closed my eyes and braced myself as Lori sped us across the water and bounced over the wake. I never wanted to forget how, in that moment, I felt weightless and free. Then my phone vibrated, and my urge to ignore the notification only lasted until I saw Jody glance at his phone. The *New York Times* had just published an article describing how I was sequestered with family and a security detail. Jody and I howled with laughter.

———

I was again secluded in a hotel room when Jody and I returned to Atlanta. Though I felt welcome and safe there, I also felt too far from home—a place that no longer existed. In my solitude, I began to understand my new reality. I wasn't waiting for enough time to pass for my life to go back to normal; I was waiting for enough time to pass to create my new normal.

Bill and Jody were now more than just my attorneys. They were becoming my dear friends, confidants, and guardians. They advised, defended, and encouraged me, and saw to it that I had the time and security to determine how and when I'd emerge from seclusion, who I would be, and where home would be. I was used to being self-sufficient. I trusted Bill and Jody, but I was still learning how to relinquish my privacy, which I had so closely guarded.

My uncertain future overwhelmed me. Working in politics had felt so natural—not just an occupation but my identity. But I hadn't really revealed who I was, outside of work, to my colleagues in the White House.

Later that week, I escaped the confines of my hotel room and had lunch with Bill at Alston & Bird. After we finished eating, he said that there was someone who wanted to meet me. We walked to a corner office suite, and Richard Hays, the firm's managing partner, stood up and greeted us warmly, framed by floor-to-ceiling windows. He extended his arm to shake my hand, but instinctively, I pulled him in for a hug. Richard asked thoughtful questions about my life before and after the hearing, many of which I deferred to Bill. I realized I had not yet discussed my experiences with anyone outside my close-knit circle of attorneys and felt ashamed for losing my train of thought.

Richard asked how my hotel accommodations were. I didn't hesitate to answer that my room was comfortable and I could never thank him enough for Alston & Bird's generosity and commitment to keeping me safe. In that moment, my yearning for a laundry room or kitchen stove felt presumptuous. The two men exchanged a glance, and Bill smiled and said that I probably would like to be somewhere more spacious. Richard sat on the edge of his desk, and pressure built in my chest as I tried to send Bill a telepathic message to stop what he was saying.

"Well, it's funny you say that, Bill," Richard began. He explained that he had a house in Atlanta that was temporarily vacant. "I thought maybe you would like to stay at the house for a while and watch over it for me. You know, make sure no intruders break in." He winked. "Take some time to think it over, if you want. Just so you know, though, Bill is close by, in case you're worried about him pestering you." Bill laughed and pretended to pull an arrow out of his chest. I was already nodding in acceptance of Richard's offer.

I thought about how, just nine months ago, I had felt out of place meeting high-powered attorneys. My autonomy was shackled to those transactional interactions. But when Bill and I left Richard's office together, I threw my arms around him. He hugged me back, and I never wanted to let him go.

In late July, I returned to Washington for my first interview with the Department of Justice. They had offered to convene the meeting in Atlanta, but I wanted to see Mom and Paul. My parents drove to Washington to have dinner with me at the Riggs and to pack some of my belongings from my apartment. Since I still could not return, Bill had negotiated to terminate my lease and would front my unpaid rent debt until I was back on my feet.

After four depositions and two hours of live testimony, speaking with the January 6th Committee had become a familiar and predictable experience. I knew Capitol Hill well—how it operated, what it expected, its predictable reactions to me. I knew almost nothing about the DOJ, except for its turbulent Trump-era history. I leaned on Jody, Bill, and Stephen more than ever. And there was an addition to our team, Alicia.

I woke up with a knot in my stomach the morning of my interview and begged Bill and Jody to reschedule, though I knew that was a useless effort. When I entered the Alston & Bird conference room, I saw that we were far outnumbered by the DOJ and FBI officials already seated at the table. I kept my head down and quietly found my seat as they stood up in unison.

"Ms. Hutchinson," the official then leading the DOJ's January 6th investigation said, clearing his throat. "Do you mind if I introduce myself? I'm Thomas Windom." I hurried to the other side of the table and shook hands with him and each of the others in attendance. A few investigators barely held back smiles as I introduced myself. The introductions helped lower my guard. Thomas asked if I had any stories to share about my life after the hearing.

"Well, I'm sort of a refugee in Atlanta. I did go to the Whole Foods salad bar last week for lunch, though. I heard a woman shriek my name and I tried to ignore her, but then she said my name again. I turned around and she started sobbing. I didn't quite know what to do, so I brought her to check out with me and prayed no one would wonder why this woman was thanking me for opening people's eyes to how much danger our democracy is in.

"And then a few days ago when I was on my way to Washington, security was escorting me through the Atlanta airport. Someone in the TSA line shouted, 'Hey, how does it feel to be a fucking liar?'" I paused, unsure of the DOJ's tolerance for profanity. "Did you say anything back?" an investigator asked. "I did. I told them I wouldn't know."

Our interview lasted eight hours, and despite my lawyers' efforts to set me at ease, I put a lot of pressure on myself to testify perfectly. I felt that a lot was riding on my credibility, and I was stressed about making a mistake or there being small inconsistencies in my testimony. By the end of the day I was completely drained, but I accepted the DOJ's offer to continue our interview the next day and prayed I could push through.

Bill, Jody, Stephen, Alicia, and I had dinner that night at Big Bear, Stephen's cousin's restaurant in Washington. I was taxed emotionally, and I pleaded with my lawyers to postpone the second DOJ interview. This time, I wasn't pleading because of my nerves—I was so physically exhausted, I knew I would not be able to focus. Bill was quiet, and Jody reminded me several times that I would feel better after a good night of sleep, and that we had to follow through on our commitment. I lost my patience. "Damn it, Jody. Are you working for me? Because it feels like you're still working for the Department of Justice!"

With that, Bill excused himself. He returned with a smile on his face. "It's done. We're rescheduling. DOJ was relieved, too. The investigator told me how exhausting today was . . ." Jody nodded in acknowledgment, and my posture slackened. Alicia handed me a glass of wine, which I eagerly accepted.

Around two in the morning, I was partially roused from my coma-like slumber by a fire alarm. The hotel had had a routine fire drill earlier in the week, so I sandwiched my head between two pillows and fell back to sleep. I woke up a second time at around five. This time, my room was flooded with blue and red flashing lights and a putrid stench that smelled like burning rubber. I peered out the window and saw that the street was soaking wet and lined with emergency vehicles. I figured a water main must have burst. Then I saw that I had twenty-three missed calls from Bill.

"Cassidy? Where are you?" Bill sounded worried.

"I'm sorry if I woke you up, but my room smells terrible. What's going on?"

"Oh my God. Cassidy," he said. "The hotel is on fire. I've been trying to call you. You need to get out."

"What?" I asked, struggling to process what he had said. "Bill, I can't leave my room now. Everyone will know I slept through the fire for three hours. That's so embarrassing."

"Cassidy," Bill said. "Get out of your room now!"

I quickly dressed, but I didn't want to go outside looking like I had just woken up. Bill called again and asked where I was. "Putting on mascara," I said.

"Oh, for the love of—get out, Cassidy!" This time I listened. I found Bill outside, and only then did I register the burning sensation in my chest and throat.

Bill and I flew back to Atlanta that evening. Three days later, the FBI executed a search warrant at Mar-a-Lago.

"Here I was, thinking my moment in time—in history—had passed," Alex Butterfield remarked to me on a Zoom call one Sunday afternoon about his own experience testifying against Nixon. He continued about the unusual parallels in our experiences, "And nearly fifty years later, I see on the front page of the *Washington Post* a side-by-side photo of us being sworn in before Congress. I couldn't believe it. I just couldn't believe it."

I had been trying to get in touch with Alex for months. We called every number we found online and even reached out to an MSNBC producer for *The Last Word with Lawrence O'Donnell* after Alex interviewed with him about my hearing, but we did not have any luck. I had begun to accept that my beloved copy of *The Last of the President's Men* would be my only connection to Alex, but Bill and I were at Reagan National Airport when he received an email from Alex's son, Alex Jr., who promised to put us in touch with his father. I pulled the book, which I carried with me almost everywhere, out of my carry-on and Bill snapped a photo to send to Alex.

When Alex and I connected that first time, we talked about the uncanny coincidences in our stories—two obscure White House staffers, separated by half a century, obligated to speak difficult truths in public about matters of crucial importance to the country. Alex was bewildered when I explained the impact his story and integrity had had on my decision to come forward with more information. We swapped stories about the White House and Camp David, our liberating yet isolating experiences with government investigations. We talked about how our proximity to power in the White House had made us both privy to many important conversations and decisions.

Alex told me that my testimony was "magnificent," noting that I was poised and articulate and came across as truthful and credible. I blushed, though I thanked him. What he thought meant a lot to me. He opened up about how he was attacked for his testimony and assumed that I would receive the same reaction, adding that it had been tough being blacklisted by friends and colleagues, who still to this day have not talked to him. When Alex said he remains friends with John Dean, I mentioned that someone had compared my testimony to his, but I identified so much more with Alex. From the moment I had read *The Last of the President's Men*, it felt like we were so similar, and like I had had a role model through such an uncertain time. Now, over Zoom, I was struck by the depth of our instant connection.

I could have talked to him for hours. In one of the most consequential moments of my life so far, when I was completely alone and overcome with fear, Alex's story was what gave me the courage to correct course. I thanked him profusely as our conversation drew to a close, calling him Mr. Butterfield. "Cassidy, please," he said. "Call me Alex. We're friends now, okay? Don't forget about me. We're friends. We'll see each other soon."

––––––

Tears rolled down my cheeks on August 16, 2022, as I listened to Liz's concession speech. I was both devastated and emboldened by the injustice of her primary loss. Her cadences and her demeanor were a reminder of the long campaign to protect and advance our founding principles. In the wake of the most vicious political battles, Liz emerged with her principles and integrity unscathed.

Bill began suggesting that I consider signing a short-term lease in Atlanta, but I resisted. As safe and comfortable as Bill and Jody made me feel, I did not belong in Atlanta. If I did not return to Washington, Trump World would have won by pushing me out. Washington still felt like home, and I was not prepared to let them take that from me. Bill reminded me that there is more to a home than familiarity with its streets, but I insisted on searching for an apartment. Bill supported my decision, and I started looking.

––––––

A few days later, I borrowed Richard Hays's spare car and drove to visit the Hunt family in Alabama. I was driving on a rural road by the time I crossed into the state, and almost every house I passed had a Trump 2020 or Trump 2024 sign on the front lawn. "Jody, if this car breaks down," I said on the phone with him, "no one here would help me. I'm going to get shot." With that, the call abruptly dropped, and I lost cell service.

The next morning, I stumbled into the Hunts' kitchen still half-asleep. Jody cheerfully greeted me and motioned to a pot of coffee and a tray of freshly baked scones still hot from the oven.

"Grab some breakfast! Your next government interview is in a few weeks, so I thought we should start reviewing—"

I asked if he was joking. He was not. So I picked out a scone and settled in at the table.

Jody and Lori had a dinner party to go to that night. They had accepted the invitation a few months prior, and had been kind enough to invite me after the fact. But when I'd learned whose party it was, I thought that my hearing was betraying me. "Rob Aderholt's birthday party? Like, the Republican congressman from Alabama?" I asked. Jody chuckled. "Yep! Do you know him?" I did know Rob—or I had known him, in my previous life. "It's probably better if I sit this one out. I'm not quite sure that's where I belong anymore." Jody agreed with me and said he'd bring home some cake.

I was sitting at the kitchen table when they returned. Jody handed me a paper plate covered in aluminum foil. "Unwrap it," he said through a wide grin. Underneath the foil was a slab of birthday cake. My body shook with laughter as Jody handed me a fork. I wished Rob Aderholt a happy birthday before digging into his cake.

We were eating lunch a few days later when our phones lit up with a text message and two photos from Bill. The first was a photo of the cover of *The Last of the President's Men.* The second was a photo of the inside, with a handwritten note from both Bob Woodward and Alex Butterfield:

Bob Woodward: *To Cassidy Hutchinson –*
Congratulations. TO THE TRUTH!

Alex Butterfield: *Hi Cassidy – I'm probably breaching some kind of literary protocol by signing a book I didn't write . . . but for you, pretty lady, I'll take my chances. You did the right thing . . . and doing the right thing is the very definition of integrity. —Alex*

I read their inscriptions over and over and did not realize that I had been smiling until my cheek muscles began to cramp. A little while later, Bill sent me another text—to let me know that the apartment I had chosen in Washington had accepted my application, and that I could move in once I signed the paperwork.

I put down my phone and watched dozens of hummingbirds drink nectar from Lori's feeders. Jody came to my side of the table and put his arm around me. I was finally going home.

———

When I was a child, moving never bothered me. I correlated moving with a fresh start and adventure, and an opportunity to embrace change and growth. But after only six nights in my new apartment, I began questioning my decision to return to Washington. On this particular night, I'd spent hours trying to fall asleep and had eventually pulled off my sleep mask in defeat. I rolled over to look out my bedroom window at the Washington Monument, and contemplated thumbing through one of my copies of *The Last of the President's Men*, but picked up my phone instead and scrolled through my emails.

I'd gone to dinner with Bill, Lacey, and their three children on my final night in Atlanta. Bill's daughter had been tempting me all summer to buy a puppy, but I needed to know where I would settle before I could make that decision. Back in Washington, it wasn't long before I thought I might need a friend after all. I'd come across an ad for eight-week-old cockapoo puppies for sale just down the road from Christopher Newport University. There were multiple puppies in the photo, but I was drawn to the largest, a clumsy-looking guy with red curls and white paws. The ad was two weeks old, but I emailed the breeder anyway. I now learned that he was the only puppy that hadn't been purchased. The next morning, I drove to the Hampton Roads area for the first time since my college graduation and picked up my new best friend.

I brought him to my second DOJ interview that week. The investigators adored him and asked what his name was. "I don't know," I said, then added, "and this time, that's the truth." Laughter filled the room.

He remained nameless for two weeks. In mid-September, I had my final interviews with the January 6th Committee. At the conclusion of my sixth and final interview, we all went into the office, which was also my makeshift puppy room. Liz hugged the puppy close to her chest and asked what I had decided to name him. "Maybe George. I think George." I waited for her reaction as she took a long look at him. "He's definitely a George," she declared. We took a photo together, and it wasn't until later that night that I noticed a portrait of George Washington mounted on the wall behind me, Liz, and George.

————

My face burned hot when the man Bill and Jody seemed to know well walked away from us at the hotel bar. I had just arrived in Atlanta for my interview with the Fulton County grand jury investigating Trump's involvement with the 2020 election results in Georgia.

"So, who was that?" I asked. They looked at me, bewildered. "The guy that just thanked you for testifying and praised your courage?" Bill asked. I nodded. They looked at each other and erupted. "Cassidy, you're trying to tell us you don't know who Charles Barkley is?!" Jody asked, but it wasn't really a question. They explained, and I had to admit I'd never heard of the basketball legend. "You're embarrassing me," I said. "Stop embarrassing me! You two know better than anyone that I can't lie to save my life!" This time, we all laughed together.

Twenty-four hours later, I was on a flight back to Washington. After six closed-door interviews and one live testimony session with the January 6th Committee, three interviews with the Department of Justice, and one interview with Fulton County, I was finished. And, thanks to Bill Jordan and Jody Hunt of Alston & Bird, I was empowered to tell the whole truth.

———

I spent Thanksgiving with Mom and Paul in New Jersey. On Thanksgiving Day, I left their house and drove to Dad's.

Dad was never very fond of holidays, even when I was young. But for some unknown reason, there have been certain holidays when I've felt compelled to check to see if he was home. There was never a holiday I found him at home. I never knew where he was, but I also never asked. And I never told him I did this.

The pragmatic and optimistic scenarios were the same, year after year. His truck would either not be in the driveway or it would be. If it wasn't, I would keep driving. If it was, I planned to stop, and hoped he would welcome me inside.

On Thanksgiving Day 2022, my optimistic scenario was that his truck would be in the driveway, and that he would agree we could talk.

As I approached the house, the first thing I noticed was not that his truck wasn't in the driveway. I noticed that other cars were.

And a U-Haul. And small children.

I slammed on my brakes in front of the house, unsure what to do.

But what I had to do was clear. I had to keep driving.

I drove until my breath choked my lungs.

He left without notice, without a goodbye or a new mailing address.

He was gone.

I stopped the car and let my tears fall, until no more remained.

And then, there was only one thing left to do: move forward.

In the throes of love and loss, bravery and fear, I found freedom.

I am finally free.

Epilogue

The pilot's voice announces we have reached cruising altitude. I look out the window to watch America unfurl below. A profound sense of gratitude to call this nation my home washes over me as I settle in for the long cross-country flight to San Diego.

Growing up, my family didn't talk about politics. Nor were my parents regular voters. And yet I had felt a calling to public service. My political views began to take shape during the 2012 election when I decided I was a Mitt Romney supporter and a Republican. I believed in the core principles of the Republican Party that Ronald Reagan had championed. I still do. The inscription I included next to my high school yearbook photograph was a Thomas Paine quote taken from Reagan's farewell speech at the 1988 Republican National Convention: " *'The harder the conflict, the more glorious the triumph.' And my fellow citizens, while our triumph is not yet complete, the road has been glorious indeed.*"

I thought I was walking a glorious road from my first moments working in Congress and the White House. For the first time in my life, I felt like I was home. I discovered I had an aptitude for managing politicians. But I would also discover that the turmoil I had previously experienced, caused by human frailties I thought I had escaped, would envelop me again, this time in the West Wing.

I had started my job with the belief that my colleagues and I were doing something important for the country. But when the president I had served wholeheartedly persuaded his supporters to reject the legitimacy of a free and fair election, I knew he was leading a dangerous assault on our political ideals and governing institutions for no other purpose than to soothe his injured pride. For a time, I resisted admitting that to myself, and I resisted being a part of efforts to hold him accountable for his actions.

Yet on January 6, 2021, President Trump's lies about the 2020 election, and the proliferation of poisonous conspiracy theories he and some of my former colleagues amplified, exposed the fragility of American democracy. The republic would survive, and power would be transferred to the new, duly elected president. But the nation would sustain wounds that have yet to heal. In the wake of that tumultuous day, I could no longer ignore the dissonance between the principles I hold dear and their abuse by powerful people who claimed to share them but sacrificed them for their own selfish ends.

I had lived in fear of a subpoena, but in my heart I wanted the truth to be known. I had seen how fragile democracy is, and my conscience recognized our duty as citizens to attend to it for its survival.

I wish I could say that I promptly and easily made the decision to come forward. After a desperate hunt to find pro bono counsel, I ended up with Trump World–funded counsel. At times I provided less-than-complete testimony to congressional investigators to assuage the concerns of those keeping a watchful eye on me. But I was ashamed of being complicit, possibly even instrumental, in an insurrection. That shame drove me to look for a way to break free from the clutches of Trump World and seek redemption by rectifying my missteps. I needed to find my way back to the right side of history. I needed a second chance.

The fortuitous discovery of someone whose name I had never heard before—Alex Butterfield—made all the difference. He had come forward to testify honestly about the Nixon White House. I would find myself in a similar position fifty years later. The account of Alex's integrity in Bob Woodward's *The Last of the President's Men* inspired my moral reckoning. Alex had served President Nixon loyally, but not at the expense of his duty to the country.

When he was subpoenaed by Watergate investigators and without hesitation disclosed the Nixon White House taping system, he saw it as an obligation of the oath he swore to the nation, not an act against tribal politics.

"Mr. Butterfield, are you aware of the installation of any listening devices in the Oval Office of the president?" the committee counsel asked moments after Alex was sworn in.

Composed, his hands folded in front of him, eyes not quite downcast, the only hint of tension the nearly five-second pause that preceded his response. "I was aware of listening devices, yes, sir," he answered, and Richard Nixon's presidency entered its twilight.

"I knew I would not lie," Alex would tell an NPR interviewer. "People were lying right and left." And those people, except for the president they had served, had gone to jail. "They were ensnared by the glitter of the presidency," Alex explained, "like it is easy to do."

I followed in Alex's footsteps, choosing to reveal the truth about what I knew about the attack on the US Capitol. I changed course, choosing to follow through on the promise I made when I swore the oath to protect and defend the United States.

I still consider myself a Republican. But I denounce the tribalism that produced the outlandish conspiracy theories and violence that some party leaders not only failed to condemn but even excused in their pursuit of power. If we do not restore responsible governing, respect for our democratic practices, and accountability for our leaders as core Republican values, I fear not only for the future of our party, but for our nation.

————

I'm awakened by the pilot's voice announcing our imminent arrival. I look out the window as we descend, soaring over desert and mountains. I glimpse the Pacific Ocean shimmering in the far distance, and the regal presence of US Navy warships resting at anchor. *Welcome to San Diego.*

I'm distracted as I gather my things and disembark, consumed with excitement to meet the man whose example had encouraged me to finally say "enough," disenthrall myself from "the glitter of the presidency," and stand up for the truth and our country.

I arrive at my hotel and quickly slip on a pair of blue jeans and a white blouse before hurrying out the door. Clutching my copy of *The Last of the President's Men*, I arrive at Alex Butterfield's condominium and am quickly ushered into the elevator—the same elevator Bob Woodward had taken years before when he visited La Jolla.

Upon knocking, I hear to come in, and as the door opens, it almost hits the nearly ninety-seven-year-old man who stands straight and dignified, just as I imagined him.

Alex.

"Don't you look familiar, pretty lady." He smiles.

We simultaneously reach out and wrap ourselves in a warm embrace. With *The Last of the President's Men* pressed against the small of Alex's back and my tears beginning to soak his cashmere sweater, I bury my face in his chest.

"It's okay," he comforts me. "It's okay, you're home now."

Bibliography

Baker, Peter, and Maggie Haberman. "As Protests and Violence Spill Over, Trump Shrinks Back." *New York Times*. May 31, 2020.

Balsamo, Michael. "Disputing Trump, Barr Says No Widespread Election Fraud." Associated Press. December 1, 2020. https://apnews.com/article/barr-no-widespread-election-fraud-b1f1488796c9a98c4b1a9061a6c7f49d.

Blake, Aaron. "Trump's Acting Chief of Staff Admits It: There Was a Ukraine Quid Pro Quo." *Washington Post*. October 17, 2019.

Carlson, Tucker. "How UPS Explained the Missing Biden Family Documents, and a Word about Hunter." Fox News. October 29, 2020.

Cheney, Liz. Remarks before the House Select Committee to Investigate the January 6th Attack on the United States Capitol. July 22, 2022.

Draper, Robert. "Cassidy Hutchinson: Why the Jan. 6 Committee Rushed Her Testimony." *New York Times*. July 10, 2022.

Goldberg, Jeffrey. "Trump: Americans Who Died in War Are 'Losers' and 'Suckers.'" *Atlantic*. September 3, 2020.

Grayer, Annie, Zachary Cohen, Ryan Nobles, and Whitney Wild. "January 6 Committee Issues 10 More Subpoenas, Including to Stephen Miller and Kayleigh McEnany." CNN. November 9, 2021. https://www.cnn.com/2021/11/09/politics/january-6-subpoenas-stephen-miller/index.html.

Hillman, Kerrie. "I Hated to Be the Guy Who Had to Tell of the Watergate Tapes, Butterfield Says." *Morning Edition*. NPR. September 30, 2022.

McGuire, Brian. "A Captain in the 'People's House': Cassidy Hutchinson Ramps Up Career in Public Service with High-Profile White House Internship." Christopher Newport University Newsroom. October 18, 2018.

Meadows, Mark. *The Chief's Chief*. St. Petersburg, FL: All Seasons Press, 2021.

Milbank, Dana. "Cassidy Hutchinson Could Read the Ketchup on the Wall," *Washington Post*. January 28, 2022.

Palmer, Anna, Jake Sherman, Eli Okun, and Garrett Ross. "Playbook PM: Camp David Guest List." *Politico*. May 15, 2020. https://www.politico.com/newsletters/playbook-pm/2020/05/15/new-camp-david-guest-list-489239.

Pelosi, Nancy. "Pelosi Statement on President Trump's Expanded Travel Ban." Press Release. Speaker's Press Office. January 31, 2020.

Reagan, Ronald. "Remarks at the Republican National Convention in New Orleans, Louisiana." August 15, 1988. Ronald Reagan Presidential Library and Museum. https://www.reaganlibrary.gov/archives/speech/remarks-republican-national-convention-new-orleans-louisiana.

Smith, Allan, and Peter Alexander. "Former Meadows Aide: Trump Lunged at Secret Service Agent, Tried to Grab Steering Wheel on Jan. 6." NBC News. June 28, 2022. https://www.nbcnews.com/politics/donald-trump/cassidy-hutchinson-trump-lunged-secret-service-agent-tried-grab-steeri-rcna35775.

Trump, Donald (@realDonald Trump). "Peter Navarro releases 36-page report alleging election fraud 'more than sufficient' to swing victory to Trump, https://t.co/D8KrMHnFdK. A great report by Peter. Statistically impossible to have lost the 2020 Election. Big protest in D.C. on January 6th. Be there, will be wild!" Twitter. 1:42 a.m., December 19, 2020.

Trump, Donald (@realDonald Trump). "Mike Pence didn't have the courage to do what should have been done to protect our Country and our Constitution, giving States a chance to certify a corrected set of facts, not the fraudulent or inaccurate ones which they were asked to previously certify. USA demands the truth!" Twitter. 2:24 p.m., January 6, 2020.

Trump, Donald (@realDonald Trump). Twitter. 5:16 p.m., October 4, 2020. https://twitter.com/realDonaldTrump/status/131286423 2711520257?s=20.

Trump, Donald. Proclamation No. 9984: "Presidential Proclamation on Suspension of Entry as Immigrants and Nonimmigrants of Persons Who Pose a Risk of Transmitting 2019 Novel Coronavirus." January 31, 2020.

Wagner, John, Amber Phillips, and Eugene Scott. "Who Is Cassidy Hutchinson?" *Washington Post*. June 30, 2022.

White House Press Office. "President Donald J. Trump Announces Appointments for the Executive Office of the President." June 5, 2020.

Woodward, Bob. *The Last of the President's Men*. New York: Simon & Schuster, 2015.

Photo Credits

Page 1
Top left: Photo courtesy of the author
Top right: Office of House Majority Whip Steve Scalise
Bottom: Official White House Photo by Tia Dufour

Page 2
Top: Official White House Photo by Tia Dufour
Middle: Official White House Photo by Shealah Craighead
Bottom: Official White House Photo by Shealah Craighead

Page 3
Top: CJH Cell Phone (Selfie)
Middle: Official White House Photo by Tia Dufour
Bottom: CJH Cell Phone (Selfie)

Page 4
Top: Official White House Photo by Joyce Boghosian
Middle: Photo by Bill Clark / CQ Roll Call via AP Images
Bottom: Photo by Samuel Corum / Stringer via Getty Images

Page 5
Top: CJH Cell Phone (Selfie)
Middle: Official White House Photo by Shealah Craighead
Bottom: Official White House Photo by Shealah Craighead

Page 6
Top: Photo by Al Drago / Bloomberg via Getty Images
Middle: Official White House Photo by Andrea Hanks
Bottom: Photo by Jabin Botsford / *The Washington Post* via Getty Images

Page 7
Top: Photo by Oliver Contreras / Sipa USA (Sipa via AP Images)
Middle: Photo by AP Images / J. Scott Applewhite
Bottom: Bill Jordan's Cell Phone

Page 8
Top: Bill Jordan's Cell Phone
Middle: Bill Jordan's Cell Phone
Bottom: Bill Jordan's Cell Phone

About the Author

CASSIDY HUTCHINSON is a former special assistant to President Donald Trump and his chief of staff Mark Meadows. She received national attention after being a key witness to the hearings led by the United States House Select Committee to Investigate the January 6th Attack on the United States Capitol. Hutchinson previously worked for the White House Office of Legislative Affairs and interned for Republican leaders Steve Scalise and Ted Cruz. She was born and raised in Pennington, New Jersey. This is her first book.